P9-BIG-206

The Story of
DAN LYONS S.J.

by John D. McCallum

Books By

JOHN D. McCALLUM

The story of Dan Lyons, S.J.

The Gladiators

College Football, U.S.A.
(with Charles H. Pearson)

Going Their Way

Six Roads From Abilene

That Kelly Family

Everest Diary

This Was Football
(with Pudge Heffelfinger)

The Tiger Wore Spikes

Dumb Dan

Scooper

Beginner's Book of Fishing
(with Dave Stidolph)
and other books . . .

The Story of DAN LYONS S.J.

by John D. McCallum

Published by

GUILD BOOKS

A Division of Catholic Polls, Inc.

86 Riverside Drive

New York, N.Y., 10024

Benedict A. Horvath

FIRST PRINTING, 1973

Published by Guild Books, a Division of Catholic Polls, Inc.

Library of Congress Catalog Card Number: 72-94967

Manufactured in the United States of America
by Craftsman-Metropolitan Press, Seattle, Washington

Man is not made for defeat. Man can be destroyed but not defeated.

—ERNEST HEMINGWAY

Contents

Preface

To do this profile of Dan Lyons, S.J., I have covered thousands of miles. The work started in New York, took me to Seattle to the neighborhood where he grew up, then to Gonzaga University, in Spokane, on to Los Angeles, back to Washington, D.C., and up to New York again—with a small fortune in telephone calls between. Almost all of the material you will read came from his friends, his enemies, his teachers, his neighbors, his family, his childhood companions, his staff, and his fellow priests.

I cannot reduce the man to any concise common denominator and the reason is that he has lived many lives, not just one. I believe that every writer lives as many lives as he has written stories, and that this must always be so when a man writes from a sincere dedication to cover the times and get down to the truth.

You might suppose offhand that Father Lyons is a "super hawk," judging from *Newsweek* magazine, the liberal press, and his own column. Actually, in person, this isn't the case.

He is one of the most exuberantly warm and open-hearted human beings it has been my pleasure to know in more than 20 years as a biographer of famous people. Few people of stature I have known can match his candor. While I was writing this book there was no subject on which he said, "I'd rather not get into that," or, "Let's leave that out." He never stopped to calculate his words so as to put the best possible interpretation on potentially controversial matters.

He never uses obscure words when clearer words will do. But he uses words carefully and correctly. When he wrote that two certain well-known sex-education specialists were "moral degenerates," friends of his thought he would be sued. "Don't worry," he reassured them, "I am not referring to their conduct, I am referring to their moral code. A moral degenerate is one who lowers prevailing moral standards. That is what I accused them of. I wish they would sue me. I would love to go to court and prove how much they are causing our moral standards to degenerate."

Father Lyons is not an argumentative man by nature. But he will debate with anyone at the drop of a hat. A former debate coach at Gonzaga and Seattle Universities, he has appeared in debates at more than a hundred college campuses across the U.S., from Berkeley to Dartmouth. He comes prepared for battle. Once, while debating the dean of the chapel at Boston U., his opponent declared, "We have to accept the fact that some countries have chosen Communism." Father Lyons in his cross-questioning asked him to repeat the statement. The dean did, and Father had the opening he had been waiting for. He said, "Can you name two or three countries where the people have chosen Communism?" Long pause. The dean started to say, "China . . ." but quickly broke off the sentence. More silence. Finally, Father Lyons said, "Name just one." The dean couldn't. Father had made his point.

As Father Dan's reputation has grown, fewer people have been willing to debate with him publicly. He says, "From the anvil of discussion fly the sparks of truth."

At Fairbanks, Alaska, one time, his opponent was a Japanese professor. He recalls that the best line of the night was uttered after the debate was over. The Japanese professor was the father of a tiny daughter, and Father Lyons asked him if she had been born in the United States.

"No," the professor replied. "Like it says on so many things, she was made in Japan."

Father Lyons has a keen sense of humor. It is a part of his personality the public seldom gets to see. Often he will embellish his conversation with humorous anecdotes. He spent four years going to school in Ireland, and some of his funniest yarns are drawn from that experience. Sample:

"Paddy Murphy had been courting Katie O'Reilly for twenty years. Finally one evening, as they started out for a walk, he popped the question: 'Will you marry me, Katie?' And Katie said, 'I will.' They walked on in silence for the next half-mile. Then Katie said, 'You're awfully quiet, Paddy,' and Paddy replied, 'I've said too much already.' "

Another Father Lyons' story? Listen:

"Michael Waldron, another country Irishman, had been courting Bridie Sweeney for many years. Bridie finally asked him one night, 'Do you think we'll ever get married, Michael?' And Michael replied, 'Ah, who'd have us?' "

On all phases of Father Dan's life, I notice that he doesn't try to fool anybody, including himself. In our interviews for this book, the details flowed out of him with characteristic spontaneity.

If there is anything you don't understand about Father Lyons when you have finished this book, it won't be because he tried to hold information back from me. He doesn't draw many conclusions about himself, but the various facets of his character are implicit in his personal testimony.

For example, take the big question: What is his philosophy about life after death? In this angry, atheistic, uncertain new world has he kept the traditional faith? You will see from the evidence herewith that he is a very devout man who puts his religious beliefs into practice. Pinned to hard work by more commitments than it seems possible to meet, except by tireless work, he has the God-given faculty of being able to juggle his schedule so that he can do a dozen tasks at once.

Judging from my personal observation of Father Lyons this past year, he is never too busy to help a person in need. Offhand, I can recall two specific instances. I remember we were in the middle of editing the final draft of this manuscript, when his office phone rang. The caller was a lady from Brooklyn whose sister had a serious drinking problem and needed medical attention desperately. Could Father Lyons advise her as to what to do? On inquiring, he learned that the sister's liver was enlarged. Her health had been so badly damaged by liquor that she would live just a few more months if something wasn't done.

Father Lyons told the phone caller, "There is only one

place in the U.S. I know of that can cure your sister's alcohol addiction and restore her health."

"Where's that?"

"Schick Shadel Hospital, out in Seattle."

"If you say so, Father."

Without daring to tell her sister why they were going to Seattle, the woman agreed to get her there.

Father Lyons said to her, "I'll meet your plane in Seattle."

It was a 6,000-mile round-trip to and from the Coast, but Father Lyons didn't flinch. He flew to Seattle ahead of the two sisters and was there in time to meet their plane and accompany them to the hospital. The patient, however, balked at signing in. She demanded to be escorted back to the airport. Father Lyons tried to reason with her, but she wouldn't listen. Finally, after a half-hour of cajolery, in which Father Lyons convinced her she had only two choices—Life or Death—she agreed to stay.

The 14-day medical treatment cost $1,500. Father Lyons personally guaranteed the payment. This for an alcoholic women he had never met before.

Several weeks later, Father Lyons repeated this act for a woman in Denver whom he had never met. At the request of a close friend, he was on his way to Seattle and stopped off in Denver and made arrangements for a 41-year-old woman alcohol addict to be admitted to Schick. At Denver, he learned that the woman had just been committed to 90 days in the psychiatric ward at one of the local hospitals. He was told it would take legal action to transfer her to Seattle. So he arranged for Mr. Richard Casey, a lawyer-friend in Denver, to represent her. Father Lyons spent two hours in the psychiatric ward talking to the woman. Afterward he phoned Schick and got the doctors to agree to receive her. Father Lyons agreed to guarantee payment again. Then he talked the government psychiatrist in charge of the woman's case in Denver into letting her go to Seattle. As it developed, the lawyer was instructed by Father Lyons to put her on the plane, and someone from Schick met her at the gate in Seattle.

Curious, I asked Father Lyons why she had been committed to the psychiatric ward in the first place, and he replied, casually, "Because she tried to kill herself with a shotgun. She thought her situation was hopeless. But she was perfectly sane. She was simply addicted to an intoxicating drug, alcohol. She is all right now."

I told him, "You saved her life—and that first woman's, too."

"No, I didn't," he said. "The hospital did."

Father Lyons doesn't pretend to be anything more than what he is. Nor does he pretend to be anything less. When he speaks of his work, his goals in life, he does so without making much of it, though he knows he is dealing with important issues. His tone is sincere and matter-of-fact.

When word finally got around that I was writing this book, letters crossed my desk from the four corners of the U.S.

"I'm writing to say I will be glad to help you in any way I can . . ." The note was signed by William F. Buckley Jr., the most prominent Catholic layman in America. Another distinguished Catholic who wrote me was Dr. Stefan T.

Possony, director of international studies at the Hoover Institution on War, Revolution, and Peace, at Stanford. The author of many scholarly books, former professor at Georgetown, former advisor to the French Air Ministry and to the Pentagon, Strategy and Military Affairs Editor of the American Security Council, he had this to say:

"I have known Father Lyons for nearly ten years and there are many points about him which have impressed me greatly. I would like to share them with you.

"Father Lyons is extremely knowledgeable about world conditions. In fact, he is about the best informed priest I know here or in Europe. He has traveled extensively in all parts of the world. He has kept up-to-date on the conflict in Southeast Asia and is one of a few American civilians who has met virtually all the important political figures in Vietnam. He is well informed about China, the conditions which exist on the Mainland, and on the great progress that has been made in Taiwan. In my experience, his judgment on Asian affairs has been impeccable.

"Father Lyons has deep understanding of the ideological confrontation between the various varieties of communism and the Free World in general and the U.S. in particular. His awareness extends to the intellectual dangers which threaten the Church, most of which derive from a false identification of Christianity with the unrealizable communist utopia.

"I would like to suggest that Father Lyons is a modern ecclesiastical diplomat of the highest caliber—not in the sense that he is a diplomatic negotiator, but in the sense that he is a political expert of international stature. He understands the impact of the ideological struggle on religion and the theological aspects of world conflict.

"Father Lyons is a very unique man, possessing great physical, mental and moral strength which is so necessary for the successful realization of the types of missions the Society of Jesus was founded to accomplish. He is an excellent writer, a good editor, and a fearless person who tells the truth as he sees it, but who is always willing to listen to the other side.

"I am happy to count myself among his friends and admirers. And if I may say so, I am convinced that St. Ignatius would have loved and appreciated Father Dan."

Other scholars like Dr. Anthony Kubek and Dr. Anthony Bouscaren also came forth to offer their assistance. "We believe in Father Lyons," they told me. "We are very enthused about his work." Another who made himself available as an adviser was author Vic Hurley, a retired lieutenant commander in the Navy and one of the recognized authorities on the peoples of Southeast Asia. An outstanding military historian, four of his books remain classics: *Southeast of Zamboanga, Men in Sun Helmets, Swish of the Kris,* and *Jungle Patrol.* He is part of a vanishing breed, one of the last of the old Asian hands.

Father Lyons, while mild-mannered in nature, can be a fighter, too. He is a man who stands up to be counted when sides are to be taken. Obviously such a person has made some enemies along the way. They are vocal. They lash out at him in public print. They talk about him in Congressional committees. They speak of him on radio and television. They do not always fight fairly. Yet one of the notable qualities of his character is his total lack of animosity toward these detractors. He seldom expresses even mild resentment, and in no case have I been able to find where he harbors any lasting feeling of ill will. He is the same way in private conversation. He doesn't go in for backbiting and running people down. Malice and spite are not part of his makeup.

His manner is the same with anyone he meets, from an obscure rice farmer in South Vietnam to Presidents. He is never overawed by celebrities, even before he became one himself. He doesn't try to overawe anyone else.

I have many pictures in my mind of Father Lyons. One of my favorites is of that Sunday in August, 1972. He had flown out from New York to be my house guest at my Tacoma, Washington, summer home. Next morning we got up for early Mass. Several churches were considered. I suggested going over to the chapel at Bellarmine Prep, since it was Jesuit and Father Lyons was sure to know some of the priests there. This was rejected, however, on the grounds that he didn't want to get tied up in lengthy conversations afterward.

He told me, "There is nothing I would enjoy more than spending the day at Bellarmine, but we have so much work to do, we are going to have to work all day on the book. We were in Seattle yesterday with the printer. I would have loved to spent the day at Seattle U. The president, Father Louis Gaffney, is an old, close friend. And the vice-president, Father Joe Perri, has been one of my best friends since grade school. The other vice-president, Father Tim Cronin, is one of my former students and debaters. Yet we did not have the time. I just hope they will understand."

We finally settled for St. John of the Woods, a little country parish hidden in the forest not far from my home.

"That will be perfect," Father Lyons said. "I don't know anyone there, and we can come back as soon as Mass is over. Easy in and easy out."

On the way, Father Lyons mentioned that he should offer to say one of the scheduled Masses, to help the pastor out. The Jesuits have been trained to assist at parish churches whenever they can. I stopped the car in front of the rectory. Father walked up to the front door and knocked, prepared to introduce himself. A husky, white-haired priest opened the door and stared out at him.

"DANNY LYONS!" thundered the deep voice. "WHAT ARE YOU DOING WAY OUT HERE?"

Father Lyons found himself being pulled through the door by Father Barrett Corrigan, S.J.—his old geometry teacher from Seattle Prep days (1935)!

It was indeed a small world.

Later, I expressed my amazement to Father Corrigan about the coincidence of their meeting like that. "I mean," I told him, "look at the odds. Here was Father Lyons, at this little church out in the woods 3,000 miles from New York, and the first person to greet him was someone he knew."

Father Corrigan laughed.

He said, "*Everybody* knows Father Dan!"

Now you can get better acquainted with Dan Lyons, S.J., too. Just turn to the next page and read on.

PART I

CHAPTER 1

Battle Fronts

Mid-April, 1972 . . .

North Vietnam's five-phase offensive had begun in the sky. It started with a shattering barrage of at least 12,000 rounds of rocket, mortar and artillery fire across the Demilitarized Zone separating North and South Vietnam. This was followed by a ground attack. More than 25,000 North Vietnamese troops, using Russian-built tanks and artillery, swept down through Quang Tri province like marauding locusts, sending 50,000 refugees fleeing south and U.S. advisers scurrying to their helicopters.

As President Nguyen Van Thieu's stunned military forces struggled desperately to regroup, the South Vietnam leader appeared on TV to deliver a grim ten-minute speech.

"This," he told his anxious audience, "is the final battle to decide the survival of our people . . ."

Hanoi had launched its biggest offensive in South Vietnam since *Tet* 1968. The North was plainly seeking a decisive military victory that would both display the impotence of Thieu's regime and politically embarrass President Richard Nixon. For Washington, and indeed for Saigon, it was the first genuine test of Vietnamization, a policy that the American Administration had pursued relentlessly in order to buy time until the South Vietnamese were strong enough to defend their own soil.

There was no argument that the Communist offensive was serious. How to face up to it was debatable. What should the United States do? President Nixon provided the solution two weeks later. His decision: Mine the harbor at Haiphong. His logic was to cut off Hanoi's main supply route from Russia and China.

The President's decision split U.S. Asian experts into two camps. One argued that the mining of Haiphong harbor represented an act of aggression. "Sure as hell," they shouted, "it's going to bring Russia and Red China into the fighting. World War III is just around the corner."

Nixonites retorted: "It's a stroke of genius. It's been long overdue."

Back at 86 Riverside Drive, in New York City, Dan Lyons, S.J., sat at his typewriter, smiling. He was very pleased with the President's announcement. For six years now, hadn't he been telling Americans in his weekly column in the Catholic press, on radio and television, and from the lecture platform, that the only way to stop Communist aggression in South Vietnam was to mine the harbor at Haiphong? Indeed, he had. On Wednesday, February 16, 1966, he had also told a Congressional subcommittee on The Far East and the Pacific in Washington, D.C., his views on this.

Then there was his lengthy private meeting with Richard Nixon at Taipei, in 1966. Father Dan, serving as Secretary-General of the Free Pacific Association for the United States, wrote a newspaper series during a visit to Taiwan that was published in papers all over the world, including Taipei. Nixon was visiting Taipei at the time and Father Lyons' articles about Vietnam in local English-language papers caught his eye.

"Find this Father Lyons for me," he told an aide.

"Where?"

"Phone every hotel in Taipei until you locate him. But get him. I want to talk to him."

The aide finally located Father Lyons at the Grand Hotel, the hostelry owned by Madame Chiang. A meeting between the two men was arranged for that afternoon. They met at Father Dan's hotel and talked for nearly four hours. They talked about South Vietnam. They talked about North Vietnam. They talked about the extent to which American troops should be involved. *And they talked about the mining of Haiphong*. Nixon agreed with much of what Father Lyons said.

"We also talked about President Diem," Father Lyons said. "We both shared the same position that he had been the victim of false propaganda back in the U.S., and that Nixon's old friend, Ambassador Henry Cabot Lodge, had been taken in by it. Hence the handle—Henry 'Sabotage.' I told Nixon that when I talked to Lodge, all he could say to me was: 'Mistakes were made, and I do not care to discuss them.' Not that Lodge wasn't cordial. I had had lunch with him and his wife at their home, and later visited with him at the embassy. But on the subject of President Diem, he was significantly silent."

On the day that President Nixon went on national television and told the American people he had decided to give orders to mine Haiphong harbor, I sat with Father Lyons in his office. After the President had finished making the announcement, Father turned to me and said: "The only difference from the advice I gave him six years ago and what he is doing now is that he's mining the harbor in the name of the United States. I had recommended that it be done in the name of Saigon, and thus reduce the inevitable criticism of U.S. policy. On that detail, I think I was right.

"We have only ourselves to blame if we do not have enough Vietnamese pilots. The way Nixon is doing it, so massively, is taking a lot of pilots. But I still feel we should at least do it in close cooperation with the Viet Air Force. The U.S. should play as subsidiary a role as possible. It boils down to the old propaganda game. Who wins that, wins the war."

The strong stand of Father Lyons against Communism has earned him the sobriquet, "Father Hawk," among his critics. He visited Vietnam for the first time in 1964. Since then he has gone back sixteen more times.

Father Lyons became a familiar figure in Saigon, with its two million people. One million refugees of war. Three hundred thousand carriers of tuberculosis. Two hundred thousand juvenile delinquents. One hundred thousand black marketeers. Fifty thousand prostitutes. Thirty thousand U.S.

soldiers. Saigon. Bomb shelters grown over with grass. Seven hundred thousand wheeled vehicles plodding through 356 kilometers of streets. Oriental women in European brassieres. European women in American brassieres. Two million black garbage rodents running at dusk. Twelve-hour working days. Thirty-seven and one-half years average life span. Saigon. Father Lyons saw it all. He saw it and smelled it and heard it. And when he returned to America, he told and wrote about what he saw and smelled and heard.

"There is no longer any way out of Vietnam, unless we decide to win the war," he started telling his audiences in 1965. "But we lack the will to win, if our present policy is any indication. Some thought it was going to be easy to win, once we escalated. Some thought the other side would soon give up. But the Commies know our Achilles heel: they know we have no policy of winning. Nor have we had such a policy since World War II. A little country like North Vietnam would not dare war against us if it thought we would try to defeat them. Ho Chi Minh knows that we can, but he doubts that we will. And he has every reason to doubt it. We are fighting in Vietnam because we let the Reds take China, then North Korea, then North Vietnam, then Cuba. They know that our policy is one of stalemate. . . ."

People began to listen to Father Lyons. Some agreed with his views; some did not. The publisher of a Catholic magazine even listed several writers who should "shut up." Heading the list were Taylor Caldwell, the noted Catholic novelist; General Curtis Le May, former Air Force Chief of Staff—and Father Lyons. Retorted the padre: "I might have said the same thing about the editor, but it would have been impolite. Besides, he seldom says anything, anyway."

Father Lyons, of course, had his supporters, too. Thousands of them. One, Francis B. Smith, a former Naval Intelligence Officer in World War II, wrote to him, encouraging him to "stay in there and fight the good fight." After reading Father Lyons' weekly column in *Twin Circle,* the national Catholic newspaper, Smith wrote:

> "Your information as presented in *Twin Circle* is far more knowledgeable than the majority of so-called and often self-styled military analysts. I was recalled to active duty in the Korean War, and served in the Pentagon. At that time we estimated that 60 per cent of the State Department desks were suspect and insecure. We were able to prove security leaks by counter-espionage intercepts of courier dispatch material en route from Paris to Moscow. Because of Civil Service protection and compromise problems we were unable to oust even the professed Communist sympathizers. . . ."

As a means of sampling public opinion, Father Lyons organized Catholic Polls, Inc., and began polling his readers, viewers and listeners several years ago. He used such controversial questions as the Pentagon papers and the Vietnam war. He sent the poll to random homes of 500 *Twin Circle* subscribers, half priests and half laymen. Replies were all grouped together. They are still on file in his New York office for anyone who wants to inspect them.

The first question read: "Do you feel *The New York Times* had a right to violate U.S. security laws by publishing the Pentagon papers?" Four said yes; 170 said no.

"The liberal press, radio and TV have tried to convey the impression that the vast majority of Americans approved of what *The New York Times* did," Father Dan told his readers. "Our poll, which as far as we know is the only poll taken on the subject, shows that overwhelming numbers of people condemn *The Times* for its action. The propaganda has been so bad in our news media against the role of the United States in Vietnam that we asked the second question: 'Do you feel that the United States is the aggressor in North Vietnam?' Seven said yes; 183 said no. Yet the Left Wing would have us think that many millions of Americans condemn our government as the aggressor.

"Our third question covered the other side of the issue: 'Do you feel that North Vietnam is the aggressor?' 173 said yes; seven said no. Again, it shows how strongly our readers oppose the aggression of North Vietnam. There is almost unanimous agreement that North Vietnam, not the U.S., is committing the aggression. The fourth question read: 'Do you feel the United States sought to gain any territory by fighting in Vietnam?' Our readers replied with four yeses and 173 noes. The fifth question: 'Who do you think bears the responsibility for starting the war in Indochina?' Two said the U.S.; 170 said North Vietnam."

Dan Lyons was gaining wide support now for his pro-American stand. In the minds of many, he was a wanted man and a needed man—and a stout man to have on our side. He was wanted and needed by that great, often too-silent majority who have life patterns and ideals that call for the preservation of what we have and not its destruction. His blood runs hot when he hears such militant civil rights leaders as Father James Groppi say: "We will use whatever tactics are necessary to attain our ends. We have used the brick, the bottle and the match and it has been effective on some occasions. And, along the way, Stokely Carmichael and H. Rap Brown have been our Patrick Henrys, George Washingtons and Paul Reveres. . . ."

"It is for such morally reckless, unjust and unpriestly opinions that I oppose the tactics of Father Groppi," Father Dan told us. "Such conduct is disgraceful and demeaning to the Church."

Dan Lyons believes that America is great today because it is populated by great people. He is a conservative, but he is a man of strong convictions and he will express them any time, any place. On the night of February 8, 1965, thirty-six hours after American planes first bombed North Vietnam, he received a long-distance telephone call from a student at Berkeley, California, then the scene of campus riots. "The Left Wing is demonstrating all over the campus," said the unknown voice at the other end of the line. "We want to challenge them to a debate. Can you come down?"

"I'll debate anybody the Leftists can put up—anywhere—any time," Dan said. He was Dean of Students at Gonzaga University, in Spokane, Washington, at the time, and coached the debate team. Two days later he was at the University of California debating Dr. Peter Scott. A thousand students were there, and the front rows were filled to overflowing with baited questioners. "It is obvious," Dan Lyons told the hecklers, "that some of you would rather live under Communism. But you are so few that you should pick a Communist country of your choice and go there, instead of trying to sabotage our country." He made his point. The heckling ceased.

He had just published a new book, "The Future of Vietnam," and the Berkeley students purchased 800 copies of it. Two weeks later, when the student council tried to pass a motion censuring U.S. action in Vietnam, his book was quoted from incessantly in the council chambers. P.S.: The motion lost by a 9-to-9 deadlock. Wrote the telephone caller, who turned out to be a Jewish boy from Brooklyn: "Whew!"

When James Jackson, the Communist editor of *The Worker,* was to speak at Eastern Washington State College, Father Lyons was asked to reply. "If freedom of religion means nothing to you," he told the students in his summation, "if you don't care about freedom of speech, freedom of ownership, freedom of family life, or freedom of movement—then perhaps you could get along under Mr. Jackson's system. But in that case you are a slob—S-L-O-B!"

Three thousand students cheered him.

Communist Jackson called Father Lyons "a twin brother of Rasputin," to which Father Dan replied: "The Church is an anvil that has worn out many hammers."

The President of Gonzaga asked him a few days later why he used the word "slob." "For effect," he said. "The students loved it, and it has been quoted on the radio ever since I used it."

Publishers of conservative Roman Catholic newspapers have long looked upon Patrick J. Frawley Jr., the Los

Angeles millionaire and former chairman of Eversharp, Inc., as their most reliable patron saint. For years his company was the major national advertiser in the Catholic press. It was therefore a natural step for Frawley to move directly into Catholic newspaper publishing, in 1967. At the urging of Father Lyons, he put up the money to start a new national weekly called *Twin Circle.* Appropriately, the sixteen-page tabloid published its first edition in November of that year during the Soviet Union's 50th-anniversary celebration of the Communist revolution.

Star Columnist, Editor-at-Large, and general factotum of *Twin Circle* was—Father Lyons. The new editor was Frank Morriss, who had resigned as news editor of Denver's nationally-circulated *Register,* the second largest Catholic paper in the country.

"The Soviets are celebrating 50 years of militant disbelief," Editor Morriss told a press conference at the unveiling of *Twin Circle.* "We aim to answer with an effective voice of equally militant belief."

The new paper owed its beginning and much of its hard-rock aggressiveness to Father Lyons who, as head of the New York-based Free Pacific Association, spent much of 1967 writing and lecturing around the country in support of the Vietnam war. Two years earlier he had become president of the Twin Circle Publishing Co., a new Frawley subsidiary which publishes paperback books.

Father Lyons told *Newsweek* magazine: "One reason for *Twin Circle* is that many conservative Catholic newspapers—and some Catholic bishops—have recently swung to the left on the Vietnam issue. As we see it, our paper will combat liberal Catholics who either question church dogma or erode absolute moral standards. In particular, we will give a greater voice to the Pope as the chief teacher in the Catholic Church."

Twin Circle had an initial circulation of 100,000. Every Catholic pastor in the U.S. received a trial subscription, and every Catholic grade school was offered cash for each subscription their pupils sold. Later, Father Lyons added a weekly TV series (40 cities) to his schedule, and a daily nationally-syndicated radio program in 560 cities. Now millions of Americans were feeling the Lyons influence.

Father Lyons quickly became a watchdog for the conservatives. He went after such pessimists as columnist Walter Lippman: "He seems to be the Lord Macaulay of the Twentieth Century—that is, everybody reads him, but no one believes him." To Senator Fulbright's charge that American servicemen "have made a brothel out of Saigon," he retorted: "Fulbright should be censured by Congress. One could say the same thing about government employees in Washington, D.C."

He attacked Drew Pearson, the mendacious partner of Jack Anderson, for falsely claiming, among other things, that he fought in World War I, forcing the flame-throwing syndicated columnist to defend himself weakly in this manner to Hodding Carter III, Editor of *The Delta Democrat Times,* Greenville, Mississippi: "I tried several times to enlist but was not able to make it because of a knee injury I suffered in my youth. Finally, as the war progressed and they lowered the physical standards, I was able to join the Student Army Training Corps, the equivalent of what is now the ROTC. It was a standard part of the U.S. Army, and I have an honorable discharge to prove it."

Father Lyons was the first writer in the national Catholic press to attack the policy of the diocese of Baton Rouge, Louisiana, of allowing remarried Catholics—those who were divorced and not remarried in the Church—to receive the Sacraments. His columns in *Twin Circle* and *National Catholic Register* reached the attention of official Vatican quarters. Subsequently condemned by Rome, the Baton Rouge policy was stopped six weeks after it was condemned in Lyons' columns.

Father Lyons' personal philosophy is essentially simple: "The future does not belong to those who preach hatred and injustice. The future belongs to those who love and who practice justice." By justice he means observing the absolute moral laws of God, then loving and serving Him.

He has no tolerance for so-called "doves" when faced with aggression. He asks, "Do you know my definition of a dove? It is a pretty bird that has no defense against a bird of prey. The only flight for the doves we see today is from reality. They have no defense against aggression. They never come up with any realistic conclusions. They never tell us where they would draw the line. They never say what countries they would abandon and what countries, if any, they propose to defend. They never say why getting out of Vietnam would be fair and square for the Vietnamese, or why such an abandonment, however polite, would lead to world peace. They never admit that surrender might encourage other wars of liberation against free peoples."

One of Father Dan's staunchest supporters is a Presbyterian minister from Montreat, N.C., named Calvin Thielman. He is Billy Graham's pastor. Rev. Thielman accompanied Father Dan to Vietnam on one of his trips in 1966. They went to the war zone as personal representatives of President Lyndon B. Johnson. Rev. Thielman and the President were fellow Texans. Before entering the seminary as a young man, he had campaigned hard for Johnson in Texas. So when Rev. Thielman returned from Vietnam, the President told him, "I'm going to make you Chaplain at the White House." The appointment carried with it the grade of full colonel in the Air Force.

"The President, however, didn't keep his promise," Father Lyons told me. "A newspaper columnist for one of the Washington papers got wind of it, criticized LBJ for it, and the proposal was dropped like a hot potato. Johnson let a local news columnist intimidate him, in other words. That was too bad. Rev. Thielman would have been an excellent influence for good around the White House. He's a great and devoted Christian."

After Father Lyons and Rev. Thielman had finished making their report to the President, the latter stayed on as a guest of LBJ's at the White House for several more days. One morning, he bumped into the President in the hallway.

"Mr. President," he said, "that's a splendid suit you're wearing. You look mighty sharp."

The President said, "I don't feel so sharp."

Later in the day, Rev. Thielman missed his lunch while waiting to get in to see the President, so he asked one of the White House servants to bring him a roast beef sandwich. The sandwich was an hour in coming. When the servant did bring it, Rev. Thielman was in with the President and never did get it.

That evening, Rev. Thielman had an 8:30 dinner appointment with the President. When they were finally seated, the President confided to the pastor that he usually ate dinner at 7:30, but that he had had a roast beef sandwich at 5:15 and thus was eating an hour later.

He said, "Say, Calvin, wasn't that your sandwich?"

"Yes, Sir—and you ate it!"

"Well, I didn't know what else to do. The boy brought it, asked me who it was for, and I said I didn't know, but I'd take it."

"But your family has you on a strict diet."

"If you won't tell, I won't tell."

The President considered that sandwich a victory of sorts. With the way the war had been going in Vietnam, victories were few and far between.

Father Dan and Rev. Thielman have built a warm friendship over the years. The Presbyterian minister's respect for the Jesuit priest was revealed recently in this letter:

"Dear Danny:

> I wish you would come and see us. The family often speaks of you and nothing would give us a happier lift than to have you come to Montreat for a good visit.
>
> Last Saturday, I read an account in our local newspaper by some religion writer, regarding you and the *Twin Circle* and Patrick Frawley. I know how you feel. You can remember when Aubrey Brown of the

Presbyterian *Outlook* did me in—I want you to know that you are in pretty good company, having incurred this particular liberal's wrath. He regularly tromps on Billy Graham and anyone else who happens to be evangelical or conservative. So please don't be bothered about it.

Danny, this morning Mrs. Billy Graham telephoned me to say that she is to participate in a television panel dealing with the damage that pornography is doing to America's young people. You had some of the finest articles on this I have ever read, and if it is not too much trouble, could you please send copies of these to me and I will see that Mrs. Graham gets them. I know she will appreciate your help, and I want to commend you and encourage you again on your work.

Your friend in Christ,
CALVIN."

Father Dan once commented to Presbyterian Dr. Thielman that his parents must have been very religious to name him Calvin. "Yes, they were," he replied. "I was named after Coolidge."

Few Jesuits in recent times have purposely embroiled themselves in more public controversy than Father Lyons. In May, 1972, he formed an organization called United Ireland, and asked for participants to help him tell the story of the persecution of the Catholic people in Northern Ireland.

When you live with the Irish for four years, as Father Lyons did, you come to know and love them. He said, "No pen can capture the special blend of hospitality in Ireland because it is spiritual. They do not greet you or bid you goodby. They bless you, coming and going. I have heard hundreds of Irish blessings, usually in very few words. This is what they say or mean to say: 'May the Saints protect you, and sorrow neglect you. Bad luck to the one that does not respect you. The top of the morning to all that belong to you. Long life to your honor! That is my song to you.' Now you know what they mean when they say, 'God bless.' "

Some years ago, Father Lyons visited John Hearne, the Irish Ambassador in Washington, D.C. He told the ambassador, "May the wind always be at your back." From the vantage point of 70 years, the ambassador replied, "Ah, Father Dan, it's always in your face, after fifty."

Dr. Anthony T. Bouscaren, author of many books and a professor of political science, points out that history is made by human beings and not by blind economic forces and chance. He told me, "Churchill turned Britain around in 1940. DeGaulle twice did the same for France. And William F. Buckley, Jr., made conservatism popular in America, beginning with 'God and Man at Yale.' Now Father Lyons has rallied the traditionalist and loyalist Catholic forces in the U.S. almost alone. And he has done it at a time when the Church has been under siege. He is an inspiration to thousands. He is demonstrating what ONE man can do."

In 1967, Father Lyons organized what is today known as the National Committee for the Liberation of China, Inc. His national council included such distinguished Americans as Dean Clarence Manion, Taylor Caldwell, Father Raymond J. De Jaegher, Dr. Walter Judd, Dr. Anthony Kubek, Maj.-Gen. Thomas A. Lane (Ret.), Eugene Lyons, Dr. Stephen C. Y. Pan, Brig.-Gen. Clyde Watts (Ret.), Dr. Stefan T. Possony, and Fred Schlafly, among others. When their attorney appeared in Albany, New York, for the purpose of incorporation, he was asked by state officials, "Does Father Lyons have any troops?"

The lawyer replied, "No."

"Oh. In that case, it will come under the heading of Education."

One prominent Jesuit, a Dean at Seattle University, feels that Father Lyons is the logical answer to the Father Berrigans of the Church. He made the following comparison:

"The courage of Lyons in espousing an unpopular position recalls the distinction between true and false prophets in the Old Testament. One criterion of the false prophet is that he told the people what they wanted to hear and not the frequently unpleasant, upsetting Word of God which was good for them. If Berrigan has become the idol of so much of the secular press (such as *Newsweek*), the reason may well be that he is this type of false prophet —uttering what they want to hear rather than what is true! Berrigan, in my opinion, is a pop martyr, glorified on the covers of national magazines. He has shed not a drop of blood for his mod views.

"Lyons stands for the traditional Christian values of self-sacrifice, self-discipline, the mystery of the Cross, and redemptive suffering (unpopularity, humiliation, etc.). It takes courage to undergo the lot of the true prophet. Father Lyons will never appear on the covers of mod magazines.

His justification of loyalty to and defense of country are not mod ideas for those who will not suffer any inconvenience to defend family, friends, and nation, because of their selfishness, indifference, and lack of character. *No greater love has a man than to lay down his life for his friends*—St. John's words still hold for Lyons; whereas Berrigan says no principle is worth a human life. Christ might have 'saved' his life acting on the Berrigan principle. And Christ might have avoided insisting on the truth of his mission.

"Lyons defends the Church; Berrigan always attacks it, mocks it, in his prima donna fashion. Lyons is not seeking himself. His style is ordinary, not theatrical. Lyons is consistent with his collar. He is loyal to the institution he represents. Berrigan is financially sustained by an institution which he is consistently discrediting in his exhibitionistic fashion. Patriotism, loyalty to nation and Church are Lyons' qualities: love of neighbor. Berrigan loves far-off neighbors (Communists, etc.) but not his *real neighbors* in the U.S.A. and Church.

"Berrigan tends to make Vietnam the world's only moral issue. Lyons sees that Christian living involves many moral principles. He is more democratic in that he listens to the voices of the people of South Vietnam, Formosa and elsewhere; Berrigan would rather achieve 'peace' by letting the Reds have them. Berrigan ignores the people in affliction; whereas Lyons is compassionate.

"According to Father James Schall, S.J., of the California Province, Lyons and his associate, Ken Baker, S.J., probably have more genuine influence in the United States than any other Jesuits of their Oregon Province; among U.S. Jesuits, they'd rank in the Top Ten. Lyons is the spokesman for traditional values, for community as opposed to prima donnaism in the Church and politics. He is for traditional American and Catholic values of work, sobriety, collaboration, integrity, and community. His great service lies in representing views many of his confreres are afraid to represent for fear of opprobrium. He contributes to the democratic process of debate by representing positions held by the majority of Americans not in control of the national media. He contributes to freedom by contributing to the great debate with his radically clear statements on moral, social, religious and other issues. He balances off Berrigan in Jesuit circles. He prevents Berrigan from becoming the sole spokesman for U.S. Jesuits and all Catholics."

Father Lyons has not been shy about lambasting the Berrigan brothers in the national press. On February 9, 1971, the Manchester, N.H., *Union Leader* carried this headline: "BERRIGAN BROS. 'PATSYS' FOR REDS, SAYS PRIEST." Father Lyons had struck again. "The Berrigans," he said, "are a strange mixture of exhibitionism and anti-Americanism. How can they, as priests, be so indifferent to the take-over of one-third of the world by militant atheism? Democracy is bad, they say, but Communism—well, it's not so bad.

"The Berrigans are patsys for the Communist line. Is there any way in which their position differs from that of Hanoi? No, there is not. Do they have any sympathy for the people in South Vietnam who want to stay free? No, they do not. For six years I have been invited to debate

Father Daniel Berrigan. I have always said 'gladly,' but he has never been willing to debate. He is convinced, I am told, that he gets his information directly from above, so that he does not have to defend it. On the other hand, I have debated Father Philip Berrigan a number of times, principally at Purdue, Notre Dame, and the University of Cincinnati; but it was hopeless trying to keep him on the subject. His arguments wouldn't hold up in any debate beyond the freshman level. He deals not in discourse, but in diatribe. As for his brother Dan, let's stop pretending he is brilliant—he is not even balanced!"

The life of Father Lyons is the story of one man's fight for freedom. He has spoken to audiences from Dublin to Formosa, from Fairbanks to Johannesburg. To his friends he is "That Travellin' Man" who logs 15,000 miles a month when he is "at home." To United Air Lines he is a million-miler; to his associates he is perpetual motion. To the tens of thousands who have heard him lecture, to the millions who have heard him on radio and TV, he is the voice of freedom crying out against Communism.

He is a voice in the wilderness of compromise, demanding that Vietnam, East Germany, Cuba and Red China be set free "as a start." He is chairman of the Free Pacific Association, Inc., and the Asian Speakers' Bureau. His columns are the most widely-read feature in the Catholic press. His hard-hitting, pull-no-punches views are carried anonymously by 1,250 newspapers through the U.S. Press Association, and for some years on 560 radio stations and 40 television outlets. He currently appears several times a week as a guest on TV and radio programs throughout the country.

He founded Catholic Polls, Inc., which polled every priest in America on Vietnam and China with startling results. He has visited Saigon seventeen different times in seven years. In 1965, he was sent there by the U.S. Defense Department on temporary duty. In June, 1966, he was dispatched to Vietnam by the White House to report on the work of private relief agencies. In September, 1966, he was decorated by the Republic of China for his relentless battle on behalf of freedom. In December, 1966, he visited East Germany, Thailand, Hong Kong, Macao, Taiwan, and Korea, taking soundings on Red China. In March, 1967, he visited Rhodesia and other parts of Africa.

Father Lyons is founder of the Twin Circle Publishing Company, Inc. He is a director of the East Asian Research Institute, Inc. He carries a portable typewriter wherever he goes. While traveling on the plane, or in his room after the debate is over, he is busy typing late into the night. His book, "Vietnam Crisis," written in collaboration with Dr. Stephen Pan in 1966, has sold more than 150,000 copies. Other volumes, such as "The Voice of Peking" and "Left of Liberal," have met with similar success.

Some of Father Lyons' biggest debates have come not outside the Church, but *within* the Church. He has never been shy about throwing verbal punches. In July, 1969, for example, the *National Catholic Reporter* ran this quotation in its lead article: "Until we get rid of the clergy, we cannot hope to change anything." Father Lyons answered the cynicism in his next editorial:

"The statement was supposedly made by 'a theologian.' So-called 'theologians' make a lot of damn-fool statements from time to time. What kind of 'change' did the cynic have in mind, and why was the anonymous statement so prominently featured? Doesn't NCR realize it has featured so many shocking attacks on the Church that it has lost its ability to shock?

"In the same issue, on page two, the question is asked for the umpteenth time: 'Why are virtually all the American Catholic hierarchy so silent on the war?' NCR suggests bitterly that it is because the bishops are afraid they might lose Federal funds.

"The fact of the matter, which NCR seems afraid to admit, is that all of the U.S. bishops made it very clear in their annual statement of 1966 that: (1) a nation has the right to defend another nation against aggression; (2) we should have confidence in the basic policy of our government in helping to defend South Vietnam; (3) the bishops quoted the Vatican Council to prove that soldiers who fight against aggression are 'instruments of security and freedom on behalf of their people.' The bishops have since reiterated their position. What bugs the NCR is not that the bishops have not spoken out, but that the bishops have not changed their position, despite all the confusion spread by such writers as themselves.

"Father Patrick O'Connor, an Irish Columban who spent the past 15 years in Vietnam, told me two years ago about an interview he had with NCR's reporter, Tom Fox, after the latter arrived in Saigon. 'Tom,' he said, 'I read your article about how the Catholic Church received a lot of money from the Government during the Diem administration. I was here in those years, and have never been able to pin down any facts on the subject. Would you mind sharing your facts with me?' Father Pat, the official reporter for many years for *National Catholic News Service,* was known for his conscientiousness. Imagine his disgust when NCR's reporter admitted that his only source was two college students.

"The second lead story on page 1 of the same issue was about a poll being taken of 40,000 U.S. priests who are being asked to sign what they call an 'anti-war' statement against the defense of South Vietnam. The only poll ever taken of all 59,000 Catholic priests in this country was taken by Twin Circle Publishing Company, in 1966, before our paper started. Of the 8,500 replies, 87 per cent declared the war in Vietnam should be won quickly."

The year 1969 was a year of bitter turmoil inside the Catholic Church. Father Lyons would soften that description, however. In a note to me, he referred to it as "a rather fascinating interlude." To illustrate some of the inner-feeling, he gave me a letter he had received from Dale Francis, his close colleague over the last ten years. It was dated November 17, 1969, and was written just after Dale had returned to his Huntington, Indiana, home from a certain Ohio city, where he had talked to all the priests of a diocese there.

"Dear Father Lyons:

I feel a little like the sparrow that accidentally ran into a badminton game.

I spoke on the sense of disorientation that exists among the people today, not opposing the changes but saying that the people had been disoriented in this time of change, would be more disoriented with the introduction of the new liturgy, suggesting compassion for them and the necessity of establishing new points of reference and orientation by stressing those things that cannot be changed in the Church.

I think this went fairly well, but what happened in the discussion afterwards totally confused me. First of all, most of the discussion had no reference to what I said and seemed directed to others present. For example, a young priest with long sideburns got up and said, 'Priests are judged not by what they say but what they do. The priest who gives a beautiful sermon but then shows by his life he does not practice what he preaches is considered a phony.' I can only guess that he was striking out at some priest in the group. A pastor, from the same town as the young priest, then got up and said something about priests who try to please young people without realizing they'll be older people. Then someone got up and said that it is not the young people who support the Church. Then another priest got up and said that those in authority in the Church didn't listen to their priests. All of this went on and on and I didn't know what to say. It had nothing to do with what I had said, and I don't think it was in any way directed toward what I had said.

Then there were a couple of priests who seemed at least to know I'd spoken. One said the trouble was we had to establish value systems instead of rules, but I could only say I'd not disagree, but there were value systems and value systems—that saying we should establish value systems meant nothing unless we explained what value systems we had in mind. Then another priest responded directly to me but seemed to be thinking I was a traditionalist against all change, which wasn't what I said at all and was totally irrelevant to my point.

Summing it all up, most of the hour's discussion seemed to me to be a battle between the priests, directed toward one another. It amounted to almost a brawl, because I could tell the priests were really emotional about the things they were saying. The chancellor, when he closed, said he couldn't remember any time a clergy conference had brought this much discussion, but my own feelings were that it wasn't as much discussion as internal bickering. The bishop said he liked my talk and agreed with me. I told him I didn't know what most of the priests were talking about, and he looked a little grim and replied, 'That's because they don't know what they are talking about themselves.'

I learned later that there have been three or four priests who have left in the last few weeks, a few more who have romances going on and are expecting to marry. What a night. . . ."

What has been the Church's official position toward Father Lyons and his stands? Has there ever been a move within the Society to censor him? Listen:

"When I first started lecturing in the Spring of 1964, after my first trip to Vietnam, it was the custom that when I was asked to give a lecture, I would go to my Superior, in that case the president of Gonzaga University, and he would write to the Provincial in Portland, who would then write to the bishop of the diocese where I was to lecture. The bishop, in turn, would write back to the Provincial, and he to the president at Gonzaga. If it was to be a lecture in another Province, my Provincial would write to his counterpart of that Province, and he would write to the bishop, and back again.

"But all this was after the second Vatican Council, and change was possible. I began giving two and three lectures a week in different cities, and I simply neglected to write to anyone for permission. I just cleared with my own Superior. It was a welcome change which made it easier for others.

"Similarly, when I started writing a weekly column for *Our Sunday Visitor,* I had to submit the column each week to the president of Gonzaga, who gave it to two censors unknown to me. They took two weeks to go over each column. If a change was suggested, it might have to go back for approval. It was an extremely cumbersome system, obviously not intended for a weekly columnist, particularly one who was a current affairs columnist, as I was listed on the masthead. But that was the traditional system.

"Early in 1966, I arranged with my Provincial to have the editor of *Our Sunday Visitor,* Msgr. Joseph Crowley, appointed as my censor. That made it automatic, and very quick. Later, after becoming editor of *Twin Circle,* I became my own censor. That is the way it has gone ever since.

"I have never been threatened with a legal suit, nor has anyone in authority in the Church hinted I should be censored. That charge remained for Senator Fulbright to make. I had been on the radio in Washington, D.C., every day for about two years, when Fulbright was holding hearings to investigate Gerald Smith's nomination as head negotiator for the SALT talks. As I often pointed out in my regular radio broadcasts, I had no faith whatever in negotiations with the Communists, either at SALT conferences or elsewhere.

"Fulbright had obviously been listening to my radio programs while riding to work at 9:20 a.m. daily. So when the hearings were published, this is what he was recorded as saying: 'Mr. Smith, you don't believe it is a waste of time to try negotiating with the leaders in Moscow, do you? You certainly don't agree with Father Lyons, who is on the radio every morning, who says it is a waste of time, do you? (Denials from Smith, who was looking for employment.) Yet in spite of the policy of our government, this Father Lyons is on the radio every morning, denouncing the idea of negotiations. . . .' Poor Senator Fulbright. Free speech was often not allowed before his committee, and the idea it existed elsewhere was hard for him to swallow."

Father Lyons is well aware of his national image as a "hawk." In fact, he tells a story on himself about the morning in Saigon when he showed up a little early (6:30 a.m.) for breakfast at General Westmoreland's home. While waiting for the general to arrive, he chatted amiably with a young Brigadier General, who was Westy's aide. The aide told Father Lyons that the night before, General Westmoreland had said to his two house guests, a Rear Admiral and a Vice-Admiral from Cincpac: "Do you know who the biggest *hawk* in the United States is?" One guessed Lyndon Johnson, the other someone else, but General Westmoreland said: "No! It's Father Dan Lyons—

and he's going to have breakfast with us in the morning!"

General Westmoreland endorsed the strong stand of Father Lyons. He used to give away many copies of the the padre's book, "Vietnam Crisis." He liked Father Lyons, was always most cordial to him, and on several occasions put Father Lyons up at his home overnight, sometimes for a week or 10 days, though there were only a few beds in the house.

One time when Father Lyons visited Saigon he was in town for only a few days. So he phoned Westmoreland's aide (a person unknown to Father) and told him he would like to make a breakfast appointment with the General. The aide said it was hopeless on such short notice, and explained that the General was leaving that very next morning at 10:30 for a field inspection trip.

"Just tell him Father Lyons is in town and would like to meet him at his home for breakfast."

"Yes, sir."

A half-hour later the aide phoned back and said the General wanted to have breakfast with Father Lyons at his home at 7 the next morning.

At breakfast, the General talked leisurely to Father Lyons about the war. An hour stretched into two hours. Father tried to excuse himself, saying he knew how busy the General was. But Westmoreland was most gracious.

"Come on, Father," he said, "ride with me to my office. I want to talk to you some more."

The drive to "Pentagon East," as the military offices had come to be dubbed, was about six miles and took them through downtown Saigon and out toward Tan Son Nhut airport. When they arrived, Father Lyons tried to excuse himself once again, but the General insisted he go inside with him. There they chatted some more. The General knew how Father Lyons felt about the strategy of the war: that Haiphong should be mined.

"If the political pressure is too great for Washington," Father Lyons added, "then Saigon could carry it out."

The General nodded.

"The South Vietnamese could do it," he agreed.

Then a colonel walked in, carrying maps and data to show the General what had been happening out in the battle zones. Father Lyons knew it was time, surely, for him to bow out. But no, the General pulled Father's chair alongside his, and had him take in the briefing with him.

There was something of a mutual admiration society between Father Lyons and General Westmoreland. This was borne out in a recent exchange of letters. On July 31, 1972, Father Lyons wrote to commend the General on the occasion of his retirement as Chief of Staff:

"Dear General Westmoreland:

> Particularly since our visits in Saigon over the years, I have followed your distinguished career with much interest and admiration. Knowing you, I am sure you will continue to serve our country in varied and effective ways.
>
> But at this point a word of commendation is in order: Heartfelt congratulations on a job well done!
>
> You may be interested in the enclosed clipping about our readers' reaction to the closing of Haiphong. That they responded so highly in favor is a modest tribute to our efforts to keep them informed. Much of what I told them I learned from you and your associates in

Vietnam. I will always recall with fondness your hospitality to me, and those wonderful porch breakfasts in Saigon.

Renewed congratulations!

Cordially,
DAN LYONS, S.J."

General Westmoreland's reply was dated August 10, 1972:

"Dear Father Lyons:

Indeed it was a great pleasure to receive your letter. I have missed seeing you in recent years and have often wondered how you were getting along. Quite obviously all is well with you and you are continuing your very commendable efforts to present practical problems in their true light.

Your warm words on the occasion of my retirement are deeply appreciated. The several times that you visited me in Vietnam were pleasant occasions and our discussions very helpful to me. Any extension of hospitality that I may have offered you was more than offset by the pleasure of your company.

My very best wishes to you.

Sincerely,
W. C. WESTMORELAND
General, U.S. Army (Ret.)"

Neither profit nor personal glory motivates Father Lyons. He is a responsible, seasoned newsman—a great reporter. Through his widely-read column he has become something of a national conscience. He is blunt, he is literal, he is selfless. And he is dedicated to what he conceives to be America's high destiny: Leader of the Free World. Speaking of America's potential to an audience in New

York, he said, "This country was founded on the broad shoulders of dedicated, patriotic men who were able to think clearly. Men like George Washington were no more in love with war than you or I. But he did tell us, in 1793, that to secure peace it must be known that we are at all times ready for war. The first rule in war, of course, is very simple: *Know your enemy*. But the modern-day liberal is never sure. . . .

"I speak to groups all over America because I believe very strongly in the power of the enemy through the Cold War, and that our form of government will not survive if we leave everything up to the government. Admiral Arleigh Burke has said: 'The existence of freedom will continue to depend upon the ability of free people to better understand their own national strategy in relation to the Communist challenge.'

"I believe that. I also believe that the U.S. is at the brink of disaster by men who lack faith, who are defeatists, and who tremble like cowards at the mere mention of such phony scare words as escalation, proliferation, provocation, and confrontation. Where is their courage? Where is their loyalty?"

In August, 1971, Father Lyons visited South America. It was a 15-day, 8500-mile fact-finding trip. Going along with him was Chris Manion, a graduate student in political theory at Notre Dame. The pair spent six months preparing for the journey. In their spare time, they had read and researched the countries they were visiting, kept files, and did their homework. Chris had spent a year in Mexico learning Spanish, and Father Lyons was able to lean on him as an expert interpreter.

Father Lyons is convinced that the trouble spot of the 1970s is going to be Latin America, so he wanted to update his ideas and find out all he could. He wrote ahead for contacts, both with laymen and with priests. The Maryknoll Fathers were especially helpful. The two Americans stayed with them in Peru, Bolivia and Chile.

In Lima, they had a lot of contacts, starting with the Victorero family. Their daughter Lillian has worked as secretary in Father Lyons' New York office since 1966. So her former pastor, Father Thomas Garrity, M.M., took Father Lyons and Chris to see Cardinal Landazuri, Primate of Peru. During the introductions, the Cardinal turned to Father Lyons and inquired: "Are you a Maryknoll?"

"Worse than that. I'm a *Jesuit.*"

Father Garrity explained, "He's a *periodista* (journalist)."

"Oh," the Primate said, "that is the worst of all!"

Another story? Well, Clymer Wright, a lifelong Texan and hardline editor of *The Houston Tribune,* was complaining to a small group of fellow Southwesterners at a conference how disappointed he was in the selection of guest speakers who had been appearing at Southern Methodist Church in Houston.

"The Methodists are letting me down," he groaned. "I can't stomach any more of those Leftist radicals they've been bringing in.

"So I joined the Southern Baptist," he said, "and now

look at them. They're bringing in the militants and rabble-rousers like it was a Communist holiday!"

Just then, Father Dan Lyons, S.J., walked into the room. Wright spotted him immediately and, half-pleading, said: "Father, how are things going in *your* Church?"

"You mean you want to join?" Father Dan said. "How desperate can you get!"

CHAPTER 2

A Priest's Priest

Father Ken Baker, S.J., was precise and confident. He clipped the tips from six stems of asparagus with two strokes of his knife. He chewed in careful cadence and his conversation was friendly, yet as sharply defined as the white collar he was wearing.

"I hope you're in good shape?" he said.

"Why?" I said. It's my best word.

"Because you're writing about a man whose only recreation is work. Dan works eighteen hours a day. He's been doing it for over thirty years."

"Doesn't he ever take a break?"

"Once in a while he will go to a movie—and then go back to his office and write a column about what he has seen."

"When did you first meet Father Dan?" I asked.

"In 1961," he replied.

"What were the circumstances?"

"Well, I had just returned from my studies in Europe and was assigned to teach philosophy at Gonzaga. That same year Dan was named Dean of Students there. He lived in one of the dorms and I lived in the faculty residence. Actually I didn't get to know him very well that first year. Our paths seldom crossed."

"What was his image in those days?" I wanted to know.

"He was known to be rigorous and tough on those kids who were caught drinking. But, remember, ten years ago things were different. Drinking on most campuses was not tolerated. If a kid got out of serious line at Gonzaga, Dan sent him home. Plenty of them."

"Wasn't it about that time that Father Dan began branching out a little bit?"

"Yes," he said. "He began to write a regular column for *Our Sunday Visitor.*"

"The largest Catholic weekly in the country," I said.

"Yes. With about a million readers."

"When did you and Father Dan begin working together in New York?"

"Wait, let me tell you this story first. On February 1, 1970, I became the fourth president of Seattle University. Like Dan, I was known for my strong and uncompromising views on Catholic education. I have always felt there was a need for our schools to remain Catholic. It was for this reason that I was picked to run Seattle U. One of the first persons who wrote to congratulate me on the new position—and to encourage me to make a strong Catholic school out of SU—was Dan."

"In the meantime, of course, he had written the best-seller, *Vietnam Crisis,* and had become nationally-known as a columnist-lecturer."

"That's right. I was very pleased to hear from him."

"What happened at SU?"

"I ran into problems. A number of the Regents—most of them non-Catholic—refused to go along with my efforts to make the university into an uncompromised Catholic institution. They were holdovers from the two previous administrations. And so, on November 1, I was forced to resign. I'd lasted only nine months."

"What did you do then?"

"Well, I rested for about a month at Marquette University, where I had taken my graduate studies in theology, and still had a number of friends. Afterwards, I flew on to New York to appear on Bill Buckley's popular TV show, 'Firing Line,' with Mother Elizabeth McCormick. The subject for discussion was higher education. Bill was very hard on Mother McCormick for her active role in the de-Catholicizing of Manhattanville College, in Westchester County. Incidentally, there's an interesting account of this show, from Bill's point of view, in his book, *Cruising Speed.* Well, the day after finishing the show I took the Metroliner to Washington, D.C., with my friend, Father John Navone, S.J., from the Gregorian University in Rome. Father Navone, like Dan, is a native of Seattle."

"What was the purpose of your trip to Washington?"

"Seattle University was in serious financial straits, and Father Navone and I went there to try and get some grant money for needed programs."

"Was there any specific reason for the money problems at Seattle U.?"

"Most definitely. To get me to resign, the Regents had temporarily chopped off all support. Unless I quit, they were threatening to force the school into bankruptcy. It was a very real crisis."

"Did you meet Father Dan in Washington?"

"No, New York. After finishing our work in Washington, we went back up to New York to visit some friends. The last evening there, we browsed around Saks Fifth Avenue. At 4:30, we began to think about what we should do that evening. Dinner at Fordham and a visit with old friends was one possibility. Then I remembered that Dan Lyons was living in New York and that he had just returned from Manila, where he had covered the Asian Conference of Bishops and at which Pope Paul VI attended. I told Father John that Dan would probably be able to give us some good first-hand information on the Conference. I told him, 'Let's call him and invite him to dinner.' "

"Was he at his office?"

"Where else? Not only was he at his desk, but he answered the phone. He was happy to hear from us, he was free that night, and he said he would be right down to pick us up. He said, 'Meet me in front of St. Patrick's Cathedral, 5:30.' An hour later, he drove up in front of the Church in a battered old green Volkswagen. Right on time. We drove over to the New York Athletic Club for dinner, and to catch up on the news. He told us all about his work, with gusto, and about his trip to Manila. And he told us about *Twin Circle,* and about *National Catholic*

Register. About half-way through dinner, I said, 'Dan, do you have any suggestions about where an ex-college president can find a job? I'm out of work.' 'It's tough to be a has-been,' he said, 'at 41.' I am the youngest Jesuit ex-president in the country.

"At first Dan did not give me a straight answer. Then, during the dessert, he suddenly said, 'Ken, how would you like to be editor of *Homiletic & Pastoral Review?*' I said, 'What's the deal?' Then he gave me the details."

"That's the magazine that goes out to about 17,000 priests, isn't it?"

"Yes."

"And it was up for sale?"

"Yes."

"But Dan doesn't consider himself a theologian."

"That's the point. I am a theologian, and he figured we could go together and buy the magazine for our Province. I would be the editor and he would handle the finances. I told him I was interested."

"Who owned the magazine at the time?"

"Jack Wagner. His grandfather had started it in 1898. The very next morning, Dan phoned him and set up an appointment for that afternoon. He wasted no time. He moved right in and made Mr. Wagner an offer. Apparently it was the best one he received, because, when the other bids were in, Wagner accepted. Two weeks later, I met Dan in Portland, Oregon, for a meeting with our Provincial, Father Kenneth Galbraith. Dan explained the deal to him. He was sympathetic, but told us that we were on our own. He said the Province could not help us financially. He flatly told us we would have to find our own way to finance the purchase of the magazine. Dan said he didn't need the Province's help, all he wanted was Father Galbraith's permission to close the deal. *Twin Circle* was not involved, and Dan planned to turn the magazine over to the Province, as soon as it was paid for.

"When was the sale actually consummated?"

"In early January, 1971."

"Did you take over the magazine immediately?"

"Not until March 1st."

"And so you moved from Seattle to New York."

"On January 15th, I packed all my gear at Seattle University and moved into the top floor of the residence at 86 Riverside Drive, where Dan stays. He had a room all prepared for me. It had been a storeroom, but he had it cleaned up and had bought all the furniture I needed for a simple living room."

"Suddenly you fellows were in the magazine business."

"Dan got right to work assembling a staff to help us. First, he hired his old friend, Bernard Belson, a great little fellow, to be our office manager."

"A Jew—working for the Jesuits?"

"Sure, why not? I'd say about forty per cent of Dan's staff are non-Catholic. Lillian Victorero, Dan's secretary from Peru, was also put to work in charge of our circulation, ably assisted by Dan's Haitian secretary, Claire Nelson. We all worked very well together. One of the first things Dan did was to send out a promotional brochure to 45,000 priests. This mailing produced nearly 3,000 new subscribers."

"Father Dan is quite a promoter."

"What impressed me most about him," Father Baker said, "was his decisiveness and keen business sense."

"That's something you don't normally expect to see in a Jesuit priest," I said. "Especially one who has spent his life with books, and not with hard-nosed merchants and shrewd promoters."

"But," Father Baker said, "I saw very quickly that Dan was really a great promoter himself. Give him any good cause for the Church, for the country, for the family and good morals, and he really shines."

"What was his approach to the magazine?" I asked. "Did it make money at first?"

"Dan saw immediately from the Profit-Loss sheet that the magazine was a money-maker. And judging from our early mail, he also saw that it is an instrument for much good among Catholic priests in America."

"What sort of deal did Jack Wagner give you?"

"Dan did not tell Wagner that he had no money. He simply said that we needed three years to pay off the full price. He told Wagner he felt the $100,000 he was asking was a fair price, even though he knew three or four others had tried to buy it for less. I think Dan's attitude made a point with Wagner right from the start."

"Did you make a downpayment?"

"Yes, of $5,000. Dan agreed to it without knowing where he would get it. Then he sent a copy of the magazine to his friend in Alabama, Mrs. Roberts Blount, and told her about the deal. She phoned three days later, and told Father she was sending him $5,000— though he had not mentioned any figure to her, or asked for her help. She simply said: 'Father, the idea is splendid. I just got $10,000 from the bank, and I'm going to send you half.' When he tried to thank her, she replied: 'You knew I'd help you, Father. You knew I would.' She has helped us ever since."

"How has the magazine been doing in this first year of operation?"

Father Baker smiled.

"Dan's almost got it paid off already. I told you he was a great business man."

I said, "Father Dan is becoming something of a legend, the way he uses the airplane. His office seems to be in the sky."

Father Baker said, "He makes constant use of all the inventions of the Technological Age. He is in the air constantly. He thinks nothing of flying from New York to Los Angeles or to Europe on a few hours notice. Distance is just no serious consideration for him."

"I know," I said. "Recently, he was in Los Angeles on business. He phoned me at my home in Tacoma and said, 'I'm on my way back to New York for an important meeting tomorrow morning. Why don't you meet me at Sea-Tac Airport this afternoon and I'll come around that way? We'll be able to talk for a couple of hours.' He did, too. I took my tape recorder, United Airlines gave us the use of their executive guest offices, and we spent two hours together working on material for this book. Six hours later, Father Dan was back on the phone, calling me from his office in New York. I like his style."

Father Baker said, "He's on the telephone a great deal

each day. His phone bill runs about $600 a month. He makes terrific use of long-distance calls. If it is something that promotes his work, cost is no consideration to him. He takes a plane as readily as most people climb into their cars to drive down to the nearest supermarket."

I said, "He has a lot of friends, doesn't he?"

"There's no class distinction about him," Father Baker said. "They range from the White House to the lowliest peasant. Dan makes friends wherever he goes. Many of his good friends are folk he has met on his trips; many of them on airplanes in different parts of the world. He'll do anything for his friends, too. I have seen him loan some of them money when they are short and never ask for it back. Recently, one of his very liberal friends, with whom he disagrees on almost everything except the existence of God, was desperately in need of some cash and called Dan. There were no questions, no hesitation. Dan gave him the money immediately."

I said, "Did you hear the story about the Irish priest who visited him and was robbed? Dan had loaned him his beat-up green VW, and when he returned to Dan's office a few days later he left the car parked just outside the front door. Well, he was inside for only thirty minutes or so and went out to the car to get something. He was shocked to discover that someone had broken into the car and stolen his suitcase and all his clothes. They didn't get his money, camera or passport, but his clothes were gone. It was cold and he had no overcoat. So Father Dan took off his own coat and insisted the Irish missionary take it."

"That was the third coat he had given away that winter.

That's what I mean," Father Baker said. "Dan is very human. He never seems to lose his composure. He smiles and laughs a lot. Nothing seems to bother him."

I said, "Not even those national and Church controversies he embroils himself in? He can fight pretty hard."

"Sure," Father Baker conceded, "he can get terribly mad on some issues, but it doesn't last long. In a few minutes his blood has cooled and he'll laugh again."

I said, "I notice that he seems to generally be on good terms even with those columnists who attack him in their papers."

Father Baker grinned.

"Last April," he said, "he met Msgr. S. J. Adamo, who regularly attacks him in his column in *America,* the Jesuit magazine. But there was no explosion. They had a pleasant chat, laughed, and wished each other well. That's my point. I think Dan has respect for people he disagrees with. He keeps his professional and personal feelings separate. Personally, he is very gracious to them, while he may be very sharp in his written attacks on their ideas or proposals. He did say, though, that he was glad Msgr. Adamo did not have those initials 'S.J.' after his name."

I said, "I don't think I've ever met a priest with more important irons in the fire than Father Dan. He has to be the busiest priest in all Christiandom."

"He once commented," said Father Baker, "that if he took some of those irons out of the fire, the others would get hot. He's involved in so many different activities it's impossible to keep track. He used to have calling cards for all his different operations, but now he has done away with that and just has a simple card with his name, address, and phone number. He claims he has more fronts than the Communists."

I said, "There is lots of talk these days among seminarians and young priests about getting out of the sanctuary and into the world to influence it. Wouldn't you say Father Dan is a shining example of this?"

"Very much so," Father Baker said. "He's been doing this for more than ten years. It's nothing new to him. He's leading the parade."

I said, "Father, if you had to sum up Father Dan's life in a sentence, what would you say?"

"Well," he replied, "he's a man who is very loyal to God—to America—to family—and he has dedicated himself to the kind of work that will help them to prosper and grow."

CHAPTER 3

Priest-Commando

Father Dan Lyons, S.J., is six-feet tall and weighs a muscular, neatly-distributed 185 pounds. His walk is erect as a lance, and his regular, clean-cut features and handsome profile convey a sense of youthful, indomitable vigor. Today, he is acclaimed as "the most widely read priest-journalist in America." Those close to him love and revere him, know him among themselves as "Danny," and repeat with affection the legends that have grown around his name. His voice is soft yet incisive, his manner courteous, a model of politeness. One of his greatest assets is his warm sense of humor. He laughs easily, and when something strikes his funny bone, he tilts his head back and roars until tears roll down his cheeks.

To gather material for this book, I did not spend a great deal of time tagging after him with pencil and notebook, a minor-league Boswell, but I did receive advice from many friends of his concerning the writing of this work. Could I, I asked myself, write of him objectively? William F. Buckley, Jr., General Tom Lane (Ret.), Dr. Anthony Kubek, Father Ken Baker, and numerous others mentioned during the course of our narrative, offered to give me of their help, their time, their material. They opened their minds to me, some of them their files, as did members of Father Dan's family.

I now began to grow familiar with the many sides of Father Lyons. Gradually it dawned on me that there were many Father Lyonses. I got to know some of them. There is Father Lyons the journalist. Millions know him, and he's a talent to be reckoned with. And there is Lyons the TV personality and Lyons the radio voice and Lyons of the lecture platform and Lyons the raconteur and Lyons the Federal labor arbitrator and Lyons the hawk. Many people have grown to know these Lyonses, and each of these differs from the other Lyonses in substance and size and quality.

Then there is Lyons the business administrator—first-rate—and Lyons the teacher and Lyons the promoter (apt and fast) and Lyons the priest (deeply devout) and Lyons the globe-hopper (his "office" is in the sky) and Lyons the good Samaritan and Lyons the patriot and Lyons the conservative. Then there is Lyons the man (teetotaler, always in shape, watches his diet, quick on the conversational draw) and Lyons the hard-worker (18 hours a day) and Lyons the meditator (he considers that day lost when he can't offer Mass) and Lyons the Irishman ("Actually, we're half-Swedish and half-Irish, which, according to my late father, makes us ALL Irish").

Nineteen Lyonses. There are more, of course. But these are the nineteen that keep popping up in this book. Lyons the Jesuit is the thermostat who heats or chills the remaining eighteen. Intellectually, he is a walking encyclopedia, as befits a man who was trained by the scholarly Jesuits, and has graduate degrees from Gonzaga University, St. Louis University and Milltown Park, Dublin, Ireland. I have never seen him at a point where he could not understand the subject under discussion. He is a fast thinker, cocking his head and nodding to the speaker, anticipating what is going to be said and saying it first, or adding to it. Father Lyons has enormous power of comprehension plus a sharp assessment of his own weaknesses.

He is as honest and courageous as an urchin the night before First Holy Communion. His memory is, in a way, his greatest single asset. He remembers almost everything he ever learned.

And yet, this is overanalyzing, oversimplifying the man. He is real. He is regular. He is sincere. He is earthy.

Dan Lyons is aware of his public image, but he rarely thinks about it. He has too much spirit, a too brisk carriage, and too much determination in his eyes to be mistaken for anything other than "Father Hawk." There is nothing halfway about him. He is not afraid to speak out on the unpopular issues of the times. In this day of double-talk, his candidness, his total honesty, is refreshing. "An expert," he insists, "is an ordinary man a long way from home. Any person who puts credence in his own press clippings is heading for a fall."

The fact that Father Lyons is a Jesuit says a lot about the man. No other group of men has, down the centuries, furnished so much material for hot controversy. By far the largest and, in many ways, most influential of the religious orders of the Catholic Church, it is also the most feared, the most suspected and the most maligned. For 437 years the Jesuits have had to contend with enemies inside the Roman Catholic Church as well as outside. There are those who still believe that every Jesuit has horns and cloven hoofs. Others will swear no Jesuit can look you in the eye, and children have been known to run off yelling when greeted by a friendly Jesuit.

Wars, revolutions and intrigues have often been laid to their doorstep, and almost everything a Jesuit may say is automatically taken by some to be double talk. The very name, "Jesuit," originated as a defamation, implying a great show of sanctimony, and nothing is more typical of the defiant spirit of the order than its adoption of the taunt to designate the members of what is still officially and formidably known as the Society of Jesus—"S.J." Hence, Father Daniel Lyons, S.J.

What is the official function of the Jesuits in this world? A body of religious men devoted to the spiritual perfection of themselves and others, they may exercise their apostolate in a variety of ways, including teaching, preaching, missionary work, and social action. The order's Latin motto, *Ad Maiorem Dei Gloriam*—For the Greater Glory of God —places the emphasis on "greater." Their minds fixed on this single purpose, the Jesuits have, through the nearly four and a half centuries of their existence, contributed no end to the great forward rush of Western civilization. The order's history glows with the names of brilliant scholars, as well as those of some thirty saints and many martyrs. There is no more striking proof of its appeal to modern Catholics than the fact that its membership has doubled since the First World War.

Of the world's 37,000 Jesuits, no fewer than 7,600 are Americans. They form the largest and, in some respects, most vigorous national group within the order. And though the headquarters of the society remains in Rome, a stone's throw from the Vatican, the weight of the American contingent is making itself felt, increasingly.

In the United States, the Jesuits are looked upon as one of the most active and most influential elements within the Catholic community. Best known for their great string of colleges and universities—among them Georgetown University in Washington, D.C.; Fordham University, New York; St. Louis University, St. Louis; Marquette University, Milwaukee; the University of San Francisco; Boston College; Santa Clara; and Loyola Universities of Chicago, New Orleans, Los Angeles and Baltimore—they are now in charge of more than 150,000 students. However, education is by no means their sole interest. American Jesuits run houses of retreat, service Catholic parish churches, publish newspapers and magazines, and operate radio and TV stations. Their Sacred Heart program of music, talk and prayer, has long been carried by hundreds of commercial radio and TV stations in every part of the United States.

But the United States, with its ten Jesuit provinces, is only one of nine assistancies, or geographic regions, into which the society divides itself for administrative reasons. Each province is administered by a "provincial," and each assistancy is represented at world headquarters by an "assistant." Horizontally, the order is divided into three main categories—some 18,000 "fathers," or priests; some 10,000 "scholastics," or future priests; and some 6,000 lay brothers employed largely at clerical and domestic chores and subject to a relatively short, informal training.

Father Lyons belongs to the Oregon province, with headquarters at Portland. It covers the Northwest states.

There is, at first sight, something baffling about Jesuits. Although they form an order, they are neither monks nor friars, but "clerks regular." They do not live in monasteries but in houses. Father Lyons, for example, lives in quarters in upper Manhattan, at 86 Riverside Drive. The five-story building was once the elegant private town house of the late Douglas Fairbanks, Sr., famous movie actor, and his wife, Mary Pickford. The residence is owned by Cardinal Paul Yu Pin, exiled bishop of Nanking, China. It is used as a center for Chinese students, as well as Father Dan's offices.

Father Lyons and his fellow Jesuits are distinguished by no picturesque habit. The ankle-length black cassock, with the broad, black cincture, which Jesuits wear in the streets of Italy and other European countries, becomes in the United States an indoors garb. Out on the street, the American Jesuit is dressed like any other priest, and the magnificent, cartwheel Roman hat deteriorates into a commonplace black felt hat. In hot countries the Jesuit wears white. And, when a delicate assignment calls for it, he may confront the world in civvies. Father Lyons, incidentally, wears no hat. He "left it somewhere" twenty years ago.

This singular adaptability is very much in keeping with the character and purpose of the order. Founded in 1534, by Inigo de Onez y Loyola, a Spanish nobleman and soldier known to the world as St. Ignatius, it was conceived as a spiritual shock battalion, a light cavalry of the Roman Church. Ignatius had been wounded by a cannon ball at the siege of Pampeluna and, convalescing, had vowed to lead the life of an ascetic, devoted only to the Church.

Desirous of creating a brotherhood whose members would be ready for immediate action at the Pope's command, in any sector of the world-wide front, he organized his "Company of Jesus" along military lines and freed the brethren from all time-consuming ritual, such as the choral recitation of the Divine Office.

He ordained a form of government closely resembling an absolute monarchy. According to his Constitutions, valid to this day, the order's highest legislative organ is the general congregation, or parliament. However, its chief function is the election of a general and his cabinet of personal "assistants" who advise him. Having installed them, parliament goes home, leaving the general to rule supreme during his lifetime. He is addressed as "Your Paternity." Visitors may kiss his hand, and his tremendous power, combined with his black garb, has earned him his grim nickname—the Black Pope. (The real Pope, or Holy Father, who wears white, is the Black Pope's only superior among men.)

Under its chief executive, the society moves as one body, with orders coming down through the provincial and local superiors appointed by the general, to the individual Jesuit—whose job is to obey, to do, and, when the need arises, die a martyr's death.

Deep in this vein, Father Lyons was expected to obey and to do after being told by his Provincial, John J. Kelley, S.J., of the Oregon Province, that he could not give up his position at Gonzaga University in 1965 and go to New York to be Secretary General of the Free Pacific Association. Father Kelley's decision was contained in a letter to Father Lyons:

"Dear Dan:

I am very sorry that I missed you when you were here in Portland this week-end to talk at St. Ignatius. It was probably my fault as I just took it for granted that you would drop in to see me. I am sure a visit vis-a-vis would be more fruitful than this letter.

After long prayer and much consultation, I have decided that you are to remain at Gonzaga University in the primary capacity of teacher and that your talks should be limited to the local area in such wise that they do not conflict with your regular teaching load. You may, of course, continue your weekly column for *Our Sunday Visitor*.

I have definitely decided against your going to New York to be Secretary General of the Free Pacific Association. I will not here go into all the reasons that have prompted my decision, but I shall be happy to give them to you in detail when we next meet. In fact, if you wish to come down to see me concerning this you are most welcome. Be sure to call ahead of time, however, as I will be in and out of the office in the days to come. I am writing to Archbishop Yu Pin to notify him of my decision.

I wish I could have happier news for you, Dan, but this is the way I see it before God, and I must follow what I think is right. I know you will accept this decision with the proper attitude and as a true and obedient son of St. Ignatius.

Wishing you all of God's blessings, and begging a remembrance in your prayers, I am,

Sincerely yours in Christ,
JOHN J. KELLEY, S.J.
Provincial."

Father Dan was torn between two factions. On the one hand was his dedication to the ideal of obedience; on the other, he felt he could not give up the huge opportunity waiting for him in New York. What to do?

"It was the greatest personal trial I've yet faced," he told me. "My work—writing extensively, lecturing, frequent appearances on radio and TV—seemed terribly important. Frankly, it looked like I wouldn't be able to have it both ways. That is, stay in the Jesuit Order and continue in this work."

I asked him, "Are you saying that you actually considered leaving the priesthood?"

"Not the priesthood—the Jesuit Order. It would be impossible for me to leave the priesthood. But I did think I might have to leave the Jesuits and attach myself to someone like Cardinal Yu Pin, who had asked that I be loaned to him. He would have allowed me to go on with my work, because he was convinced as much as I that it had to be done. So, yes, I did consider leaving the Society.

"The very thought of such a move was extremely serious, and I was deeply concerned about the prospect.

I had grown totally attached to the Jesuits. Still I believed the work I was doing had to be done. I felt it was absolutely urgent. So I must confess to you that I did consider leaving the Order and becoming a Diocesan priest to be free to go on with the work. Thank God, that wasn't necessary. After several talks, my Provincial changed his mind. He finally relented and assured me he would not stand in my way to do the work that had opened up for me in New York.

"Other than that one time, I have never found it difficult to do what I have been assigned to do. As a matter of fact, the Order doesn't invoke a command except as a last resort. That's something we never think about. We do what we are told. In my case, it was not a question of disobeying the Order; rather, it was a question of whether I might have to ask their permission to leave the Order to be free to carry on with what I considered was very important work at the request of Cardinal Yu Pin, who convinced me that Asia would be saved or lost, depending on the propaganda war in the United States."

Much of the fifteen years it takes to make a Jesuit is spent, you could say, in rearranging a young man's personality. No Jesuit can forget that St. Ignatius himself described obedience as "a holocaust in which the whole man, nothing at all excepted, is offered up."

Where ordinary obedience is a matter of subjecting one's own will to that of the superior, the Jesuit variety affects will, intellect, and judgment.

Indeed, the Jesuit, in St. Ignatius' words, "must offer up his understanding . . . that he may not only will, but also think the self-same with his superior. . . . Obedience comprehends not only the execution, so that the person do that which is commanded, and the will, so that he do it willingly, but also the judgment, that whatsoever the superior commands and thinks good, seem just and reasonable to the inferior, so far, as I have said, as the will, by its force and vigor, can bend the understanding."

Hence, perhaps, the old superstition that, to a Jesuit, white must be black if his superior tells him so. In point of fact, Jesuit discipline has a deep spiritual meaning, as the obedient subject sees, in his superior, the Lord Himself. Still, when St. Ignatius, in the order's Constitutions, orders the brethren to obey "as if they were a dead body which suffers itself to be borne to any place and to be treated in any manner whatever," the outsider may wonder whether this degree of discipline can actually be maintained. The answer is, it can.

Time and again, the Jesuit, engaged in a scientific project or a stimulating and useful job, is suddenly told to pack up and go far, far away. The president of a great university may find himself, tomorrow, the head of a remote and modest house of studies, or a hospital. A brilliant scholar may be ordered to teach small boys arithmetic. A young man may be sent—for the rest of his life—to a small mission station in the tribal lands of South America. He may be ordered to speak, henceforth, in another language, or change his nationality. And he is not expected to reply with a "See here. . . ."

Obedience to any command, it's true, is void if it conflicts with moral or religious law, or with the evidence of patent truth. St. Ignatius thought of it: "If anything occurs to you different from the superior's opinions and it seems . . . that it ought to be declared, you may propose it to him."

Obedience has a sister, Poverty. As the society is, technically, one of the mendicant orders, living off alms—and, thanks to a papal dispensation, tuition fees—austerity is part of every Jesuit's life. He may own nothing. What he possessed in civil life, he has disposed of, like a dying man, in a last will and testament before becoming a full member of the Order. If he earns a salary as a teacher, writer or administrator, he turns it over to the community and is, in turn, allotted what modest funds he needs for certain specified necessities. Father Lyons, for example, sometimes earns $1,000 a night for lecture appearances, yet gives the fees to the Society, or to projects approved by it.

Like most Jesuits, Father Lyons enjoys only the bare essentials in his living quarters in New York. There's a modest bed, a closet, a bookshelf, a desk, a typewriter, and a washbasin with running water. After five years in New York, he finally installed his own portable shower, which he considers a great luxury.

When fulfilling his apostolic mission in the outside world, he travels a lot. He belongs to United Airline's "Million Mile Club." If traveling by train, is he entitled to a sleeper? The rule of thumb says that, if a good night's rest is necessary for the performance of his work, he may indulge. But Father Lyons frowns on liquor or tobacco of any sort. And so it goes, through the myriad small temptations and conveniences of our century. "The Society frees us," said Dan, "from the tyranny of having or wanting things. We are the freest people on earth, free to dedicate our lives intensely, effectively and responsibly."

How does an American get to be a Jesuit? About 350 young men join the society in this country every year. Nineteen years of age, and sometimes older, they come from every social stratum, and search for something that no worldly job, career or business can give them. Their serious intent, known as "vocation," should rest on something more than reason. One senior Jesuit admitted that what the order is really looking for is a supernatural motivation. Apart from that, good health, a virtuous life, a high-school education, a well-adjusted personality and a good brain are all that is required.

The grinding process starts immediately—to last for fifteen years. Donning the habit, the novice joins a group of about twenty others at a secluded Jesuit establishment in spiritual preparation for his life in the society. His day is organized from five A.M. to 10:30 P.M. and the routine includes instruction, prayer, and a good deal of humble, menial work.

It includes, too, a thirty-day retreat—the series of deep self-examinations based on the classic document of Jesuit introspection, the Spiritual Exercises of St. Ignatius. At any time, before the first two years are up, the novice may be told he is not fit to be a Jesuit and shipped back home; by the same token, he may turn in his cassock on his own volition and walk out the door.

But at the end of the two-year novitiate, the young man takes the triple vows of perpetual poverty, chastity and obedience. He's in the army now. And he moves upward (leaving lay brothers behind at this point) through a two-year liberal-arts course, to a Jesuit college for priests where he spends three years studying philosophy, in Latin. A three-year "regency" of active teaching at a Jesuit high school or college rounds out a memorable and decisive decade.

The pressure, all this time, has been terrific. While senior Jesuits do not deny that some fine boys do crack under the strain, the miracle is that it happens to so few. Day in, day out, the student is closed in by the unyielding framework of a highly organized and regimented life. His study program is a heavy one, additional hours are spent in mental prayer, his character is put to many tests, his conscience is kept on a continuous alert. His teachers and superiors, closely observing him, report to their superiors and, in the end, the Society knows more about him than he does himself.

And now the student, having come this far, narrows his field of vision to concentrate on the Divine. Transferred to a theologate, he studies for the priesthood. After the third year of this four-year course, he is ordained a priest, and it is only now that Mr. Lyons, S.J., turns into Father Lyons, S.J. A fifteenth year of spiritual preparation, the tertianship, once more at a secluded place, puts on the spiritual polish.

Still—there is one more step. All fathers must, some two years later, take their final vows, implying the definitive binding of the Order to man and man to Order. However, those who have proved themselves the fittest in the long, painful process of selection, add to the standard vows of poverty, chastity and obedience, a fourth—that of perpetual obedience to the Pope. This fourth vow is the celebrated Jesuit refinement. Those asked to take it—one out of every four or five—henceforth form the elite of "professed fathers," and they alone may hold high office.

What kind of man is Father Lyons as he emerges from his monumental incubator? He is, for one thing, an extremely learned fellow. He has read everything from Aristotle to Jean-Paul Sartre. He knows the ins and outs of philosophy, theology, history and sociology. He can converse in Latin, and he is, as a rule, at home in several other languages (though Father Lyons confesses he cared more for political science, sociology and labor relations than he did for languages).

After fifteen years, the young Jesuit's personality is formed in line with the established pattern of the order. Down to the tips of his sensitive fingers, he is a Jesuit. While it would be absurd to say that the long grinding process had erased his individuality, a certain norm has been achieved. Our Father Lyons knows how to think, to reason, to obey, to do without. Inhabited by a strong will, he is, at the same time, the perfect instrument of a superior will. A powerful *esprit de corps* links him with every member of his brotherhood. He is used to being baited by his enemies, and watched by his superiors. And he is honest with himself to the extent of formally examining his conscience for fifteen minutes twice a day.

With such a man, the order can take chances. It can send him, alone, to the end of the world, and know he'll be out there working, as ever, "for God's Greater Glory."

Such a man is Father Lyons.

Such a man can talk for hours about Catholicism in general and the Jesuits in particular. He can tell you what the "S.J." after his name really means. Listen:

"St. Ignatius, the founder of the Jesuits, had been a military officer, a captain in the Spanish army," Father Dan said. "He was, in fact, a Basque, the only one to head the Jesuits until a few years ago, when our present Father General, Father Pedro Arrupe, was elected. In my meetings with Father Arrupe he reminds me very much of what I have read about St. Ignatius, and pictures of him. He spent 20 years in Japan. Father Arrupe is very familiar with the work I am doing with our publications, and has been very encouraging to me. I know that he will be among the readers of this book. His assistant general for the U.S.A. is Father Harold Small, whom I have known since he was newly ordained, and I was in high school. He was president of Seattle University 30 years ago, then Provincial (i.e., superior) of the Oregon Province. I have met with him in Rome on numerous occasions.

"I have also met with Pope Paul in Rome and in Manila, and Cardinal Yu Pin has told him about our work several times.

"Of the four large Religious Orders in the Church (Benedictine, 6th century; Dominican, 12th century; Franciscan, and 13th century) the Jesuits are the most recent. We are highly centralized, far more than the others. Every college president and religious superior is appointed from Rome. The General can give orders—e.g., to have 30 missioners sent to Japan, and have them immediately implemented. Also, since most of our men are engaged in education, we have the longest course of studies. In the U.S. we run about 45 high schools (all college prep) and about 28 universities. Best known are Georgetown, Fordham, Boston College, Holy Cross, St. Louis U., Marquette, and four Loyola U.'s. Incidentally, at Georgetown, a porch still stands where Gen. Washington stood and addressed the students."

One of America's long-time literary giants, James Warner Bellah, was raised an Episcopalian but was educated by the good fathers of Georgetown University, where he took a Masters degree in history in 1945. He is a great admirer of the Jesuits, their goals, and their scholarly approach to life. As one who has written nineteen novels, more than a hundred motion pictures, and whose famous short stories appeared in virtually every popular magazine in the U.S., Canada, and England, including more than 100 issues of the old *Saturday Evening Post,* Bellah was awarded the Georgetown Medal of Honour at the school's 175th Anniversary celebration.

In World War I, he served as a pilot overseas in both the Canadian Royal Flying Corps and Royal Air Force. In World War II, he started as a lieutenant, 16th Infantry, and finished as a colonel on the staff of Admiral Lord Louis Mountbatten in Southeast Asia. As a war-toughened military man, he appreciates the strong stand the Jesuits traditionally take on controversial issues.

Bellah told me, "It is significant to the pattern of continued American living, to remember that when savage campus unrest swept the country, it did not sully the Jesuit colleges. The reason that it did not, rings clear. The Jesuitical approach brooks no distortion of objective thinking—no corruption of the purity of reason—and rioting is as far from objectivity and reason as was the volley at Kent State that was ultimately necessary to stop it.

"Proof of that necessity is that that volley wrote *finis* to violent student demonstrations, nation-wide.

"All of us know that those campus riots were Communist engineered—but the Jesuit faculties knew at the time—that they were, for the tradition of education is of as long-standing—or longer—in the Jesuit Discipline as it is in the Episcopalian and the challenge of the tradition is to feel out its traps and deadfalls in advance.

"The Society of Jesus was founded by soldiers and gentlemen (the latter being a much misunderstood word, inasmuch as it derives from *gens,* the people, rather than gentle and denotes in its purest sense men with a concern for the people) and in time of crises soldiers and gentlemen are indispensable—for the one is a disciplined man trained to controlled action and the other has an innate obligation to people—people who, in the mass, in time of crisis invariably enter into uncontrolled, unreasoning, self-destructive courses of action—until leaders appear.

"Of such leaders, in our day, Father Dan Lyons, S.J., is among the foremost—a Christian soldier marching in the footsteps of Ignatius Loyola and Francis Xavier, across the world, head up and heart strong to bring the world peace!"

Father Lyons picks up the Jesuit story:

"The Jesuit Order was started at the time of the Protestant Reformation, so it became a counter-Reformation. It operates in Provinces. When a Province gets about 1,000 it is divided into two.

"The original name was 'Company of Jesus' in Spanish, French, Italian and Latin. St. Ignatius organized it very much along the lines of an army, hence the military unit, company. It would have been mistaken for a business term in English. But 'society' is a very inadequate translation.

"Because of our mobility and unity, and because we take a special vow of obedience to the Pope, we are often referred to as the shock troops of the church. We are never allowed to accept ecclesiastical honors, such as the title 'Monsignor,' and if any Jesuit is nominated to be a bishop, our Fr. General must ask the Pope to 'remove this evil from the Society' (a policy laid down by Ignatius). Rarely, the Pope insists, e.g., in Northern Alaska, where nearly all the priests are Jesuit missionaries, a Jesuit bishop is appointed.

"The Society is often attacked, and our enemies make us out to be 'wily.' We have repeatedly been accused of teaching—and practicing—that the end justifies the means, meaning that we justify an immoral means. This is completely false. But if the means is not bad, and the end is not, that is another story. It is traditional for us to seek maximum influence, and that often means working behind the scenes. Frequently it means writing books, and teaching in prominent seminaries such as the Gregorianum and the Biblicum in Rome. Most theology and philosophy texts have been written by Jesuits.

"An example of quietly using influence occurred in Indonesia several years ago. The population is mostly Moslem, and the Moslem religious leaders had the revised

Constitution being written in such a way that Islam would have become united to the government. Some of the top political leaders, though Moslem, did not want that, so a Jesuit in Jakarta was secretly asked by them to rewrite that part of the Constitution, so it could be presented and adopted, which it was, stressing freedom for all religions. Only a couple of people knew about it. The Jesuit who did it was not Indonesian, but he had followed the Jesuit rule that 'we must learn the language of the country where we reside.'

"The spirit of permissiveness, of doctrinaire liberalism, of situation ethics, relativism, secularism—the crisis of faith, the decline in spiritual values which places so little value on patriotism and freedom—the spirit of rebelliousness that is so rampant in the free world today—all these things have taken a terrible and a terrifying toll within as well as without the Church.

"Some Jesuits say the Order today is not the same Order they joined. I find that conclusion too pessimistic. It is the same Order essentially, even though it is not the same as it was in many ways. The General and other superiors have lost a lot of their authority—some of it has atrophied from lack of use. Our job is to recapture the spirit we had, to get back what we are in danger of losing, and have been in the process of relinquishing, through confusion and in some cases a spirit of rebellion. We have to rally the forces of good, the forces of enlightenment around us. With men like Father Ken Baker we can do it, with God's help.

"God's nature is such that He must be served, He must in justice be honored. Hence I do not think He will allow the forces of evil to take over the world. The future must belong, not to those who hate God, but to those who love Him. But we must do our part against evil forces."

One of Father Dan's favorite stories has to do with the early Jesuit missionaries who settled in his own Pacific Northwest. They were largely Italians from Milan who had been expelled from Italy by Garibaldi. Before they came to the Rocky Mountain mission, they prepared themselves with special skills. One was the first medical doctor in Montana. One built the first church in Idaho, still a very impressive structure. One of them, the famous Father Cataldo, founded Gonzaga University, where Father Dan later taught and was Dean of Students. Another, a lay brother named Carigiano, became renowned as an artist. His greatest work is still preserved on the ceiling and walls of St. Ignatius mission in Montana.

As a boy, Brother Carigiano had seen the Sistine chapel in Rome. It was an advantage the Italians had and still have. They grew up surrounded with the master works of art, and they emulated them. Brother Carigiano painted, as part of his Bible history course in oils, a graphic illustration of the Last Judgment. When the Indians gathered around that evening to study the work that had just been finished, they noticed with great delight that there were no Indian faces among the souls of the damned. *They had it made!* Or so they believed.

The Indians weren't the only ones who caught the oversight. That night, Brother Carigiano toiled with paints and brush far into the morning. After the Indians had gone to bed, he went to work and touched up the faces of those suffering in the eternal fires. He dabbed here and brushed there, darkening half the faces, and he added a few Indian feathers for good measure on some of the scalps. Bright and early, Brother Carigiano was back on the scene, as some Indians came to show their brothers that all the souls in hell were *white*. Their smiles quickly lapsed into frowns, however. Lo and behold—the Indians had joined the palefaces in hell during the night!

CHAPTER 4

This Business of Being a Descendant

Funny, this business of being a descendant.

If you believe, as many people do, that prenatal influences are the main governing forces within us, then we are agreed that the fused and reconciled traits of his forebears form the core of the average man's character. And environment, generally speaking, is no more than the shellac which overlies these passed-on heritages. Accepting this basic premise and still not giving our progenitors all the credit nor yet all the blame for what you or we may be, we say it's fair and proper that a man should look to his traceable antecedents for slants and trends when he begins sorting out his reactions to life.

We are sure that Father Dan's love for the place where he was reared is not altogether due to the circumstances of his being a native son. We are sure it goes deeper than that, for into it enters the elemental fact that his parents established themselves in Seattle nearly sixty years ago, bore two sons and four daughters there, and were pillars of the community. Father Dan can scarcely remember a time when he did not rejoice in his birthright nor fail to boast of it. Indeed, he was parentally encouraged to do so. His Irish father would tell him, "You're half-Irish and half-Swede, so you can run for any office in the State of Washington!"

Washington was part of Father Dan's ancestral fiber. To cite conspicuous examples of an American's birth place, being a Virginian is a profession, and being a South Carolinian is a trade to be worked at in season and out, but in the Pacific Northwest corner of the country, Washingtonism is an incurable disease; a disease, though, to be proud of. On the other hand, we've rarely heard a man brag about coming from Armenia—or Arkansas. But a Bostonian of the older stocks would brag, or a Californian, either of the Forty-Nine breed or the Spanish breed; and a Texan, surely; and likewise a Louisianian, especially one whose people dated to the first French settlements or the subsequent admixture of the Arcadian exiles. Practically all Danes are like that, too, and most of the Scandinavians, and invariably the Scots and the Irish. Since Father Dan is part Irish and part Swedish and all Washingtonian, he can offer several valid excuses for his vainglorious behavior in this regard.

Facts on his ancestry reveal that of his four grandparents, only one was born in the United States: his maternal grandmother, Johanna Matilda Linnell. She was born on January 1, 1855, at Chisago Lake, Minnesota.

The man she married was John Daniel Linnell, who came from Sweden, where the two Linnell families were related.

Grandfather Linnell was the only one of Father Dan's grandparents that he knew, his father's parents having remained in Ireland, and his maternal grandmother having died in the Seattle flu epidemic of 1916, four years before Father Dan was born.

Jarlath Lyons, Dan's older brother who was killed in a plane crash in World War II, was named after the patron saint of the west of Ireland, where their father, Patrick, attended St. Jarlath's College, in Tuam, County Galway. People always took for granted that "Dan" was an Irish name, and his mother capitalized on it by insisting year after year that her husband have "Danny Boy," the Irish folk song, sung at the Irish banquets in Seattle.

The truth is that Father Dan received his name from the *Swedish* side of the family. It was his grandfather's second name, and the name of Dan's great-grandfather. At Hovmantorp, Sweden, there is still a tree on the family property known as the "Daniel Tree."

Father Dan's grandfather worked as a farmer and a carpenter throughout the Pacific Northwest, where Dan's mother was born. She was born in the little town of Buckley, near Seattle, on September 16, 1891. Her father later farmed in Alberta, Canada.

The one grandparent who was born in this country comes from pioneer stock, and her older brother, O. M. Linnell, provided a graphic account of those early days in Minnesota.

It was in 1917, at Grove City, Minnesota, that Dan's

great uncle, his grandmother's brother, wrote the account of his life in Swedish, after repeated requests from his children and grandchildren, to whom he dedicated his memoirs.

Fifteen years older than Dan's grandmother, he was born in Sweden, April 21, 1840. His reminiscences were written in the Swedish language. They were intended, he said, "solely for the immediate family," but some of his observations deserve a wider audience.

In the spring of 1852, his father, Magnus Jonason, and family set out from Karlshamn, Sweden, for Gothenburg in a small sail boat, manned by two men and a boy. It took seven days to reach Gothenburg, where they waited three weeks for a sailing ship, the *Ambrosius,* which was carrying a cargo of iron to New York.

Twelve men comprised the crew. They reached New York after 51 days, on August 3, 1852. Being just 12 at the time, Dan's great-uncle, who wrote the account, was thrilled with the adventure and could not understand why there was so much "fussing and weeping" as they said goodbye.

When they arrived in New York, they had to go to Chicago by boat to Buffalo, by rail to Dunkirk, then by boat to Detroit across Lake Erie, then by rail to Chicago. There was no railroad from New York to Chicago. Ordinary freight cars were used for transporting the immigrants, and Linnell reported that they had not been cleaned very well since they were last used for hauling swine. Benches of bare planks just eight inches wide were put in for seats.

Arriving in Chicago, they found it to be only a little village on a low, muddy plain. A canal boat took them to LaSalle and then by team and carriage to Andover, Henry County, Illinois. It was a two-day journey. From there they went to Knoxville, Illinois, where they were given circulars about the Chisago Lake area in Minnesota. As land was selling around Knoxville for four dollars an acre, they decided to push on to Minnesota, where land was selling for $1.25 an acre.

Dan's great-uncle decided it would be easier to form a colony in Minnesota, "where the danger of mixing up with other nationalities would not be so great." The time was perfect, for hundreds of Swedish immigrants started pouring into Minnesota in 1853-4. Many of them came as a result of his father's letters. The Linnells left Illinois by river boat up the Mississippi to Minnesota. It took two weeks of tedious traveling, with low water often causing the boat to go aground.

The immigrants were given quarters on the boiler deck, among the cattle and miscellaneous freight. "However," wrote Linnell, "to be among the cattle and swine was not nearly so offensive as to be subjected to the shameless treatment some of the party received from the crew. Two of the women were especially annoyed. One, a sister of mother, Sarah Helena, was a large woman and very strong, accustomed to the work of a large estate in Sweden. When one of the crew attempted to annoy her one day, she sent him reeling with a stiff blow on the ear. He left her alone thereafter."

They were happy to see the houses of St. Paul as they

rounded a bend in the river. It had a population of about 3,000, which was a third of the entire population of Minnesota. Linnell, Sr., went down to the Chisago Lake area to look for land. It was encouraging to find there were no stones. It was a welcome relief for the Swedes, after all the stones they had in their homeland. There were a lot of trees, but they meant homes and a source of income. "Besides," they said, "stumps would rot in time, but stones never."

Every man was his own carpenter, and the families were in log houses before winter. Wrote Linnell: "The bark on the roof was cracked in places, so when it snowed hard there was snow on the floor. When it rained we had to mop up the water. During the coldest part of the winter we had to keep a fire going hard all night or everything would have been frozen solid. I was thirteen years old now and it became my task to keep the stove supplied with wood.

"I had to pick up the wood wherever I could find it, and at times it was almost more than a boy of my years could do to drag the heavy loads home. We had to go eleven miles on foot to the Falls for anything we had to buy.

"The only means of transportation was an old work-ox owned by a Peter Berg. The owner was so extremely careful of his ox that the weather had to be just right before he would allow the ox to be used for hauling. There were only five families living at that time in what is now (1917) the largest Swedish settlement in America."

In the spring of 1854, Rev. Erland Carlson came from Chicago to organize the Chisago Lake Swedish Evangelical

Lutheran Church. Each family gave about two logs for building a church. Young Linnell took a job for six dollars a month, but was paid in merchandise, not in cash. For nine months he was too far away to attend church service. "My only spiritual food," he said, "was found in an old psalm book, and the Bible." In the following year his youngest sister, Johanna, Father Lyons' grandmother, was born.

None of the children attended school, which explains why he wrote his biographical notes in Swedish. "Yet," he wrote, "the time I could spare from my work I gave to reading books on travel, history, biography, etc. I had no textbooks until I was twenty."

In the fall of 1859 he went to Louisiana, with five other young men, to look for work.There he got his first look at slavery: "We landed one evening at a town known as Grand Gulf in the state of Mississippi, about seventy miles below Vicksburg. The following morning there was to be a slave sale at the market. We walked up there and watched the selling of four young men and a young mother who had two small children. When she had been sold she pleaded and wept that the one who had bought her would also buy her children. She got down on her knees, begging that at least they might buy the youngest child.

"I have never been able to forget that scene, the poor mother on her knees, begging, with tears. It seemed, however, to make absolutely no impression on the unmerciful slave owners. Some of us, following this experience, determined, when the call came for volunteers, to go if needed, to fight slavery."

By the summer of 1862, he had enlisted. It was the second year of the war, and many had already been killed or wounded, returning home crippled for life. "Those who were going now had vivid object lessons of what the war meant. It was hard to see husbands and fathers parted from their wives and children. Many of the women cried uncontrollably, a few fainted."

They were called the Lumbermen's Company of the Seventh Regiment, Minnesota Volunteers. After training for 13 days at Fort Snelling, they were dispatched to Fort Ripley in western Minnesota to fight Indians who were killing white settlers. His company publicly hung the 38 leaders of the Indian rebellion who had been captured.

After a long bout with illness, he was discharged on August 4, 1863. By October, he was able once more to work in the woods. The following June 24, he was married to Caroline Anderson, to whom he had been engaged for nearly two years. Caroline had come from Sweden by herself in 1859, at the age of 19.

He described his bride beautifully but simply: "I first saw this girl who was to be my wife on the day she was received as a member of the church. She was a consecrated Christian, having gone through a real conversion shortly before. She wanted to live now wholly for Christ. She had been endowed with unusual beauty and a quiet, even temperament. Several suitors tried to win her but I was the one to whom she finally gave her heart.

"She was my loving and faithful companion until she died. Our married life was very happy. I received her as a gift from God and thank Him for her many years with me and the memories I hold of her. I hesitated for a long time to ask her to marry me, but the first time I ventured I received the hoped-for answer. Our marriage was blessed with eight children, four boys and four girls, born between the years 1867 and 1884." The children were first cousins to Father Dan's mother.

Looking back on his earlier years, Linnell went on to write that he spent seventeen springs working on the river for the lumber companies. "We camped out on the river banks in all kinds of weather, rain or snow, never inside a house as long as the work went on in the spring. If I fell off a log into the river there was no time for a change of clothing. It had to dry on my back.

"Sometimes we did not even have a tent. When it rained or snowed we stuck a pike pole into a tree, hung a blanket over it and crawled under. Soft pine branches or brush was what we had to lie on. With wool blankets we tried to keep warm."

In looking back over his life, Linnell admitted modestly: "Although my family was never in want for food or clothing, I have had no great success financially. It was often extremely hard and my plans miscarried. I believe that God saw it was best for me not to have much of this world's goods. I have so much to thank God for, first for salvation through Christ, good health, and the fact that none of my children ever fell into open and gross sins as so many parents have had to grieve about. We have never striven for riches nor tried to gain anything from another's hurt."

For various reasons, he decided to leave the area around

Chisago Lake "where we were so well known and where so far as I know we had not an enemy." Lumbering was diminishing, and he decided to move to western Minnesota. He bought a farm near Acton, with 160 acres. He soon added another 160. But in 1877 the Rocky Mountain grasshoppers were so numerous they destroyed the area's crops, reducing farmers to begging for a living and for a little seed grain.

During all this time his parents were living with him and his family. There were good years and bad. At times his debts seemed overwhelming. His son Albert returned from the Spanish-American war. They invested $5,000 in cattle and machinery, only to see the price of cattle drop from five cents per pound to two cents. "Skin disease broke out among the cattle," he said, "and practically every farmer in the state went broke. I lost $5,000, but Albert had put in six years of hard labor for nothing. He had to walk off with little more than his clothes."

Friends advised him to let his farm be foreclosed, and they would bid to buy it back and deed it back to him after six years, when his debts would be outlawed. "I owed $6,000 to friends who had trusted me without security," he said. "I could not have faced that disgrace. . . . Many, many times I had gone into the woods alone, in tears, to pray. I did not want my children to feel that their father had been a defaulter."

He sold all of his holdings to pay off his debts. The sale netted $32,960, just enough to pay all of his debts. "I was so tired of carrying the heavy burden of debt that I closed the deal. Everything seemed to have gone against me. At the time of this writing (1917) those lands are valued at $120,867, but I am glad I could sell and close the books without owing a man a dollar."

O. M. Linnell was not only a strong church member, he served in local state-wide government for many years as well. He never sought office, but was made chairman of Acton township, then elected county commissioner. "There was no courthouse," he commented, "and each commissioner had to provide out of his own funds for taking care of the county records."

In 1880, he was elected Representative to the Minnesota State Legislature. "It was a surprise to me," he said, "as I had never considered myself fit for that position. I had no funds to carry on a campaign, and questioned the wisdom of the nomination."

Yet he took his duties seriously: "The first term I spent in learning to know the ropes and getting acquainted with older members, on whom I might call to help me put through some bills later." He was re-elected in 1882 and served as chairman of the House Committees on Agriculture and Manufacturing. He served as second-ranking man on the Committee for State Lands and Reformatories. "I sponsored several bills for my district," he recorded simply, "without having a single vote cast against them."

For the sake of his posterity, he wrote of his wife's last illness. She could not lie down for her last nine months. "Twice before the last night she had told us all farewell, asking to be forgiven for all her failings. She went to sleep on Sunday morning, February 1, 1903, at half past one, and I feel assured that she, for Jesus' sake, did awaken there, where she is enjoying an eternal Sabbath.

"Her constant prayer," he wrote, "had been for grace to be patient during her suffering and that it might be her Lord's will to take her home as a poor sinner saved by grace. The funeral was held on the 5th of February. She was dressed as she was when a bride, to meet her heavenly Bridegroom (according to her wish). Burial took place in the Swedish Evangelical Lutheran Church cemetery in Grove City, to rest until the day of resurrection. She was 63 years, 2 months and 19 days old."

Thus wrote the great-uncle of Dan Lyons, S.J., the brother of his mother's mother, a man who was also related to his mother's father. Dan never knew any of his Swedish forebears except his grandfather. But he knew him well, as he lived in the Lyons home in Seattle for many years after giving up homesteading near Edmonton, in northern Alberta, Canada, in 1933, at the age of eighty.

Dan knew him as a very placid, quiet and peaceful man, patient and good-natured. Their favorite game together was cards, especially cribbage.

"A chip off the old block" was the old expression. The story of one family, multiplied by countless thousands, is the story of our nation. The story of a family is also the story of one person, heir to the influences and the strains of character that have gone before.

CHAPTER 5

Bringing Up Dan Lyons

The first chapter of life really dates back to a man's first memories. For the record, however, Father Dan Lyons was born at Columbus Hospital (now called Cabrini), not far from the heart of downtown Seattle, and only a few blocks from Seattle University, where his brother and four sisters later attended college, and where he would one day teach.

The date of his birth is noteworthy: *Friday the thirteenth!* August 13, 1920.

Superstition might try to make something out of that—but Father Dan will forever count it among his lucky days.

He was christened simply Daniel Lyons, with no middle name, and was the third in a line of two sons and four sisters. Seeing him in his mother's arms for the first time, a neighbor lady whispered, "He looks like little Greengoose. The pretty lad in the story book."

The time was still four-and-a-half decades away before

baby "Greengoose" would find the appellation changed to "Father Hawk," by his critics. His birth certificate states that his father's occupation was working on a barge.

Seattle was a grand old town to be born in, being a colorful seaport and lumber capital and a city with character and individuality. And surely that flat-faced, high-shouldered, two-year-old five-bedroom house that his father had bought when Dan was only six months old was a splendid place for a boy to spend a childhood. With six children eventually, the Lyonses became the hub of their east side neighborhood, a gathering place for all the youngsters of the area. The house had a beautiful view of Lake Washington, the Cascade mountain range, and Mount Rainier. A frequent visitor, Father Michael O'Malley, S.J., used to say, "When you sit down to dinner with the Lyons, you never know who you'll end up with before dinner is over."

The times in which Dan Lyons was born found America still caught up in the hangover of war. The Roaring Twenties had not yet begun their mad, whirling, chaotic rollercoaster ride. But fun, fanfare and frolic were in the wings, ready for the cue. Meanwhile, life went on. A restaurant in downtown Seattle featured a seven-course luncheon for seventy-five cents, with music. One of the good buys in automobiles was the seven-passenger Abbott-Detroit at $1195. A men's clothing store was selling overcoats for $15, several worsted suits for $21. For men the collar was Ide, the ale was Olympia. A 10-room house with a half-acre of property cost $5500. The favorite cigarettes were Fatima, Sweet Caporal and Piedmont, although only callow weaklings smoked them.

The era in which Dan Lyons spent his boyhood was a time of superlatives. An age of exaggeration. Everything that was done right was done more right and bigger than ever. The same applied to everything that was done wrong. Men who had been casual drinkers now had to get drunk. Women weren't satisfied with the role of attracting the male to marriage and making a home for him. They had to be his equal on the public forum, in politics, in the office. It was a time of giants, too—Dempsey, Bobby Jones, Tilden, Babe Ruth, Owney Madden, Dutch Schultz, Capone and Johnny Torrio. A smart man saved his money and acquired $25,000; a clever one played the stock market and had a million—or nothing. Cars were being made bigger and faster; trains were cutting a day's time off the run between Seattle and Minneapolis; men sat in their homes with earphones and heard real live music come out of the air. As a small boy, Dan remembers going to his mother's cousin's home, Glendon Strand, who had one of the first radios in town. It was a battery set, an Atwater-Kent. The time was three o'clock on Sunday afternoon, and as Mr. Strand dialed in vain for a radio program, the conclusion was obvious: nothing was being broadcast at the time.

There were flagpole sitters, marathon dancers, cross-country walkers, and the balloon tire was the newest thing in auto travel comfort. At home, small boys fought over which one could be first to play "Poet and Peasant" by pumping the pedals of a player piano.

What an era! What a world! What a country!

Patrick Lyons had been in America fifteen years at the time of the birth of his second son, Dan. He had crossed the sea from Ireland to America in the spring of 1905. He was born on a farm at Skeghard, near Ballyhaunis, County Mayo, in the West of Ireland, only a few miles from the place where Cardinal Gibbons, America's first Cardinal, was raised. Patrick studied at St. Jarlath's College in Tuam, County Galway, a prep school. He also attended a year at All Hallow's Seminary, in Dublin. Pat and several other students were dropped from the seminary, however, for betting a shilling on a horse race, and that was strictly forbidden. For reasons known only to himself, he never mentioned to his children that he had ever gone to the seminary. Years later, when Dan went to Ireland to study, he found out about it from his Aunt Mary Higgins.

Pat Lyons was born on March 29, 1882. He grew up in a family of five boys and three girls, somewhat the reverse of his own family in Seattle of two boys and four girls. Pat and three of his brothers emigrated from Ireland to America, as did one sister. One brother is still living, Michael. Michael Lyons, 97, spent most of his life in Chicago, and now lives in St. Petersburg, Florida. Nephew Dan visited him twice in 1972, and made sure he had received the Last Sacraments. The landlady spoke to Dan about funeral preparations, owing to the old gentleman's age, but Uncle Michael said to him instead, "Dan, why didn't you tell me you were going to Ireland last fall? I would have gone with you. Maybe we can take a trip over there together next summer. I'll buy two tickets." Dan visits Uncle Michael several times a year and takes him for a drive.

Dan's father was a devout man. He had a very deep

faith. When his children were small, he took them to Mass every day before trotting them off to school. There was Patricia, the oldest, and Jarlath, Dan, Eileen, Noreen, and Sheila. They attended the Carmelite Convent chapel, located on 18th Street, three blocks north of Madison. Father John Moffatt, S.J., was then a young priest from Seattle Prep and said the Mass at Carmelite. He was to be Dan's Novice Master, 10 years later.

Another priest who offered daily Mass there in those days was Father Edward Flajole, S.J., destined to be Dan's Rector (Superior) at Mount St. Michael's in Spokane, 15 years later. Dan surprised him one day as a seminarian by quoting from a sermon he had heard Father Flajole preach, 15 years before. Father Flajole dug in his sermon notes and found the sermon Dan had quoted from. He had quoted word for word. It was but one of countless times people around Dan have marvelled at his memory.

While Patrick Lyons herded the family to Carmelite for 7 a.m. Mass—or, at times, to St. Joseph's Church for 7:15 Mass—Alice Lyons, the mother, stayed home and prepared their breakfast. By 8:10, they'd be scurrying off to school. Jarlath and Dan went to St. Joseph's grade school, and their sisters attended Holy Names Academy. Their father drove them to Mass each week day, and when a special feast day came along on Saturday or during the summer he would call upstairs to their bedrooms: "JARLATH—DAN—GIRLS! IT'S THE FEAST OF CORPUS CHRISTI! WE DON'T WANT TO BE LATE!" and off to Mass they all went.

They never felt there was any compulsion to attend

Mass, as their father was the persuasive type, not compelling. Never one to act quickly, he would always say, when his children wanted to do something in the future: "We'll see," or, "Next summer is a long ways off," or, "Ask your mother." That did not mean that her decision was final—and then they would go back to their father for his answer.

Patrick Lyons had a keen mind.

"I might have known he had been in a seminary," Dan said. "He used to help me with my Latin in high school, and I had four years of it. I think he knew Cicero and Virgil better than I ever did later. He also helped my brother with his college math."

Pat Lyons was nine years in America before he married. He spent a year in Philadelphia, a year in Boston, a year in Montreal, and a year or two in Chicago. Dan asked him one time how he got to Seattle. He replied that he went to Butte, Montana, and a man was shot to death in the hotel room next to him on the very first night that he, Patrick Lyons, was in town. So he went to the railway station, put what little money he had on the counter, and said to the ticket agent: "Here, how far will that take me?"

"And that," he said with a straight face, "was how I happened to end up in Seattle."

His children could never tell when he was giving them the facts, or just teasing them. He also had a favorite story about how he packed to come to America.

"When I was leaving Ireland," he often said, "I noticed other people had suitcases, so I picked up an old suitcase and put all I had in it—an old pair of shoes."

Patrick Lyons arrived in Seattle in 1910. For the first five or six years he worked as a longshoreman. Then he graduated to checker on the waterfront. His job was to keep track of what the longshoremen loaded and unloaded. He became a charter member of the Checkers' Union, and taught Dan not to cross a picket line. For helping form the union he was blacklisted at times, which meant he could not get a job at certain docks.

"Dad also worked as a supercargo," Dan said. "That's the guy in charge of loading an entire ship. During World War II there was no export business, so he went back to working as a supercargo. He was offered a government job in 1942, but he felt nothing was more important than sending supplies to our fighting men in the Pacific, including his oldest son, Jarlath, a Navy commander."

Patrick Lyons earned his education the hard way. For eight years, he worked all day on the docks, and went to school in the evenings.

He was often heard to say, "The best thing about America is free night schools." He studied English, mathematics, history, and even Latin. When he considered himself well educated, he went to work in the offices of the Pacific Steamship Company. "Dan," he told his son, "you never get paid for working. The harder you work in this country, the less you get paid." He was referring to using your back instead of your head.

From the steamship business he went to work for Douglas Fir Export Company, owned by 80 lumber mills in Washington and Oregon, and handled all of their export lumber sales. He wasn't with them more than a year before being named the Seattle office's traffic manager, and six months after that he joined with George Inouia, a native of Japan, to form a lumber export firm called U.S. Trading Company. The company operated until World War II, when all exporting was terminated for the duration. They had offices in Tokyo, Osaka, and Kobe, and usually in England, Germany, and mainland China. Their customers extended all over the world, but principally in Japan.

This was back in the 1930s, before the days of freeways, and on one occasion Patrick was driving back to Seattle from Vancouver, B.C., with two customers from Japan. His passengers told him they had to be in Seattle by 7 p.m. As Patrick drove along they kept urging him to go faster. Finally, his patience boiled over. He pulled off onto the shoulder of the road, stopped, turned to his Japanese guests in the back seat, and said: "Do you want to be in Seattle at 9 o'clock—or in hell at 7 o'clock?"

"SEATTLE! SEATTLE! NINE O'CLOCK!"

Whereupon Patrick Lyons resumed driving at a safe pace.

His approach to life was highly original. When there was a strike in the mills or on the docks, sometimes lasting for as long as six months at a time, he'd go downtown to a second-hald bookstore and buy such books as Prescott's history of Peru, or a volume of Longfellow's poems, and read until the strike was settled. He went to work, 9 to 5, just as regularly all during the strike. He was imperturbable. None of the family ever knew his income. When asked how business was he invariably replied that it was "quiet" or "all shot to pieces." Once, when it was booming, he admitted "it's not so bad."

The young woman that Patrick Lyons chose to be his wife was a lovely Swedish girl from Buckley, Washington. Her name was Alice Linnell, the daughter of an immigrant father, and whose mother's parents also emigrated from Sweden. Her mother died before Dan was born, but he can yet remember his maternal grandfather very well.

Dan told me, "While I never met my father's parents, Grandfather Linnell lived with us at times in his latter years. I remember him as a very pleasant, patient old man in his 80s. He had farmed, worked as a carpenter, homesteaded in Alberta for a while, retired at 80 and lived until he was 97. Mother had three brothers and a sister. We were close to all our uncles and cousins, and never seemed to run out of second and third cousins. We frequently visited our relatives."

Alice Linnell was a strict Lutheran. When she was 14, she had been sent back to Minneapolis for a year of religious study, preparatory to being confirmed in the Lutheran Church. Nine years younger than Patrick, she was working in a candy store at Bellingham, Washington, when a girl friend arranged a blind date for her with him. He came down from Vancouver, British Columbia, for the double date, and after he had gone back to Canada, 30 miles away, Alice told her girl friend, "I'm never going out with that Pat Lyons again. He's too Irish—and, besides, he's a Catholic!"

Two years later, they were married.

Today, when her children remind her of what she said about their Dad having been Irish—and *Catholic*—and yet she married him, she says, "Yes, but he wrote such beautiful letters!"

In 1916, two years after she married Patrick, in Vancouver, B.C., Alice Linnell Lyons was converted to Catholicism, shortly after their first child, Patricia, was born. According to her version, two hours after she was baptized in the Cathedral in Seattle, the dome of the cathedral collapsed. "And they're still waiting for me to rebuild it," she says, "but I'm not going to do it."

Patrick and Alice Lyons sent all their children to parochial schools. That was *his* influence. He visited a lot with Irish priests and was very active in the St. Vincent de Paul Society, helping the parish poor. Alice often told him, "You should have been a priest." She never knew he had once been a seminarian.

Since their mother had not been educated in Catholic schools, much of what they learned about the Church came from their father. He had an enormously powerful faith and passed this on to them. He never preached to them, he didn't have to. They could *feel* his faith. It was always there. Once, when Dan was spotted by his father going to Mass without a prayerbook, the father told him he should never be found in Church without his prayerbook or rosary. Patrick said, "None of us is that good."

The mother also had a big influence on the children. She never missed Sunday Mass. She often said, "It would be unthinkable." Religion, husband, children were very important to her.

During those earlier years, Alice Linnell Lyons took such a savor out of life, although because of the Swedish reserve which was her inheritance, you might not always have guessed it. Either great grief or great joy would freeze her to immobility. Afterward, in privacy, she might give way to her emotions but never while outsiders looked on. Nothing seemed to perturb her. Her daughter, Pat, remembers coming home from school one afternoon and was shocked to find a big red firetruck parked in front of the house and hose-carrying firemen frantically climbing all over the roof. Pat rushed through the door, frightened. She found her mother standing at the kitchen sink—nonchalantly cleaning strawberries. "MOM! MOM! WHAT'S GOING ON? WHAT'S THE FIRE ENGINE DOING HERE?" With calm indifference, Alice Lyons said, "Oh, there's a fire upstairs," and she went on cleaning the berries. The roof had caught fire, but the firemen took care of it, as Alice figured they would.

Another example? Well, once when the children's Uncle Henry was a young boy he was out chopping wood and cut off his finger. He ran screaming to Alice. She told him, "QUICK, GO GET THE FINGER!" Moments later, Henry dashed back into the house, shouting, "I'VE GOT IT! I'VE GOT IT! I HAD TO FIGHT THE KITTY FOR IT—BUT HERE IT IS!" Calmly, she sewed the finger back on, and he still has it today.

Like her husband, Alice Lyons read a great deal. She discussed many things, but not neighborhood gossip. Before getting married, she had taken a secretarial training course at Bellingham Normal (now Western Washington State College) and then worked for a while as secretary to Judge Kellogg in Bellingham. After her children grew up and left home, she worked for several more years during World War II as a civilian secretary at the Army offices in Seattle. ("We had to make five carbons of everything," she said. "But nobody read them. Then the war ended—and we had to make only four copies of everything.") Dan and his sister Pat remember that their mother "typed all of us through school." In her 80s today, she can still take shorthand and type fairly well. She typed Dan's first book manuscript for him. Pat remembers that when she wanted to take a course in typing in high school, her father said, "You can learn to type at home from your *mother*." And she did.

All her life Alice Lyons has had such fine small vanities. Even today her complexion is that of a healthy schoolgirl. She is very proud of this. And although in her mid-life her hair turned gray, it never did take on that brittle, lifeless look which so often comes with age. It curled on her head and shone with a lovely luster. She loved little adornments of dress, loved bright colors. On the provocation of a special occasion, she would spend hours down at the local department stores in Seattle—she loved to shop and made something of a ritual of it—picking effects in costumes. She had a positive gift for creating comfort and the feel of luxury out of simple possessions. She could have been living in an attic or a basement and somehow still have made it homelike.

Without being offensive about it, she never avoided speaking her likes and dislikes. But she stopped short of talking about people. She detested gossips. When you told her something confidential you knew it would go no further. For company she preferred young or youngish people. She was frank to say old infirm people bored her to distraction; they wanted to discuss their symptoms, wanted to waste their time—and hers—on small gossip and petty chitchat. Above all, she refused to listen to pessimistic predictions. Everything would turn out all right. It usually did, and meanwhile, she saved herself a lot of worry. Mrs. Lyons was a solid Scandinavian housewife who knew her place and duty in life. That place was the kitchen, the duty to feed and look after her family. She insisted that her children come home every day from school for a hot lunch, and when they walked into the house at 3:30 after school, she was always there to greet them. She always seemed able to time a cake coming out of the oven just as school was letting out.

The Lyons family was typically early American in the sense that they were tightly-knit and affectionate toward one another. Even though Patrick and Alice Lyons were engaged in a struggle for existence during the Depression, they made time for the sentimental relationship between parents and children that marked our American families in those days. Often when any of the girls went to their rooms, they'd find such tidbits as this taped to their mirrors: "Any girl can be gay in a classy coupe . . . in a taxi she can be jolly . . . But the girl that's worthwhile is the one who can smile . . . when you're bringing her home in a trolley." There was charm in the way Patrick Lyons made a point with his children. He often told them such witty little sayings as: "Sophistication is the art of being wise without having wisdom," or "Anyone who swears or uses dirty language does it because he hasn't the proper vocabulary," or "Don't read trashy books, because there's so much good literature printed you'll never read it all."

While he was gentler with the girls, Patrick Lyons could dole out the corporal punishment to Jarlath and Dan. He often harangued them about the importance of saving their money. He'd tell them, "You shouldn't hang around with boys with no ambition. I don't want you going with fellows who aren't going to college." Once, when he heard Jarlath complaining about going to Seattle College, he snapped, "They've graduated better men than you'll ever be." The mother overheard his reprimand, and said, "What a way to talk about your young *hopeful.*"

Sure, Dan Lyons, S.J., remembers the Nineteen Thirties, the terrible, troubled, triumphant, surging Thirties. He and his brother and sisters grew up in them. He can't think of any decade in history when so much happened in so many directions. Violent changes took place. America was modeled, lives remolded, the government rebuilt, forced to function, duties and responsibilities it never had before and can never relinquish. Looking back, the decade seems to have been as carefully designed as a play. It had a beginning, middle and end, even a prologue—1929 gave contrast and tragic stature to the ensuing 10 years.

Father Lyons remembers '29 very well. A lot of his father's friends in Seattle thought they had it made. He remembers the drugged and happy faces of people who built paper fortunes on stocks they couldn't possibly have paid for. "I made ten grand in ten minutes today. Let's see—that's eighty thousand for the week."

In Seattle, bank presidents and trackworkers rushed to pay phones to call brokers. Everyone seemed to be a broker, more or less. At lunch hour, store clerks and stenographers munched sandwiches while they watched the stock boards and calculated their pyramiding fortunes. Their eyes had the look you see around the roulette table.

Then, suddenly, the bottom dropped out, and for the next few years millions of Americans were on an intimate basis with cold and hunger. Dan was only twelve, but in 1932 he found himself involved with loss, too. The bank where he had been putting his savings—money he had earned from odd jobs—went broke, and Dan's total assets, $80, were gone. His father lost $30,000 in savings. Patrick said nothing about his own loss, but felt terrible about his son's setback.

For the next eight years, however, Dan kept receiving checks for the amount of eight or nine dollars from the bank. He got his $80 all back—and with interest. His sister, Pat, remembers that he was the hero of their neighborhood. He was the only one of the kids with any money. They envied him for it. "I don't know why they envied me," he said. "I'd gone out and *earned* the money."

Pat said, "Dan should have been a banker. I don't know how he did it, but he always seemed to have a job. There just weren't any jobs to be had during the Depression—but Dan had one. All the time. He was always putting his money in the bank. He was the only one of us who had steady income. I remember that he had enough money to afford a gray mohair sweater. I loved that sweater. The style in those days for girls was long sweaters with pleated skirts, and I was always trying to borrow Dan's sweater. One day, while he was away, I dressed all up to go out and thought I'd snitch that sweater. I snuck into his room, only to discover he had slipped his bicycle lock through the sleeve and neck and locked it, making it impossible to wear. My brother knew all the angles."

Apropos to that story, the first air trip Patrick and Alice Lyons ever took together was on June 21, 1937. It was a wedding present from their children. The occasion was a sentimental one to Vancouver, B.C., where they had been married in 1914. On the way to the airport, their mother said to all her children, "It might have been your idea to send us on this trip—but I'll bet it was *Danny's* money!"

That marked her first time in the air, and she kept saying, "It's a beautiful day for flying." And Patrick said, straight-faced, "We'll never get off the ground, there are *clouds* in the sky."

The good old days!

CHAPTER 6

The Games Boys Play

Early in life, Father Dan became imbued with a sense of adventure. It was a part of him which he never really overcame. He was a good-sized boy for his age, strong and sharp-witted. Those days when he joined hands with life became happy memories.

He now entered upon a bouncing behaviorism. There was youthful mischief in him, yet never a grain of malice. He was simply all boy.

Sometimes, as the years whirl by faster and faster, there are those who find themselves wanting to stop, if only for a little while, and look back at all that has gone before—all that has brought us to where we are now. My own brother, Pat, who teaches in Spain and who earlier wrote the splendid play, "The Last Summer," has several lines in the narration which go: "They say that the human body renews itself every so many years; if that is so, then I am not, physically, the same person I was forty years ago. But what about that intangible something within, that *me* that no surgeon with his scalpel can ever find? How wonderful it would be to call out of the past the person that was, to talk to him and ask . . . so many, many questions. If such a thing were possible I'd want to talk to a very important self in my past—the boy of summer, 1932."

Well, what about the Dan Lyons of summer, 1932? What sort of life was it for him then?

It was this sort of life. . . .

He used to swim nearly every day during the summer, usually at Madison Park on Lake Washington. But sometimes at Madrona Park, or Mt. Baker Park, or Seward Park; or at Alki Point, in Puget Sound. Like the word Seattle, Alki was an Indian word, given to the Point when the first white settlers arrived there. The full name given was "New York Alki," Alki meaning "by and by." Those first settlers were the Denny family, who arrived in the 1840's. They had their little son with them, a child in arms. Dan met and visited with that child, when he, Mr. Denny, was past 90, a real link with the history of Dan's native Washington, which did not become a state until 1889, some 31 years before Dan was born.

The Lyons family frequently went for extensive rides in their Buick on Sundays. In 1927 they had their first glass-enclosed car, instead of curtains. In 1929 Mrs. Lyons learned to drive. Teaching her how was an experience right out of a Bob Newhart comedy skit. One afternoon, Patrick took her out for a lesson. She was driving around the tower in Seattle's Volunteer Park—a one-way road—when suddenly another car popped up in front of them, coming the wrong way.

"Pat!" she cried. "What shall I do?"

"You're at the wheel," he said.

Alice Lyons made her decision. She crashed into a light pole.

At that time, *The Seattle Times* was running a contest entitled, "The Worst Bawling Out I Ever Got From My Husband."

Alice Lyons won first prize!

When he was satisfied she could do it, Patrick urged Alice to take the car and drive the children to California. They went all the way to Mexico, visiting most of the old Spanish Missions along the way. Dan learned to drive on the ocean beaches on that trip, sitting on a pillow so that he could reach the clutch. The trip made a lasting impression on the children, according to their ages. Dan was just old enough to bring back many memories of Oregon and California, the latter especially, along with Mexico, striking him as such a different part of the world.

The long days of summer always rolled by on greased axles for him. He was twelve now, and there was always something to do. In June, he and Jarlath went to Wickersham, in the northern part of the state, where their Uncle Roscoe Tibbles had a farm and three sons. It was a stirring time of year. School was out, the sun had returned to warm the woods country, and there was always something to do. Not only house doors and windows, but cellar doors, the attic window, and the great barn door were open now, day and night. Barefoot boys, no longer handicapped by school hours, were free to roam at will, wading streams, peering into squirrel holes, feeding small birds in the hollows of trees, following trails far into the forests, digging in sandbanks, and playing baseball.

There was nothing formal about their games. They played baseball, for instance, wherever they happened to be when the fancy took them. Someone would raise a hand and yell "scrub one," and he'd be the first batter. Scrub two would be the catcher, scrub three the pitcher, and so on. They just marked out a home plate in a cow pasture and picked the nearest convenient tree for first base. The only restriction they ever observed was to move a good distance away from any plate-glass windows. They had only one real problem in their games. That was getting a ball. They used a ball until there wasn't any ball left. When the cover came off, they wrapped it in black friction tape. When it got lopsided, they stopped the game and pounded it back in shape. When it started unraveling, they rewound it. Sometimes it would unravel too much and get so small they could hardly see it. Then they would fuse it together with the remains of another ball and make a new one. Such was country baseball in 1932.

Another of their diversions was to go to the nearest stream and play roughhouse, such as swinging themselves across the water by means of a stout rope tied to a limb. Sometimes they fished for bullheads and trout, sometimes they went about searching for "buried treasure," and sometimes they went whooping and prancing along the water's edge, chasing each other round and round, shedding clothes as they went, until they had peeled down to their underwear, and then continued the frolic in the water, against the stiff current, which tripped their legs from under them and greatly increased the fun. Now and then they stooped in a group and splashed water at each other with their palms, slowly moving toward one another, with averted faces to avoid the strangling sprays, and finally gripping and struggling until the best man ducked his mate, and then they all went under in a tangle of white legs and arms and came up blowing, sputtering, laughing, and gasping for breath at one and the same time. When they were completely exhausted, they, would run out and sprawl on the dry, hot sand, lie there and cover themselves up with it, and then, gaining another surge of energy, would break for the water again and go through the original performance all over again.

By July, the countryside was laden with tall grass new-cut and drying in the sun, the corn knee-high was ready for hoeing, potatoes, squashes, and pumpkins in bloom, sweet peas climbing up chicken wire to cover the shed wall with pink, white, red and lavender; lettuce, radishes, and cucumbers were for the picking, and the pea pods were full. The nights were short and the dark was thin and soft, a-twinkle with fireflies, heavy still with the heat of the sun, and rich with the smell of fruit and flowers and fir. It was a glorious place for a 12-year-old to spend part of each summer.

In the waning days of the season, when the corn silk was ripe and reddish, the boys would suddenly get a hankering to smoke. Now smoking in the early Thirties was regarded as a vice. Cigarettes were called "coffin nails," and the users known as "fiends." American women did not smoke. When a boy began this habit he had to go through more dodges in hiding his bronchial debauchery than a writer of bad checks. So when Dan first saw Jarlath roll up the "makings" in a piece of newspaper and light it, he caught at the idea and said he would like to try it, too. The young brothers found a place behind their uncle's barn a comparatively safe sanctuary for their trial smoking exercises, and Jarlath rolled Dan one of his super-duper lung-foggers and handed it to him. Dan had never smoked before, and his brother showed him how to put a torch to it and puff.

Soon they were stretched out on their elbows and puffing in earnest. The smoke had a bitter taste, like burnt weeds, and they coughed and gagged a little, but Dan said, boldly: "It jes' takes a little gettin' used to."

Jarlath nodded in agreement. He said, "It's easy. I don't feel sick at all."

Dan said, "Neither do I. I could smoke this stuff for a week without stopping. I bet some of the guys couldn't though. Two puffs and they'd faint dead away."

Jarlath said, "I wish I could see them tackle it just once."

"Oh, don't I," Dan said. "Jes' one little ol' snifter and they'd have to be carted away."

"They sure would."

"Yeah."

The talk drifted on. But by and by it began to dwindle somewhat, and grow a trifle drowsy. The silences widened. The spitting grew more prevalent. Both Jarlath and Dan were looking very pale and miserable now. Their tongues felt like charred liver, their nostrils could barely bail out the smoke fast enough, and sudden retchings resulted every time little overflowings escaped down the wrong hatch. Jarlath's burning ash dropped from his shaking hand. He moaned, "I don't feel so good."

"Me neither," Dan said, his face ashen-colored. "I think I'm gonna throw up."

"Me, too," Jarlath said.

Around the dinner table that evening neither Jarlath nor Dan were very talkative. Something told their uncle that if they had had any trouble during the afternoon they had got rid of it. They both had a humble look, and they were not forced to eat.

Dan had learned his lesson. He never smoked again.

With the approach of harvest came one of Dan's favorite events on the year's calendar, the annual Western Washington Fair at Puyallup, 30 miles south of Seattle. There was something very exciting about those old Fairgrounds, and Dan and Jarlath and their sisters looked forward to "Seattle Day" every year. Located on a large tract of ground at the south end of town, the old wooden fence encircling the grounds had been whitewashed once upon a time, but by 1932 the rains of years had washed the fence to a wispy gray, so that in the dusk the long warped panels stood up in rows, palely luminous. The rust had run down from the eaten-out nailholes until each plank had two staring eyes on a wooden fence. The ancient grandstand was of wood, too, and had stood there in all weathers until its rheumatic rafters groaned and creaked in the senility of advancing age. Behind the grandstand stood the buildings that housed the agricultural exhibits; squash the size of green boulders, stalks of corn fourteen feet long—well, eight feet anyway; families of chickens domiciled unhappily in wooden coops.

Dan and his family always tried to get to Puyallup for the Fair early in the morning, when the familiar pattern took form. The fairgrounds had their own concerto. There were first the sounds of birds chirping, chicken legs frying, and the distant crack of a hammer. Soon the barns came alive, and then, like the strike of a match, everything seemed to be one big scene of activity. Everyone was busy. Over in the stables the grooms were pitching hay, lugging pails of water and shouldering sacks of feed. The trainers were meticulously preparing their horses for workouts.

Morning crawled toward noon. The beat of the fair quickened. People from miles around were arriving, pouring through the front gate. They came afoot, by bus, in private automobiles, and even in farm wagons that jolted whole families. From grandsire to babe in arms they were all smiling and filled with grand anticipation.

The midway was still relatively quiet, but the drama of the livestock shows was beginning to pick up. In the cool shade of the sheep tent men knelt in line, their animals by their sides, and spectators stared solemnly at them. The exhibitors, wearing straw hats, blue cotton shirts and white suspenders, knelt almost motionless. Finally, after closely inspecting each animal, the judge was ready to make his decision. The eyes of the men did not move from the eyes of the judge. When he finally announced his decision, clapping broke the stillness, and the winner accepted his blue ribbon unsmilingly. The losers just shook their heads, looked suspiciously at the judge, and walked off into the noonday sun.

The Puyallup Fair was a place for competition. It was evident everywhere. In the halls of the grandstand elderly women fussed over their needlework and their quilts and their pies and cakes, and they seemed painfully aware of the young woman down the hall who had just sprung a prize piece of pastry on them. It was not the pastry—it was just that she was so young and so pretty!

As vital to the fair as competition was the fact that it was a meeting place for old friends who did not see much of each other. Many families, the same ones every year, journeyed to Puyallup, and they lived in tents on the edge of the fairgrounds. They usually stayed for the entire week, much of which was devoted to the exchange of gossip and just looking. The men looked longingly at the farm equipment on exhibit and the women looked at each other. The small boys just stared big-eyed at the stateliness and strength of the draft horses and the skill of the men harnessing that strength. The old men, tired from the sun, wandered the halls, browsing through the pamphlets at the various booths and inspecting everything from contour chairs to the display of shaving mugs.

Over on the midway business was in full swing. The wide trail of dust that was the midway was packed with people, and the afternoon air was torn with sound, a different sound at every few steps—the crack of a rifle in the shooting gallery, the gay yet melancholy tootle of a calliope, the deep growl of the Ferris-wheel motor, the hollow pop of wooden bottles being hit by a thrown ball, the screams of young girls being jolted by twisting rides and the cry of the food dispensers. "Get 'em while they're hot! The biggest hamburger at the fair! Only a thin dime . . . just ten cents. Right this way, friends. . . ."

To Dan, the sweetest sound at the Puyallup Fair was that of the bugle summoning the horses to the post at racetime. It was a kind of racing devoid of pomp and pandemonium and frenetic jockeying for the mutuel window. There was no betting, but that was not the reason for the unemotional atmosphere; rather, the spectators, many of them local farmers, were just content to watch the animals run, to see a demonstration of courage and speed and strength. Indeed, the crowd generally appeared uninterested until the horses flattened out at the top of the stretch, and then there was just a low hum, a voice, like a high note on a trumpet, quivering: "Come on, boy! Turn it loose now!" And later, the race long over, the farmers would sit around on the grass as the evening shadows blanketed the grandstand, and savor and discuss with authority the races they had seen during the day's grandstand show.

Dan loved horses. He loved to ride them, and dating back as far as he could remember there had been a horse or two around his uncle's farm. One of his favorites had been an old plug called Sparky; nothing more than a middle-aged, slow-witted animal really, but he was a dignified old character with a mellow disposition, and Dan loved him. He even considered that old bay handsome. Sparky had a solid, stolid, heavy-footed gallop that jolted the rider hard at each bounce. His legs were thick and he never learned to lift them. He ran, sort of dragging his feet. He always hung his head low as he laboriously pounded along and he had a habit of stopping short in the middle of a gallop when he felt he needed some rest. When he stopped, Dan often kept right on going. Old Sparky stopped quite frequently, too, to indicate he was done for and weary and Dan had to shout and nudge him in the ribs before he would take up his pace again with considerable lagging resignation. But Dan enjoyed the usually amiable old horse and tolerated his moods.

Dan and brother Jarlath were the most combative of the children. They got along well, but occasionally they would have a falling out with each other. Their misunderstandings passed like thunder-clouds, however, leaving the sky clearer than before. There never was any real animosity when they clashed. Maybe they would be strolling home from school and Jarlath would suddenly turn and try to trip Dan. Dan responded by playfully jabbing back. Jarlath would return the punch, a little harder this time. Dan hit back, putting more weight into the blow. Then Jarlath would tackle him and wrestle him to the ground. Now they were fighting in earnest to protect their individual honor, rolling and tumbling in the dirt, gripped together in a tangle of arms and legs, whaling the holy dickens out of one another; and for the space of five minutes they'd tug and tear at each other's hair and clothes, punching and scratching each other's noses, and covering themselves with dust and boyish glory. Presently the confusion took form and through the fog of battle two dusty and tattered boys emerged standing, their tempers temporarily spent, glaring at each other.

"Hadda 'nuff?"

"YOU got 'nuff?"

"Asked you first."

"Don't push me."

"I can lick you."

"Can't."

"Can."

An uncomfortable pause. Then: "We're gonna catch it when we get home. Lookit our clothes."

"Well, you started it."

"Didn't."

"Did."

Now they were shoulder to shoulder again, eyeing and sidling around each other.

"You wanna 'nother punch?"

"Do *you?*"

And so it would go, all the way home. It was more of a game with them than genuine anger. Two young brothers fighting for the sheer joy of releasing their youthful energies. There was no bitterness. If anything, mutual respect grew out of their little arguments. There were only a couple of years separating their ages, and not much difference in size, and as long as the younger Dan felt he could knock his older brother's block off, he kept trying. Dan had plenty of fighting heart and courage.

Their mother was a disciplinarian about most things, but when it came to fighting she seldom interfered and allowed her sons to settle their differences in their own ways as long as they did it outdoors. She played no favorites. Her house was her castle in true Scandinavian tradition, however, and the boys were flirting with trouble if they fought indoors. Once, while she was busy entertaining a neighbor lady in the living room, Jarlath and Dan started rassling on the floor. The visitor was shocked.

"Aren't you going to stop them, Alice?" she asked. "They're going to hurt themselves."

"Just ignore them," Mrs. Lyons said. "Let them solve their own problems in their own way and everything will be better for them both." Then, turning to the boys, she said, "You know the rule about fighting inside the house. Now you go outdoors and finish your fight there. HURRY!"

Ten minutes later, Jarlath and Dan were back in the house together again, pleasantly playing in the corner, their differences forgotten.

For the most part, the Lyons' youngsters were robust and healthy. Patricia, for example, was an outstanding ice skater and won many races at the local rink. All four of the girls swam across Lake Washington and back—a mile each way. Noreen was an exhibition diver for the Washington Athletic Club. There was very little sickness in the family. Still, whenever one of them fell ill, their mother knew exactly what to do to get them up and running again. Her principal remedy was that century-old standby no home could function without—castor oil! A typical dose was a half a cupful of castor oil with a half cupful of molasses added to help it down and make it taste good, which it never did.

Doctors were not called in cases of ordinary illness. The mother attended to those. Every mother, it seems, was a doctor in those days, and gathered her own medicine in the strangest places, and knew how to compound brews that would stir the vitals of a cast-iron monkey.

Alice Lyons had no formal training in medicine, of course, yet there was one disease she was master of and could cure and the doctors couldn't. There was no sense sending for a professional practitioner when it struck, for it was a young boy's disease of a strange and traditional sort and always hit without exception early each year just as the frost was working out of the ground, and out of the air, too; just as the days were getting closer and closer to barefoot time, and marble and mumbletypeg time, and kites and baseball and fishing and hiking.

It would set a boy to sighing and saddening around the house, and it was evident something was mighty wrong with him, but he didn't know what. He would go outside by himself and mope and stroll down the block and think; mostly he hunted for a private place off on a tall hill some place, where he could sit and gaze dreamily away off to the East at the Cascade Mountains where the arc of the sky looked smoky and dim and so still, and everything was so solemn it seemed like everybody a boy loved was dead and gone, and he almost wished he was dead and gone, too, and done with it all. What was this mysterious malady? Why, it was *spring fever,* of course. And when Jarlath and Dan were younger and caught it, they wanted—oh, they didn't quite know what it was they did want, but it fairly made their hearts ache, they wanted it so!

Whenever Dan caught it, it seemed to him what he mainly wanted was just to get away; get away from the same old humdrum life of going to school every day, doing chores, taking a bath, going to bed, getting up in the morning—only to do it again the next day, and the next, and the next. It was so tedious, a boy needed to see something new for himself once in a while. That was the idea; he wanted to be a traveler; he wanted to travel far away to foreign lands where everything was strange and wonderful and full of adventure. He would like to go to Ireland, his dad had talked about the homeland so much. And if it wasn't possible to go to Ireland, he would have put up with lots less; he would go anywhere he *could* go, just so he could have a change of scenery, and be thankful of the chance, too.

There was nothing new about this condition. It had been going on for as long as they had been making little boys. When I wrote *Six Roads From Abilene,* the story of the Eisenhower brothers, I asked the second oldest brother, attorney Edgar Eisenhower, if he'd ever had spring fever when he was a lad back in Kansas. Ed grinned. "You bet," he said. "But it never lasted long. Our mother had just the cure for it, the dangest-tasting concoction you ever did see. Mom brewed it up herself. She made it from a prescription which had been passed down to her from her mother, and from her mother's mother before that. It consisted of one part sulphur and one part molasses, and no matter what my state of health was, Mom would give me a heaping spoonful of that stuff at the very first indication of the annual fever—just on general principles! Nothing known to medicine ever rid a schoolboy so fast of what ailed him."

In 1932, flying was for the wildly adventurous—or for the very rich. But train travel—now *that* was the business for Dan, Jarlath and their friends. As far as they were concerned, the train was here to stay. The sight of giant locomotives roaring across the Puget Sound countryside, trailing their pearled plumes, with a cut of thirty cars in tow, or more—this was so commonplace, their thunderous snorts in heavy labor so ordinary, the toot-toot-toot of their whistles so much a part of the American scene, that most grownups did not bother to appreciate them consciously. It was only the children who stood and wondered.

The railroads were at their zenith then, and time was standing still. Their proud engines and cars displayed heralds that were bywords of the day in the Pacific Northwest: Great Northern, Northern Pacific, Great Western, and the Milwaukee, to name only a few. Poets were inspired to sonnets by these names, and novelists put them into their books, just for the music of them.

Even freight trains were not excluded from the romance that pervaded all phases of railroading. Jarlath, Dan, and their cousin, Larry Linnell, now a sergeant with the Washington State Patrol, were familiar with freight trains, in 1933. It was during the hell of the U.S. Depression, and newly-elected President Franklin D. Roosevelt had asked the railroads to let the public ride the freights for free. Thousands of Americans took advantage of the arrangement, including children and family dogs. The Lyonses had an uncle Sabin living on a farm over in Idaho, and Jarlath and Dan rode the freights several times to see him, just as an excuse to have some place to go. Every summer they caught a freight in Seattle and traveled 400 miles over to Idaho. Their parents never tried to stop them. They accepted their sons' promise to stay out of trouble.

Once, when Jarlath and Dan started to leave to catch a freight, their father gave them a dollar. "Here," he said, smiling, "it's all the money I've got—and now I don't have that much."

Dan still remembers that trip.

"All the boxcars heading East out of Seattle were full," he said. "So we rode on top. We rode with the best of them. I was only 13 years old, and the freights were crowded with migrant workers and hoboes. During the Depression the land of opportunity was a seat on top of one of those freight cars. Jarlath and I went everywhere on them. It was a great way to travel for a 13-year-old kid. We had our Tibbles relatives in Wickersham, and we'd ride up there; there was another uncle at Van Zandt, near Bellingham; and some more aunts and uncles at Riverton, Washington, and at Sumas, close to the British Columbia border. We had plenty of places we could take the freights."

His uncle at Riverton owned the local grocery store; and a cousin of his mother's at Sumas also had a grocery and ran the Sumas Rodeo. But their favorite stop was Uncle Roscoe Tibbles' farm.

"We used to make ice cream by milking the cow, getting ice out of the empty fruit train cars, and grinding it up in the old-fashioned hand freezer," Dan said. "We had great picnics with our relatives and friends up there, and enjoyed working on Uncle Roscoe's farm. At 13, I helped put shakes on my uncle's barn at Van Zandt. Thirty-nine years later, those shakes are still on it."

It was the summer of 1933 that Dan and his pal, Herb Valentine, hitch-hiked up to Wickersham to see the Tibbles for a week, and then went on to Bellingham. They rode the freight train to Bellingham, and slept the night in an empty boxcar. The night was damp, cold, and to keep warm they built a fire inside the boxcar with newspapers. At 5 a.m., a resident nearby spotted the fire and reported it to authorities. Police investigated, found the two boys, and took them back to jail and locked them up. They spent three hours in a cell before they were released.

"Get out of town," police told them. "And when you go back to Seattle, take the boat."

They did.

A local Bellingham radio newscaster, with scant news to report, picked up the story. On his broadcast that day, he told of the two young visitors who had been lodged at the local jail, and revealed their names. Dan's uncle heard the newscast. Whenever his nephew visited him after that he told him where he could sleep: "There's a boxcar out on the track in front of the house . . ." There were a lot of remarks in the Lyons household when Pop heard about the episode. His boy in jail already, before he was 14! His companion, Herb Valentine, was to become one of the most celebrated Marine pilots in World War II, later personal helicopter pilot for President Eisenhower.

Once, while Dan and Jar had just gotten off a freight train in Idaho, they were asked if they would like a job fighting forest fires. Dan thought it would be an adventure, but his brother dismissed the idea: "I'm too hot now," he said. And that was that.

As they rode on top of the box cars, they sat on the walk used by railroad crewmen. They brought a blanket along to keep warm during the night, and put their belt through one of the boards to keep from rolling off. In those days, the engines burned coal, and there was a great deal of coal dust if you were on the first 10 cars, as it blew off of the open coal car just behind the engine. If you were more than 30 cars back, you were apt to get a great deal of smoke and cinders in your eyes, as the smoke from the engine settled back on the latter sections of the train.

On one occasion, Dan and Jar were pulling into a little town in the mountains of western Montana named Paradise, where the train changed crews. It was early in the morning, and the 75 or 80 vagrants on top of the cars had trouble keeping warm, and keeping the cinders out of their eyes. One of the more professional "hoboes" said to another: "What town is this?" The other replied: "This is Paradise." The first one remarked: "If this is Paradise, I'll take hell and a cup of coffee."

The boys laughed as they watched some of the professional riders check off points of interest as the train passed them. The hoboes had circulars issued by the railroad for attracting customers on the passenger trains. "Well," said Dan, "I hope they are getting their money's worth!"

Glimpses of Dan Lyons in junior and high school may

be gathered from letters written to us by him while we were working on this book:

"During the Depression, our family had an old car. As it got older and finally broke down, it sat in the garage for a year before it was fixed . . .

"Jar and I collaborated with Bill and Herb Valentine in buying a car for twenty dollars. We used to park it in garages of vacant houses. It never occurred to us to buy insurance, and with gasoline selling for 19.5-cents a gallon, I often drove up to the station attendant and said, 'Gimme a nickel's worth.' A nickel bought you a quart. The station manager would look at me in disgust and reply, 'Put it in yourself.' I usually spilled two-cents worth putting it into a milk bottle, so my purchase didn't mean much profit. I was only 13 years old then, still three years away from the legal age of 16 . . .

"We all had paper routes. When the circulation manager launched a drive for new subscriptions and announced that 'past records don't count in this contest,' my brother Jar would say under his breath, 'That leaves my slate clean . . .'

"We also caddied at Broadmoor Golf Club, and in my senior year at Seattle Prep I served as a chauffeur for a wealthy widow, Mrs. E. T. Greene, who lived at Broadmoor. Herb Valentine had been her driver, and when he was ready to quit the job, he phoned her.

" 'This is the manager of your employment agency,' he said, 'and I'm sending out a qualified driver for an interview.'

"Out I went. Mrs. Greene hired me on the spot. The job

required driving her around for a few hours each day after school . . .

"My Dad sometimes took me with him on business trips. Once, when we were driving back from Vancouver, B.C, he told me that the man he had gone to buy lumber from, had come to him many years before to purchase lumber. That was when Dad worked for Douglas Fir Export Company. The man had needed a lot of lumber, it seemed, with difficult specifications to come by, and before Dad assured him whether or not it was possible to get the lumber at the time, the fellow indirectly offered him a bribe. Dad told him, 'You're a nice fellow. I like you. If you hadn't said that, you might have gotten what you came here for. But I'll tell you what you can do—get the hell out of here and never come back.'

"After telling me the story, I said to him: 'Now that the tables are turned, I'm surprised you even bother to call on him for lumber.' And Dad replied: 'He has the greatest respect for me. If he had been able to bribe me, he'd despise me.'

"Dad often remarked how it was the Masons, not the Catholics, who so often cooperated with him in business. But he had no use for a Catholic who joined the Masons, since it was forbidden by the Church. He once met a man named Jack Doyle, born in Ireland, who had drifted away from the Church. The Masons had lured him to join with the promise of a better job if he would join them. He thus went from longshoreman to a checker and got to wear a dress suit. Dad walked up to him, eyed the suit, circled all around him several times, then raised one elbow and polished the Masonic lapel pin and said: 'Well, Jack, aren't we going places now! Yes sir. But I sure would hate to be where you're going to end up!'

"Another time, Dad heard a longshoreman say, 'Hitler is even trying to change the Bible!' And Dad asked him, 'What version do you read?' And the longshoreman replied, 'The King James version.' And Dad said, 'Well, he was the first *politician* to change the Bible—and politicians have been changing it ever since!' "

CHAPTER 7

The Making of a Jesuit

The smells, the sights, and the feelings of the U.S. Depression were everywhere still, in 1936, and there were even times when it threatenened to overtake the Lyons family. Patrick had lost $30,000 in the crash, all of his savings, and his meagre exchequer dwindled away to practically nothing. But he and his wife were determined and resourceful people. Their spunk carried them through. They scrimped, saved, played, laughed and prayed together.

The children never worried. Their mother never worried. And if their father ever worried, they never knew it. Somehow, Patrick kept the family fed and shod, just like millions of other American families. His wife had a childlike philosophy about money. Whatever was allocated to her was to spend. Her husband's job was to earn and to save, she felt. When she needed more, she asked for it. "That's all I have," Patrick would often counsel as he gave it to her. Her customary reply was for him to "just go down to the bank and get some more." Whether she understood the intricacies of high finance or not, if money was scarce she never complained.

Father Dan owes a vast amount of stability of thinking and living to his dad. Patrick Lyons, strong-willed, brave and tenacious, was a man with a lot of class. He always dressed well, and he had little respect for a man who might have driven to lunch in a Cadillac, but lacked the graces of good table manners.

When Eamon de Valera arrived in Seattle, in 1928, he asked the then affluent Patrick Lyons for funds to help start the Irish Press. They became lifelong friends after that. On another occasion, Patrick was riding with a Naval Admiral whom he had invited to speak at an Irish picnic at Fortuna Park, on Mercer Island, near Seattle. The Admiral asked him, "How do you know so much about the Smoot-Hawley tariff and all these other things we've been discussing?" Patrick, the immigrant from Ireland, drew himself up and said, "You forget, my dear Admiral, I was educated abroad."

One of his pet phrases about Americans traveling abroad was: "It's not that you have to dress like an American—but you have to dress like a European *thinks* an American should dress."

Patrick Lyons was Americanized in many ways, but he was unable to shake his accent completely. He spoke with a brogue. Anne Keefe, a friend of the family, worked as his personal secretary, and after taking dictation from him one day, asked, "Should I take the *brogue* out of it?" Anne later went to work at a bank, and he used to ask her to "put a cipher after my account."

His eldest child, Patricia, remembers when he returned from his first trip to Ireland, in 1930, and had his Irish cronies gathered around, telling stories. Patricia and her mother were in the kitchen fixing coffee and cakes and overheard the thick brogues chattering away in the next room. "Sure, and isn't it strange how quickly a person loses his brogue in America," someone said.

"Sure, and it is."

"Isn't it though."

Complete agreement all around.

Alice Lyons nudged her daughter. "Listen to the Irish," she said. "You can't understand a word from any of them."

When she and Patrick were young and still courting, her family, she confessed, couldn't understand why she wanted to go "with that foreigner. No one can make head or tails of anything he says!" But he attended night school to cut down his brogue.

Brogue or no brogue, Patrick Lyons had the deepest respect for education. His search for knowledge went on all his life. He believed that man uses only a small part of his mentality and that intellectual riches await the mental miner who digs deep enough. The magnitude of the universe, and man's role in it, fascinated him.

He expected his children to get good marks in school. He would settle for nothing less. Homework was something of a ritual in the Lyons home. After the dinner dishes were done, everyone sat around the living room table, hitting their books. Patrick went from person to person tutoring them. He was a human encyclopedia; no matter what the subject, he could usually come up with the right answer.

This boning up paid off for Dan. In a box of old family papers I found his original 8th grade mid-term report card. It was dated January, 1934, the one year he attended O'Dea High School, which was run by the Irish Christian Brothers. The card was signed by "W. K. O'Connell, Principal," and the grades follow: Christian Doctrine, B; Arithmetic, B; Reading, A; Spelling, A; Language, B; Drawing, A; History, C; Literature, B; Elocution, B; Physiology, C.

The "B" in Elocution was noteworthy, for his dad urged him to participate in public speaking and debating when he transferred to Seattle Prep the following year. Dan went on to excel in oratory. He blossomed out into the best debater in school and often competed in state-wide tournaments.

The Seattle Prep debate teams in those days were comprised of three students, with separate teams for the Affirmative and the Negative positions. Among Dan's colleagues were John Wright, who went on to become a noted Jesuit theologian; Mike McHugh, later rector of the Novitiate at Sheridan, Oregon, and a prominent pastor in Portland and Seattle; and John Monahan, who became a noted Latin and Greek professor, an assistant to the Oregon Provincial, and a missionary in far-off Rhodesia.

Dan remembers those days well.

"One of our opponents on the O'Dea High School debate team was a boy named Neil McCluskey," Dan recalled. "Neil and I had gone through the first grade together. We were also members of the 1933-34 eighth-grade graduation class at O'Dea, the last school year that O'Dea had an eighth grade attached to the high school. Neil entered the Novitiate at Sheridan the same day I did, and later served as

Gonzaga's Academic Dean when I was Dean of Students there. The friendship we started in the first grade has bound us for life. We still meet regularly. Father Neil is now Dean of Education at Lehman College, formerly Hunter College, in the Bronx, New York, with 155 college teachers under him."

Listening to Dan Lyons talk about his boyhood, it is difficult to realize unless you have been though it, what a fantastic amount of study, work and play can be got in by a kid with a good constitution and a willingness to be on the go from dawn to midnight. These are traits Dan has carried with him all his life.

That was some of the training Dan Lyons, future S.J., had.

Summer vacations meant steadier work and a little reserve added to the Dan Lyons bank account. And it also meant family picnics, sandlot baseball games, fishing, hiking, riding freight trains to Idaho, Montana, and the far corners of Washington. It meant, too, visiting those farms of his various uncles.

Such was life around Seattle for a poor boy during the Depression. You will find it paralleled in history by thousands upon thousands of youngsters in similar circumstances. In many ways it was an exciting and engrossing life, this battle against the biggest city in the Pacific Northwest, for education, sustenance and joy. And it also had an important bearing on Dan's character, his make-up and behavior in later life. It imposed upon him virtues that he has never lost.

Dan takes exceptionally good care of himself. He is a paragon of proper living habits. He keeps in rigid training with 50 pushups a day and is always in top physical and mental condition. His pleasures are simple. He doesn't drink. He doesn't smoke. Physical condition is a part of the American system of competition and free enterprise. The regimens whereby it is achieved are strictly self-imposed. It is acquired in direct proportion to the ambition of the boy who cares to practice it. His office at 86 Riverside is on the first floor. His room is on the fifth. There is no elevator. He considers that a blessing.

The bright and desirable prizes are held out to the youngster—a place on the team, a uniform, a letter, a trip. The coach makes the simple rules of training and points out what kind of an athlete is wanted on the team.

And the ambition of the individual does the rest. Dan likes the quotation of Red Blaik, the famous coach: "Nice guys are a dime a dozen, but an aggressive leader is priceless."

Dan's clean living has never grown out of a smugness and prudery, not alone out of a desire for personal sanctification. He always has had a stubborn, pushing ambition to accomplish something. He wants to serve God, and he wants to keep the world protected from the enemies of freedom and justice, and he has chosen the most sensible and efficient route to getting it. Since control of his mind and body is an important factor in holding himself up under tremendous tensions and pressures, he takes care of his physical and mental machinery in an intelligent manner.

Habits formed in youth are apt to last through life. Dan's have. He has never made a parade of his virtues, or even considered them as such. He merely lives the way he likes to live. And that means no liquor. He keeps away from spirits, not because of any prissy notions or righteousness that it is evil or wrong to take a drink, but because he has a driving, non-stop mission in life. Anything that interferes with that ambition is poison to him.

Home training had much to do with this, besides the sound soul and spirit of the boy, but the early habits of his life were also greatly responsible. The matter of time takes on a great importance; time, and the manner in which he spent his boyhood.

Even if a boy was basically sound, there was plenty of trouble for him to get into around Seattle in the Thirties, especially if he lived in a middle-class neighborhood, where some of the kids tended to drift into bands, or young gangs, groups that started as a rivalry to the bunch down the next block, and which could have easily drifted into pilfering, window-smashing and other petty offences which later could have led to the higher brackets of misdemeanor and crime.

But Dan Lyons avoided these pitfalls, for there were just so many hours to a waking day, and every minute of them was occupied with working, attending school, or playing on some kind of team. There was simply no time left for mischief.

Young Dan was an unusually sensitive sort of boy during

this formative period. At 16, he was even then showing a strong kinship toward religiosity. Wilfred P. Schoenberg, S.J., the Gonzaga historian, told me a story about the young Dan Lyons that illustrates how far back his concern for his fellow human beings goes.

His Seattle Prep days were the days when so-called "Skid Road" was still a part of the city. It was a scabrous area, two blocks of blight. First impressions of a place often prove misleading, but in this instance they showed a melancholy accuracy. The Skid Roads of America can never be things of beauty, and the lower south side of Seattle's business activity was certainly, in the local idiom, "a rough place." In such an environment Dan volunteered to spend his Saturday nights, walking among the derelicts and disenchanted, bringing spiritual comfort to those who would listen, and regularly passing out 150 copies of *America*, the Jesuit weekly magazine.

The standard of men down in that part of town was for the most part lamentably low. They were mostly lonely loggers, hundreds of them; some were out of work, some had merely come to town from down out of the hills to find sanctuary in a tavern, or perhaps the brothels. They'd roar into town, blow their winter's take in a week, and then walk back into the woods for a summer of near starvation. The light of the mountains and the light of ignorance burned brightly in their eyes. Slave laborers, if you will, condemned by modern economics to work as long as their brawn lasted.

These men were raw men. The instinctive despair that maked for killing was close beneath the surface, for they knew no different life on which to base hope. But the humanity that makes for living was there too in a primitive fifth distillation.

When they fought they used their feet, circling each other like rutting moose, lashing for kneecaps and vitals with steel-calked pacs, feinting for in-kicks, lashing to kill. I heard of one man who used to walk among the damned on Skid Road who built a reputation by his skill in kicking off kneecaps. He could lift them neatly and drive them up to mid-thigh, leaving his opponent writhing in agony, stiff-legged for life.

Young Dan's appearance on the street caused no commotion at first and his welcome was both chill and apathetic. Yet beneath their dark and gnarled exteriors the men were not bad fellows, at heart. Once their distrust of the boyish stranger was overcome, Dan discovered they could be intensely receptive. His sincerity, his clean-cut looks, seemed to create a favorable impression and, while still gazing at him askance, some of the Skid Roaders began to wonder, hopefully, if they had "got a half-decent young chap" at last who cared about them.

Despite his age and frequent rebuffs, or perhaps because of them, Dan felt those Saturday night hours on Skid Road were worthwhile. He had a queer pride in his responsibilities, a rising exultation in the hope and promise of the work. And he was convinced that he was getting somewhere when, after missing a Saturday, he'd be greeted the next time with: "Gee, Danny, where were you last week? We missed you."

A familiar figure on the street was an unemployed skipper of a fishing boat. He was short, with all the pomposity of short men. He wore a black sweater, a battered derby hat, and pince-nez. He was always removing the lenses and wiping them on his trousers the way one would wipe a fish-knife blade. Then he'd put them on again and squint to right and left, trying them out for distance. At the one end of materialism there was the fact that he owned his boat. At the other extreme of spiritualism, if all else failed, there was prayer. Somewhere between the two his life was lived.

"I bought the glasses," he'd say, "from a catalogue."

"Can you see with them?"

"No," he said.

"Can you see without them?"

"No," he said.

Dan's interest in life on Skid Road took root after hearing stories about a well-known lay street preacher named Theodore Dorsey. Dorsey had been commissioned by Bishop Gerald Shaughnessy to preach about Catholicism to the men of Skid Road. Much of his financial support came from the Ancient Order of Hibernians, headed by one Patrick Lyons, who often accompanied his son on those trips to Seattle's lower south side.

Another important influence in young Dan's life, Father John McAstocker, S.J., also encouraged him in his work on Skid Road. "If you're going to be a priest," Father McAstocker told him, "it will be good training for you." It was through Father McAstocker's connections in New York that Dan was able to get free copies of *America* sent to him in volume for distribution on Skid Road. The lumberjacks loved the magazine, and later copies of it were found showing up in many of the little mill towns dotting the Olympic Peninsula in Western Washington.

In this way, Dan was learning compassion for his fellow human beings very early. And the derelicts needed compassion, for they were losers, a motley bunch. Their damp bodies carried the scars of too many years at the woods trade—chronic arthritis, sprained and lacerated limbs, coughs, colds and asthma—all the minor ailments of humanity. And when those worn-out bodies could go on no longer, they'd ask Dan to bring the priest, for they deserved a bit of dignity in that hour of dying.

That Dan Lyons was going to be a priest, there was no doubt. . . . A writer? There was some doubt. He wrote an article entitled "Skid Road Reads *America*" and mailed it in to the editors of *America.* It came back rejected. Something told him he still had more basic work to do before he could call himself a writer.

Still, newspaper life and newspaper people enchanted Dan. He was convinced that somehow, some day, he wanted to be a part of the fascinating world of communications; a galvanic news hound, a word-smith, the flag officer of the literary fleet. Big or small, he wanted to be a part of it.

Perhaps Wilfred P. Schoenberg, S.J., the Gonzaga University historian and a close friend of Dan's, came closest to the truth. He saw in him a young man of imagery, philosophy, spirit, and perception. "I think," he remarked to his fellow Jesuits at Gonzaga years ago, "that Dan is

Benedict A. Horvath

marked with something special. American journalism shall reckon with this good fellow one day."

The first great bell-beat of crusading journalism sounded for Dan Lyons in 1937, when he was only 17. The sudden, bold harbinger of things to come was wrapped up in a missile he fired at the Letters-to-the-Editor column of the Seattle *Post-Intelligencer*:

"To The *Post-Intelligencer*:

In the Saturday edition of the *P-I* I was amazed, almost dumbfounded, to read the letter appearing in the 'Opinion of Our Readers' column, by one John Stitt, in which he condemned the various newspapers for their stand on Justice Hugo Black, (who had been a member of the Klu Klux Klan).

As a life member of the monstrous organization that rose vilely against the best traditions of our United States over a decade ago, Justice Black has certainly no place upon the highest court of justice in our beloved country.

The appointment of Justice Black is the most barefaced attempt to make a mockery of American justice that has ever been foisted on the citizens of this free land!

Born of hate, nurtured by envy, breeding in the grime of inflexible bigotry and existing in its perverted viciousness by ignorant passions, a self-confessed member of this horrible organization, an organization alien in thought, concept and principle to American ideals, has no place in American life, let alone in an American Court of Justice!

It seems almost too much to hope that a man who

has fostered racial and religious hatred in his breast can forget these traits by a mere retraction. The very fabric of his being has been stained too deeply.

In reply to Mr. Stitt, who says in part, 'I wish we had a hundred such justices,' let me, as a high school student, say that the appointment of Justice Black, and his confirmation by the Senate, must be considered as a 'slap in the face' not only to Catholics, Jews, and Negroes, but to every right-thinking person in the United States.

Dan Lyons,
Age: 17."

The incendiary language of Dan Lyons was regarded by *P-I* editors as mere journalistic brashness of the young. They saw in his letter no world-shaking implications. It was not printed.

Partly because a football knee injury ruled out sports, Dan developed total interest in amateur radio during his spare hours. He soon became a "ham" operator and got his kicks talking via Morse code to other amateurs around the world. For two years, he attended night school classes absorbing all he could about amateur radio. He even considered signing up as a ship's radio operator on Alaskan freighters in the summer. He felt he could earn enough money from the job to put himself through college.

No one dreamed much of orbiting the earth in 1936, but Dan discovered he could talk around the world with the transmitters he built at home. He also built his own receivers and could pick up signals from such distant places as London, Ceylon, Hong Kong, Katmandu, and Anchorage. His private world was growing smaller all the time. Like other "Hams," he had the calling cards of amateurs with whom he had talked on the air stuck all over his wall. His call letters were W7FZT.

Dan said, "I only used code, not voice, and as radio waves travel with the speed of light—175,000 miles a second—I could sometimes hear a signal coming from another amateur, when communicating with him, as it came both ways around the world. At 16, I passed the government test for a commercial radio operator of sending 20 words a minute, which meant we sent the signals at a rate of five or six dots or dashes per second, and when coming around the world both ways, it would cause a noticeable time-lag one way over the other, making it hard to read the dots and dashes at that rapid speed.

"Since the same signal came both ways it would sometimes take a tenth of a second longer one way than the other, causing all sorts of confusion for the receiver. Ham radio was a thrilling hobby in those early days. On Friday nights, I sometimes stayed up all night working my transmitter, catching other Hams in different countries before they went to bed or when they got up. My workshop was just off my bedroom. Many a Saturday I would have breakfast with the family before going to sleep for the night. Dad and Mom didn't mind, though. My interest in radio kept me out of mischief. I had to buy and repair my equipment, so I learned how to repair radios to earn money."

Amateur radio was a lifesaver for Dan. It served as the perfect substitute for sports. Sure, he liked sports, and even went so far as to earn places on his eighth grade and frosh football, basketball and baseball teams. Then, in his sophomore year, he smashed his knee in football scrimmage and developed a severe case of water on the knee. With no sulfa drugs to prevent infection, the doctors were not as sophisticated in the Thirties as they are now, and they were reluctant to tap the knee. Instead, they had him soak the injured joint nightly with hot compresses for six weeks. The physician told Dan, "Stay off the leg for the rest of the season, Son," and that ended the scholastic football career of young Mr. Lyons.

"Perhaps it was just as well," Dan said. "My future in athletics had been doubtful, even before the injury. I lacked speed. In fact, my brother Jarlath, who did make the football varsity, was told by the coach what a slow runner he was. Jar replied that he could run faster than I could. 'Gosh, Jar,' the coach told him, 'I never knew you had a crippled brother.' He wasn't referring to my bad knee, either."

Dan was by birth and habit an independent thinker and a man of action. He was no procrastinator, no dreamer. As he has demonstrated in his work today, when creative urgings stir his will to action he will rise to prodigious efforts, undergo drudgeries to achieve results that make an impact.

When he was a senior at Seattle Prep, a human force, perhaps more stimulating to Dan's mind than anything the material world had to offer, began to rouse in his spiritual consciousness the powers long hidden deep inside him. He listened to wise words from within, and acted upon them.

You are given sincere testimony from Dan himself as to what persuaded him to go into the priesthood.

"I think I first wanted to be a priest at the age of five or six," Dan recalls. "I always thought of being a Jesuit, as we lived in a Jesuit parish. The thought never left me for long, and though I thought of other things, such as joining my father in his export business, or possibly becoming a lawyer, I always felt *called* to the priesthood.

"The first time I could enter the Society of Jesus was when I finished high school, and I felt I would always regret it if I did not do so. Somehow, I knew it was what God wanted, and I had an obligation at least to try it. I accepted the fact it was going to be a 13-year course to Ordination. I was particularly influenced by the Jesuit teachers who had taught me at Seattle Prep. But it was years before, as a small child around St. Joseph's Church, that I first felt the urge to be a priest."

Dan felt, however, it was not a subject to discuss with his parents. In January of his senior year, he applied to enter the Jesuit Novitiate, at Sheridan, Oregon. There had not been the slightest pressure on the part of the faculty at Seattle Prep for him to enter the priesthood. They limited their role to simply telling the students that applications were being accepted. So knowing it was his own decision, Dan applied. That night, when he told his father, Patrick Lyons grew quiet.

"I think you have made a wise decision," he said, with that vast understatement of the Irish. Then he added, "I would rather see you a priest than President of the United States."

Dan agreed. He felt to be anything else would have been much less worthy than joining the priesthood.

When his mother asked him what college he was going to, he said quietly, "I'm going to Sheridan."

"That was the first I knew Danny was going to be a priest," she often remarked later.

Dan was a senior when he began dating a girl from Immaculate High School. Mary McCoy was pretty in a fresh, round-faced sort of way with rich dark hair and sweet eyes. At 17, she was a gay, light-hearted creature with considerable impish humor, many friends, and a fondness for young Dan Lyons. The antennae of her instincts began to yield messages broadcast by Dan that he liked her, too. At parties, the other girls were saying, "Gee, Mary! What did you do to Dan Lyons? He never looks twice at a girl and you had him following you around all evening."

But Mary didn't need the girls to tell her that Dan was interested. What intrigued and then bothered her was that SHE was feeling a little strange herself. Dan was a young man of personal charm.

Patrick Lyons was quite concerned about the courtship. One evening, he took Dan aside and counseled him: "If you're going to the Novitiate to study for the priesthood," he said, "you must forget about any romantic entanglements."

That's all he said. The question was dropped. Dan got the message. Several months before he entered the Novitiate in Oregon, he broke off with Mary. What became of her? "She later went steady with another student—only to see him join the Novitiate, too," Dan recalled. "This happened to her three or four times in succession. She kept losing her beaus to the priesthood. But the story of Mary McCoy has a happy ending. She later married a fellow student at Seattle University, John Katona, and became the mother of six children."

None of the boys in Dan's senior class at Seattle Prep talked much about joining the Jesuit Order. It is a deeply personal step, something between a boy and his conscience. There was no pressure from their teachers (Jesuits). The procedure was very informal. When the Provincial, Walter J. Fitzgerald, S.J., made his annual trip to Seattle Prep from Portland, he sent for the applicants individually and interviewed them in the privacy of a closed office. Everything was very confidential.

Dan told us: "None of us seniors knew who was going to the Novitiate, but a few months after we applied we were notified and told whether or not we had been accepted. In the interim, however, nothing was said, least of all by us, and it was only when the Jesuit faculty sponsored a dinner for those who had been chosen that we gathered together and learned for the first time which ones had been tapped from our class.

"Some of the boys didn't make it, but out of my class of 80 at Prep, we proudly list the following: Father Mike McHugh, now pastor of my boyhood parish in Seattle; Father Joe Perri, today vice-president and Jesuit superior, Seattle University; Father Ernie Bertin, professor of chemistry and former head of the department, Seattle University; Father Jack Wood, noted Alaskan missionary; and Father Howie Moran, parish priest and hospital chaplain, Lewiston, Idaho. Two others in our high school class became priests as well: Father Jack Donohue, a diocesan pastor at

Black Diamond, Washington; and Father Frank McHugh, an Oblate Father now stationed at Castle Rock, Washington, and chaplain at St. John's hospital, Longview.

"A few others in our graduation class began the long course of studies at Sheridan, only to discover it was not their calling. Dick Corrigan comes to mind, he never made it but has two brothers who are priests. Dick left the Novitiate and later married the sister of Father Joe Perri. Harold McChesney was another; he left after a few years of study and is now happily married and the father of a large family. None have left after Ordination."

Commencement exercises at Seattle Prep were held in late May, 1938. Since Dan was not required to report to Sheridan until mid-August, his parents decided to drive him and his sisters to Chicago to visit two of their father's brothers, Tom and Mike Lyons. Jarlath could not go because he had a summer job in Seattle. The Lyonses felt that in the normal course of events Dan would probably spend the rest of his life in the Pacific Northwest, as a member of the Oregon Province. They wanted him to have one more good trip around America before he entered a restricted life.

Thinking about that grand gesture today, Dan's mother smiles. "Now he just flies *over* Chicago," she says, in obvious reference to the more than a million miles he has logged in the air since starting *Twin Circle*. Little could she and her husband have foreseen the crowded, globe-jumping schedule their Danny-on-the-spot was destined to lead in later years.

The summer flew by. Suddenly, it was August 14, 1938,

the day after Dan's 18th birthday. It was the day when Dan Lyons, civilian, began walking the long road toward becoming Dan Lyons, S.J. His parents drove him down to Oregon. The Novitiate was located 50 miles from Portland. And why August 14th? What was so special about that date?

"We entered the Novitiate on the 14th so that we could take our first vows, two years later, on August 15th, the Feast of the Assumption," Dan explained. "Eighteen was an excellent age to enter the Novitiate. Some of our group were older, but mostly it seemed harder for them to be remade in the image of St. Ignatius Loyola, founder of the Jesuit Order."

The novicemaster at Sheridan was Father John Moffatt, S.J. This modest priest, respected for his piety and admired for his scholarship, governed the novices with an iron hand. He was a taskmaster and demanded absolute perfection. He had written more than 30 books, though writing came hard for him. He also encouraged his novices to write. In his lectures he told them, *"Verba volunt sed scripta manent,"* which translated means, "Words fly away but what is written remains."

Father Moffatt had an austere face like that of Saint Januarius. Upon it stood an ample nose, a weather vane of his moods. But size was not its chief attribute. His cut-water drew attention mainly because of its ability to change expression. When he would call a novice into his office for consultation, Father Moffatt would sit in an un-cushioned chair, close one eye, roll a pencil beneath the flat of his hand on the desk, and mutter an approving,

"Yes. Yes." Or an admonitory, "Well, now." Or a low-voiced prohibition, "Oh! Oh! Oh!" An interview that went well found Father Moffatt's nostrils dilated, as if smelling flowers. A split infinitive brought severe lines, like a fallen frown, to either slope of his promontory. He had made a long study of the written word and correct diction and the relation of words to meaning. He had deep reverence for the word. He had a quarrelsome ear that was easily outraged. His training was far from mechanical. Thought and soul had to find their way into vibrations of depth and beauty. It was beyond sight and sound. It was communication of spirit.

"Father Moffatt was the greatest apostle of the Sacred Heart I have ever come across," Father Dan said. "He kept pounding into us that we should strive for sanctity. He said it was the only goal. He had a point. How can one set out on the long road to becoming a Jesuit without intending to give God his best? Not that we would succeed all the time, but the intention was what really counted. He hammered away at this constantly, night and day, and he tried to stress his spiritual points just before lights out so that we could sleep on them. When we awoke at 5 a.m., he wanted us to think about them some more during the regular hour's meditation. Each day opened with early-morning meditation. There was also a half-hour meditation every afternoon.

"Father Moffatt was well-liked by all of his novices. We revered him. Sure, he had his little idiosyncrasies, but we were young and hardly noticed them. His knowledge of the Sacred Heart devotion was very profound and deeply personal. He lived it every minute of the day. In some ways, I suppose you could say he wasn't practical. For example, he did not think we should read novels. But such adjustments were easy to make. What he did give us was solid spirituality: plenty of prayer and mortification and all the rest. We were not there to see 'a reed shaken by the wind.'

"Father Moffatt lasted as novicemaster for only five years. Some people, the liberals, felt he was too much of a hardliner. They believed he was too uncompromising and kept crying out for his removal. In 1943, they got their way, and for the next 29 years he worked long and hard, giving retreats to nuns. He lived as though he were on retreat all that time himself. He was spurred on by his conviction that the service of Christ called for 'not his bit, but his utmost.'

"Life at Sheridan was all very rigid. To see that we obeyed the rules, a second-year novice was assigned to each of us. He was called a 'guardian angel.' We had to speak Latin all day, except during recreation. We were given three recreation periods: after lunch, during the afternoon outdoor period, and for 30 minutes after supper. But when we were indoors, we weren't supposed to talk in the corridors or seldom any place else. We never saw a newspaper or magazine, and were limited on the number of letters we received. We even had to ask permission to write a letter home. And we had to get permission for a haircut.

"But 'had to' is not the proper description. We were told what the rules were and were motivated to obey them. Griping was out. No one complained about the food, because we were told not to complain about the food. The only complaint I ever heard about the food was when I went to see Brother Lacey, the Infirmarian. Anyone who suggested he wasn't feeling well was told: 'Did you eat any of those turnips? What did you eat those for! No wonder you don't feel well!' "

Time marched on. After the first six weeks at Sheridan, Dan and his fellow Novices began the Long Retreat. This consisted of 30 days of silence, prayer and meditation. Not a word was spoken to anyone, except to the Novice Master in their weekly personal colloquies with him. Only three "break days" were allowed during the month of Long Retreat—on the 10th day, the 19th, and the 26th. On those three days the Novices went out on 90-minute walks in the morning and afternoon.

One of Father Dan's favorite stories about retreats features the well-known Pacific Northwest preacher, Father Tom Sherman, of the Oregon Province. He died in the 1920s. Father Sherman was the son of the renowned general, Tom Sherman, who did not become a Catholic until his declining years, but the priest's mother was a Kelly by birth and a devout Catholic.

Originally, young Tom had gone to West Point. He decided that professional soldiering was not for him, and he switched to the Yale Law School. Finally, he decided what he really wanted was to be a Jesuit missionary. He had met the Jesuit missionaries in Montana on his summer vacations, was deeply impressed, and so he joined the Novitiate at St. Ignatius Mission, in western Montana.

His father, by now retired from the Army, traveled out

from the East to visit him. General Sherman said he had been hearing a lot about those Long Retreats. "What does a Novice do on them?" he asked. The son, a Novice himself, said, "Well, we're in silence for 30 days. We are up at five every morning. We make an hour's meditation. We continue a series of meditations through the day—and we hold our silence all through the 30 days except for what is called a Break Day once a week."

General Sherman said, "Hell, Tom, that's no retreat—that's a *campaign*!"

The 30 days passed fairly quickly for Dan, and he was soon caught up in the daily life of the Novitiate. His training was rigid. He washed dishes, set the tables, gave a sermon to his fellow Novices at dinner time, and took turns reading aloud at table. He also learned to become a barber, along with several other Novices, and was taught how to operate a sewing machine; not fancy tailoring, just quick repairs and patches. Dan fills us in on the rest of the routine:

"By most standards," Father Dan says, "it was a Spartan life. We were up at the crack of dawn every day of the year except Christmas, when we attended Midnight Mass. We never gave much thought or complaint to the rugged schedule. Our general attitude seemed to be, God must have wanted most of us to stay, so He made it easy. Time moved swiftly along. We were always busy. We never chose our companions. They were assigned to us. We seldom talked at the dinner table. We had books read to us, and when any of us who were reading mispronounced a word we were corrected by one of the faculty, lest others learn the wrong pronunciation.

"It should be explained that there were others living in the same building with us, but in another wing. These were the Juniors. We were never allowed to speak with them or even nod, though we had gone to high school with some of them; never, that is, except on 'Fusion Day,' such as Christmas or Easter, when we chattered away to all of them in one great big noisy gathering. Why weren't there more Fusion Days? Why couldn't we do things this way instead of that? Such questions never occurred to us. In what seemed like no time at all, the first year passed and suddenly we were the 'guardian angels' for the next year's batch of raw recruits.

"Ever since the fifth grade, I liked to write. In fact, I attribute much of whatever success I have gained in writing to date to the Sisters, and, later, to my teachers at Seattle Prep. They taught us well in the art of writing good compositions. Mainly, they taught us by having us write themes every week end, and by encouraging us with the keen interest they took in what we wrote.

"The first article I tried to get published as a Novice was written while I was still at Sheridan. It was all about an old cemetery I found in the hills, 10 miles from the Novitiate. It was called St. Patrick's Cemetery. Each tombstone bore the hand-carved words: 'Born in Ireland.' Most of the Irish buried there had come around the Horn, after the Irish famine in 1848-49. They had kept sheep in the Oregon hills, and, I suppose, the Pacific Northwest rain and pretty green scenery had reminded them of Ireland.

"Well, I wrote up the cemetery for the *Catholic Sentinel,* which was the official paper of the Archdiocese in Portland. The Associate Editor was Jim O'Meara, now News Editor of the *Oregon Journal.* Jim wanted to print my article, but word came down from Monsignor Smith, editor of the *Sentinel,* that Archbishop Howard did not want the cemetery publicized, as the fences had rotted, the cattle were grazing around the gravesites, and the grounds in general were in total need of much repair. Some Irish had promised to fix it up, but nothing had been done as yet. Actually, they had all moved away to St. Paul, Oregon.

"Not wanting the wrath of the Irish on his head, the Archbishop feared the publicity growing out of my article would bring visitors. So I wrote to O'Meara, hoping he would understand. 'Surely,' I told him, 'St. Patrick will understand. Wasn't he a bishop himself!' The article was junked."

The first two years at Sheridan were called the Novitiate. The large building, about 400 feet long, was ugly on the outside, as it had never been finished in brick, and black tar had been put on the cement to keep it from leaking. It never dawned on Brother Dan that he would later have the job of raising the money to put bricks on the outside of the building, and to replace the frame dining room wing with a $500,000 addition. But that was to be, 15 years later.

On August 15, 1940, Brother Lyons and the other 18 members of his class took their first religious vows, the three vows essential to religious life: poverty, chastity and obedience. It was what he wanted more than anything else. It was what he had been working for, what he had been looking forward to. They were now Jesuits in every sense of the word, no longer "N.S.J." (Novices of the Society of Jesus) but "S.J.," members of the Society of Jesus. The first two years of spiritual training were finished. The long years of study were about to begin.

Before classes began, however, they spent two weeks at Nestucca, on the Oregon coast. Judge Peter D'Arcy in Salem, who donated the beautiful chapel at the Novitiate, had just purchased 90 acres of land for the Jesuit summer camp, at a cost of $1,500. (Fifteen years later, Father Dan put the timber on the land up for bid, and sold it for $41,250, then replanted the land with a million free trees from the government, and free labor from the Jesuit Juniors.)

The Juniors built several large cabins on the property in that summer of 1940. Brother Lyons took charge of wiring the buildings, putting all the outside wires underground. His experience as a radio amateur came in handy, as it often has since.

During those first four years, the young Jesuits were allowed a visit from their family once every three months, though they were never allowed to visit home. They took long walks, sometimes up to 25 miles on a special holiday, but they were not permitted to walk through the little town of Sheridan, five miles away. Dan's first visit there was to the dentist, after 18 months.

When they went from the Novitiate to the Juniorate, they did not progress very far geographically: from one wing to another. But their lives were much different. They had classes every day in classical Latin and Greek, English and history. They also had lighter courses in French, German and speech.

In their first year they preached a sermon in English

during the Community dinner. The second year they preached a sermon in Latin in the dining room. Their Rector was Father Francis Gleeson, who later became bishop of northern Alaska. He was a kindly, reticent man with a quiet wit, Dan recalls. "His knowledge of the Latin poets surpassed anything we could imagine. We wrote Latin letters to former teachers just for practice. He never let them be mailed without correcting them in the best Ciceronian style."

The study of languages in the Juniorate helped develop writing skills. A person needs to study another language to understand his own. The acquaintance with the great literature of the ancients in the language in which it was written was enriching and rewarding. "But it was writing—practice, practice, practice—that made the difference. We wrote at least one essay every week, and really worked at it. A number of us started writing little articles for the *Inland Catholic Register,* which was edited by Tom Royce, the father of two Jesuits.

"The nice thing," said Dan, "is to be able to write and have it published somewhere, anywhere—to practice on the public. It gives a person confidence that he can write professionally. And it provides an incentive to write, something that is needed, as writing is hard work—rewarding, but hard. No one ever became a writer unless he wrote and wrote and wrote some more. Good or bad, it is a habit."

Four years is a long time, when you are only 18. But they were very busy years, and passed rather quickly. Dan's first-grade teacher, Sister Willasene, dropped by for a visit in the summer of 1940. Hitler was busy conquering Europe, and she remarked, having lived through World War I, that "our boys will just have to stop him, that's all." Dan thought that it was hardly the right attitude. Why did America have to become involved? Hitler would not last, he thought, whereas Stalin seemed to be an even bigger threat and represented a system that posed more of a permanent danger to the world. He had given an elocution piece on that subject back in high school: "Catholicism versus Communism." But then came the attack on Pearl Harbor on December 7, 1941, and the war was on in full force. President Roosevelt did not declare war. He simply asked Congress to admit that a state of war existed.

Late in August, Brother Dan and his class of second-year Juniors took their last long look at the Oregon hills and the beautiful valley stretching out below the Novitiate at Sheridan, Oregon, fifty miles west of Portland. They had not been home for four years, but were allowed three days to make the journey. In most cases their families came to drive them. Those from Seattle, like Dan, stayed two nights there, then drove the 300 miles east to Spokane, where he would spend his next five years. "They were a very happy few days for us," recalls Father Dan, "seeing our family and old friends again."

Dan was no longer "Brother Lyons." For the next nine years, until Ordination, he would be known as "Mr. Lyons, S.J." His home for the next three years was Mount St. Michael's Philosophate, a magnificent seminary building four miles north of Spokane, overlooking the city. It was named by a former Provincial from France, Father Joseph

Piet. Hence the name, after the famous Mont St. Michel monastery on the west coast of France.

The climate in Spokane is much different than on the Oregon coast. There is much less rain and much more sunshine, with ample snow in the winter. The Cascade mountain range that divides western and eastern Washington makes the difference. At the Mount, for the first time, the young Jesuits had a room of their own. Until then they had lived in a cubicle, small living quarters each with a semi-wall, six feet high. The rising hour was the same: 5 a.m., seven days a week. An hour's meditation began at 5:30, followed by 6:30 Mass. "We never felt we *had* to get up," recalls Father Dan. "It was expected of us, and we did it. I never knew anyone who ever 'slept in.' It never crossed our minds. If we had it to do over again, we would do the same."

CHAPTER 8

A Lyons Goes to War

There was a sense of sad expectancy as you look back on America in the middle Thirties. The extravagant ebullience of the social scene of the 1920s had vanished in 1929 before breadlines and bankruptcies and bank holidays during the social revolution of the following decade. The last surviving dynasties were falling in Europe, nations collapsing, politics changing, dictators ranting, and countries torn apart by internal revolt. There was a sense of desolation in the air, and with the German and Russian intervention in the Spanish Civil War, the skeleton of Communism began to flesh itself. The whole scene had a dirty feel. Sadly, Europe was again becoming the knifing street fighter, screaming in the alleys and desecrating all its ancient pretenses to culture.

William Randolph Hearst finally sold his ace war correspondent, Floyd Gibbons, on flying into besieged Madrid, broadcasting to the outside world what he saw, and then flying out again, a very sad and disillusioned man. But Floyd did the job. He came back probably the first American correspondent to sound the warning on Communism as the ultimate enemy.

He told my friend, author James Warner Bellah: "What you've got on your hands actually are the same barbaric hordes the Roman Empire had. The Communists have no civilization as we know it. So all they can do is envy and hate—but because they have a Slavic and Mongol strain of savagery, they must, some day, make a gigantic effort to destroy America in order to justify their animal hatred."

But there was to be the German war first.

A lot of people walked through the motions in the middle Thirties. Everybody still remembered the First World War and gradually was convinced it had never come even close to making the world safe for democracy. Living was like watching a film that you had every reason to expect was new—and then suddenly realizing you had seen it all before. You dined out and matched the brittle chit-chat. You attended dinners and could see the fires of war burning through the candle flames. When the college trains left the train depot after the holidays, you knew darned well that those pink-faced kids would be tooling platoons in combat before they got out of college—and that the lovely, fresh young girls who saw them off would be the female pawns of war.

Americans who visited Germany in 1936 watched the brutal build-up. Garmisch-Partenkirchen was the scene of the Winter Olympic Games that February and the quaint little Bavarian town had the appearance of an army headquarters a few miles behind the Western Front during an important troop movement. The Nazi regime converted the Olympics into a military demonstration, despite loud denials to the contrary.

As many as 5,000, perhaps even 10,000, men in various militia uniforms marched through the streets in columns of fours all during the sporting competition, and when a stranger asked one of them, as strangers often did, if he were a soldier, the uniformed trooper would reply, "Who, me? No, I'm a cobbler. All of us in the black suits are cobblers."

Even the storms and sunsets over L'aga Longa at Como were spoiled by marching patrols of Sons of the Wolf—the age of Boys Scouts in America—but carrying wooden rifles in Italy, against the time they would graduate to real ones. From disgust, Americans came back home in deep and futile anger.

On September 1, 1939, Hitler invaded Poland. In its next issue *Time* magazine introduced a new section headed "World War" with the words, "World War II began last week."

It was a reality that Patrick Lyons accepted. Indeed, the curtain was going up. History had taught him that if America dealt with the Third Reich on the basis of *appeasement* of any kind, it followed as sure as night followed day that we would pay for it in blood and tears—in the bloody end of *our* democracy.

Patrick said, "We must deal with Hitler as an enemy—an enemy of Peace, our peace." He urged his oldest son, Jarlath, to pick a branch of the service and sign up. Jarlath had just graduated from Seattle College and for months his father had been telling him that war was inevitable. He said, "Son, you might as well be prepared for it." Patrick had some close contacts at Sand Point Naval Station in Seattle, and he arranged for Jarlath to be sent to Pensacola, Florida, to train as a Navy pilot. What happened to him after that is contained in a raft of letters, clippings, and private papers I found in the family files in the basement of Pat's home in Seattle.

This personal material permits one to look inside the lives of the Lyonses during the war years. It is the most authentic record of their thinking and emotions in that period, 1939-1945, that I was able to find. There is no hearsay about it, no outside opinions, for now the witnesses themselves take the stand in their own behalf.

The mood of this material is one of great uncertainty and yearning. We find in it a variety of expression. In many ways, it typified Americans everywhere. The files are shot with wit and grassroots observation. At times there come from the closely written lines such cries as seldom are voiced except in the private letters between father and son; but the overall mood is one of concern for family and country and the role of the individual when challenged by war. The first letter, under the dateline of January 23, 1940, was Jarlath's technical description of the training he was getting at Pensacola. In it could be heard the yearling tones of a callow cadet who was not too sure about his standing in the Navy Air Corps:

"Dear Folks:

So far, I've more time in down here than anybody in our class. It's only luck, of course, just the way I happened to be picked. There are a number of fellows who have lots of previous time. One chap has about 250 hours, another 180, and another over 100. Naturally they will advance much more readily. But I'll see if I can hang on for a time. We had our solo check last Tuesday. I got by all right and that's about all I can say. About six out of the 46 in our wing missed on two checks so they got extra time. Then they'll recheck. On the first try we have to get one 'up' check. If it's a 'down' then we have to get two consecutive 'ups.' After that we can get squadron time. That allows us three hours additional instruction. Then we would have to pass two 'ups' out of three checks. From there on, one can ask for Board time. That allows for three more hours of instruction and another series of checks. If the cadet still can't make it, he can go before the commander and ask for commander's time. If he gets that he gets more instruction and more checks. But by that time he is so nervous from 'checkitis' he can't fly a kite. The Board and Commander time depend on how good a student's Flight Jacket is (the F. Jacket is merely his flying and ground school record). Very few students get anything above squadron time these days.

Next week, I'll be taking my 20 hrs. check (if the weather modifies). It is a little stiffer check, but not too bad. In it we are tested for small field landings and circle shots. We have to slip into the small field from 1000 feet and must hit 100-foot circles for four out of six shots. It is lots harder than it sounds, since we aim at the circle from 800 feet altitude and have to gauge wind and distance while making a two-turn approach.

The guy I had for check pilot gave only three 'ups' out of eight checks. One of the boys who got 'up' gave him quite a ride. On one landing he leveled out at about 20 feet altitude, then had to nose it down, regain speed, and level out again. On the way down he went into a slight slip. Then he banged it in. The check pilot looked around at him, and said, 'I told you to land it in, not stunt it.' On another landing he banked steeply on a turn and skidded out. The check pilot again looked around, and said, 'For XXXXXs sake! You're flying a plane, not wheeling a bobsled!'

The most fun of all around here is in the stunts. Almost everyone gets sick. Some of the boys just can't seem to catch on to doing some of them. They either spin out of them or end up in a vertical power dive.

So far, I haven't been allowed to enter into the difficult maneuvers, only flipper turns and slips. After the 20 hr. check, tho, I'll have to do them all. I'm looking forward to it.

Another thing we do is ground school. They're giving us a complete (if hurried) course in aerodynamics. The course has been cut down to about ⅓ of its original time but we still have to get it all. Added to that we have at least an hour-and-a-half of radio. When we have lots of extra time around here we see if we can brush our teeth or shine our shoes. So far, I never have quite been able to complete either operation without a bell ringing.

Save me a place at the St. Pat's Banquet because I'll probably be home by then.

Well, here's to easy check pilots.

J."

Jarlath's fears that he would be "busted out" of the Navy's pre-flight cadet program were groundless. He hung in there. The following was dispatched on April 14, 1940:

"Dear Gang:

So I finally got by my 33 hour check and now I'm due to stay here at Pensacola for a few more weeks. I have been doing three-plane formation work. It's a lot of work. We had to fly three hours in a row and it is certainly a long time to keep on our toes. If you dope off for even a second at 80 miles an hour, things can happen awfully fast. The wind has been quite strong and suddenly hit an up-draft and all at once you're lifted some 50 feet above the other two planes. Then comes the tough job of jockeying around for position. Just then the leader will probably signal for a cross-over into echelon so you have to pull up and skid over behind the other plane. The tough thing about that is that you lose sight of the other planes under the wing and must wait for them to come into sight. If they don't, all you can do is sit up on the sky and wait.

Leading is a lot easier but more responsible since you have all the looking around to do. The other day, I led my formation into another formation and darned near killed six pilots.

Cadet life here is quite something for the raw recruit. The old hands love to work off steam on the new men. When a new recruit is seen on arrival he is approached and slyly questioned as to whether he has seen any women lately or whether he was able to sneak any food past the gate guard. Cat-calls and cries of 'shark-bait,' 'suckers,' and 'go back before it's too late,' etc., etc., are regular greetings. One favorite act is to have one guy play like he's gone insane and has been beaten up by the others and has been tied to a bunk. It is then explained to the greenhorns that 'this is a regular occurrence—he'll be okay, he's just gone wild. After all, he's only been here for three months.'

I got a very nice letter from Tommy McHugh telling all about the St. Pat's Banquet. It must have been a swell affair.

So long,
Jar"

Jarlath's letter of April 14th crossed in the night with a letter from his father. Patrick Lyons was in an expansive mood. His "news from home" was two pages long, typewritten, single space. The highlights were:

"Dear Jarlath:

Very many thanks for your box of cigars for my birthday. 'Twas nice to be so remembered. I certainly appreciated it. So did the rest of the family, even though they will not enjoy the smoking of them as I do every evening.

Your friend Tuma dropped in the week before last and was he in high gear. Boy, how that guy can talk. In fact, he was beginning to talk just a little bit too much, when I had to switch the subject, much to the chagrin of your sisters. I might mention that the book you suggested we read, 'Dive Bombing,' is now in the Seattle Public Library, or rather it was until we took it out, and all are now reading it and thoroughly enjoying it. I have read most of it two or three times. I wish that I was young again, and, believe it or not, cloud-hopping would be my line. We all now know what an 'up' or 'down' check means, and may your checks always be on the 'up and up.'

Shipping on the Coast is all shot to pieces. There were only Norwegian, Danish and Swedish ships out there, and now they are all tied up. The shippers are unable to get insurance on them and, of course, if any of the Danes go to sea the Bull grabs them. The Canadians ordered a Norwegian ship back to port last week. She loaded at Vancouver for Japan, went to sea, and a couple of days after she sailed, the Germans moved into Norway. So the Canucks wirelessed her to return, which she did. The Japanese and American lines are the only safe lines to ship on now. The Japs are busy in the

Orient, and there are no American ships available as the owners have sold all of them to the British and French. Believe me, it is a mess. What's more, most of the mills hereabouts are either shut down, running on part-time, or else going down. The headlines in the papers report FDR as saying, 'Get Ready for War.'

Well, there will not be any going into the war in Europe until this Oriental question is settled. The American fleet is not going over to Europe whilst conditions are so disturbed in the Far East. If Germany invades Holland what will become of the Dutch East Indies? Japan will undoubtedly have, or want to have, something to say about it. And she should, but will she? If Uncle Sam will take over the Dutch West Indies, will Japan take over the Dutch East Indies? Before you get this, the situation is so serious that we may be at war with Japan. There is real danger there, at least so we think.

Because of the war mess, my export business is pretty well closed down for the duration. I'm therefore trying to get a job some place but there isn't any to be had. As far as waiting for things to 'pop' in China, there is not much else one my age can do but wait. We are about the last of the exporters left, and, boy, there isn't much left.

I am enclosing a clipping from the *Seattle Times*. From it you'll see the the *Times* readers are not much in favor of going over to the European mess; at least, we won't be until after the Presidential Election. So far, Germany is certainly winning the war. One cannot believe anything in the papers or over the radio these days. It's all the same old bunk.

Hoping you're OK. Write when you can.

Love,
Dad"

Patrick's next letter, this one to Dan, found him in excellent spirits and brimming with pride for the Irish. It was dated July 12th, 1940.

"Dear Dan:

Hurrah for the 'Glorious Twelfth'! What a day to pick to write to a Jesuit novice. Long live King William —and 'if that be treason make the most of it.' Well, even though this may be the Glorious Twelfth it is still glorious for another reason. This is also Oliver Plunket day—beatified many years ago but not yet canonized.

I sent you some of the ship pictures for the villa, or camp, or whatever you call it. I mailed all that was left of them, and if they are not in good shape it is because a foolish young boy named Dan Lyons cut them up for some reason or other, perhaps to fit some frame or mayhap to fit his frame of mind.

Frances has changed her mind—or rather, her old man changed it for her—about going to Marylhurst, so she is taking up nursing. If she has a vocation it will be good when she is of age. Frank never discussed the matter with me. He knew very well that if he had what I would have said. What fools we mortals be, or as the Swede said, 'Us mortals *am*.'

You must be very happy as the day approaches for taking your vows. Young Pete Reilly wanted to go to Sheridan but the folks opposed it; at least, so I heard. He was a very good young fellow and received the last Sacraments before he died. The old man goes out to the cemetery nearly every day. I asked him why. If he wants to do something real for Pete he should go to Church and pray for his soul. The old man is all shot to pieces and if he does not pull out of it he will be out in the cemetery himself inside of a year. Such foolishness. After all, we are here to 'know, love and serve

God,' and young Pete was faithful to those, what shall I call them, *injunctions*. He died fortified with the rites of the Church, and instead of grieving over him Old Man Reilly should thank God for His goodness. The average young man and woman spend a lot of time preparing for 'success' in this world. And what does this world really amount to? Ask the millions of refugees in Europe, or the starving millions who only a few months ago were 'well off' and now have lost everything. It is a strange world, indeed. When you leave the protection of the cloister you will find a new one vastly different from the world you thought you knew when you left home to serve God and join His army. But here I am preaching (?) again to a Jesuit. Wot a man am I!

For some reason or other I just thought of something that happened in my lifetime. I can't remember whether I told it to you before or not. Anyway, when I was coming to this country years ago as a 'greenhorn'—so green, in fact, that if I went out on an American farm the cows would eat me—I just felt I had to have a trunk. Yes sir, I was under the impression that one necessary piece of baggage when coming to the good old U.S.A. was a trunk. So I bought a trunk; it was a tin one, and when I had it the question arose as to what I was going to put in it. I didn't have anything of value and no money to buy anything. So I decided I might be able to pick up an old pair of shoes. This I did, and when the trunk was lifted at one end you could hear the pair of hobbed-nail shoes roll around inside and make more noise than the old Chev you and Jarlath had. Everything was dandy, as the trunk was stowed away in the hold of the ship, until I landed in New York and the Customs officer asked to see my baggage. Proudly standing by the famous or infamous trunk, have it your own way, I pointed out my baggage. He said to me, 'Open it.' So I opened the trunk. Well, you should have seen that bird's face when he saw my worldly possessions. He said, 'Boy, with all that artillery you should be able to conquer the new world or something.'

And so with lots and lots of love and our prayers,

Dad"

A week and a half later, it was Mom Lyons' turn to write to her sons. But before she could drop the letter to Jarlath into the mailbox, Patrick quickly sat down and typed out the following:

"Dear Jarlath:

Seeing as how your mother is writing to you, I thought I should take advantage of the happy occasion and get my six cents worth out of the airmail.

Saw one of your P boats yesterday, or at least we thought it was, and they sure are some buggies. It must be nice to swagger up to the mechanics and say, 'Fill her up.' Eileen says, 'Just imagine Jar going out with 500 gallons of gas—oh, boy!'

They surely are building a bigger and better Sand Point. You won't know it when you see it. We are all hoping that you will get home for a vacation when you get through there—and it certainly would be grand if you got located at Sand Point. Dan is taking his vows the first of August. We haven't been down to see him since a year ago July 14th. Write as soon as you can and let us know if you are coming. If you are, we won't go to see Dan until we can all go together.

I suppose mother sent you all the rest of the news, so for the present I will say many Happy Landings.

Dad"

For the next several months, Jarlath cut down on his

volume of letters to the family. The Navy had speeded up his cadet training. But on August 13th, he found some time to catch up on his correspondence.

"Hello Folks:

It seems to be about time I answer a letter or two, so here goes. Old Squadron 4 is now well behind me. I am happily back in land planes again. Squad. 5 here is merely for instruments. We have 7 hours to familiarize ourselves and all the rest is 'under the hood,' either in Link Trainers or else in the red-striped NJ-I's.

Sept. 4 is the day that we're scheduled to complete our flight training at Pensacola N.A.S. The only indefinite point now is my probable destination. I'm hoping to be stationed on the West Coast, close to home.

Today, I had a very tiresome hour of simulated flying, making turns and glides up to 5,000 feet—without leaving the ground. They say that the guy who invented that trainer is in the bughouse, and the cadets say it serves him right for all the misery he's caused us. Those trainers are a concoction of a fiendish mind in collaboration with a maniacal imagination, but they sure do teach instruments.

J.J."

It was official now. The exciting news that Jarlath was coming home was carried in his letter of August 30th:

"Dear Family:

And so today I received my orders. I will be sent to Squadron 42 VP, where I must report 22 days after I check out of Pensacola. Should I mention that VP 42 is located at Sand Point—SEATTLE, WASHINGTON? It will be great to be home again. In fact, I will probably stay at home, since the B.O.Q. (Bachelor Officer's

Quarters) at the station is pretty well filled. So look out —here I come!

Since I will be home long enough I will probably be leaving for an extended tour of the U.S.A., next Friday. As long as they expect me to die for my country, it might be well to see what I'm dying for.

On the way home, I want to stop off at Sheridan and visit with Dan . . .

Tally ho,
J.J."

October 1, 1940. Jarlath, by now, had taken up his position as a newly-commissioned Ensign at Sand Point. His Commanding Officer was Arthur Radford, who later was named Chairman of the Joint Chiefs of Staff, and with whom Dan Lyons was to serve on the staff of the American Security Council, 25 years later.

Like Jarlath, Dan had been making strides,too. He had by this time reached the status of Junior at Sheridan, after completing two years of intensive training as a Novice. For the next two years he would be deep in a course known as the "Juniorate." On August 15, 1940, he had taken his first vows of poverty, chastity and obedience. That meant he could never again own anything, he could never marry, and he was bound to carry out whatever order he was given, provided, of course, it did not conflict with the laws of God.

Dan had spent the last two weeks in August with fellow Juniors at Nestucca Bay, on the Oregon Coast. One of his projects, while there, was to install an electric wiring system for the summer camp that the young Jesuits had built.

Though you won't get it out of Dan, Father Wilfred P. Schoenberg, S.J., who was a year behind him, remembers that Dan, an excellent swimmer, rescued several Jesuit scholastics one blustery afternoon after they had been caught by a powerful undertow and washed back out over their heads into the ocean. He later attempted a similar rescue at the mouth of the nearby Nestucca River when he heard the shrieks of a young man who was clinging desperately onto the side of a small boat. The youngster was torn from his grasp, went under, and when Dan reached him he was unconscious. Dan brought him back to shore, administered artificial respiration for more than an hour, but was unable to revive the waterlogged victim. Though his efforts had been fruitless, the young man's parents and his bride of only a few weeks stopped by a few days later to personally thank Dan for his try.

Dan's studies now were largely Latin and English, with stress on Greek and history as well. Life was changing in other ways, too. As a Novice, Dan and his classmates had not been permitted to talk with the Juniors, with whom they shared separate wings of the same building, except for four or five special days of the year when they had a two-hour recreation period called "fusion." All was confusion, Dan explained, as everyone tried to talk to everyone else at the same time, pouring out all that conversation they had been storing up inside them. Now the positions were reversed. As a Junior, he could not talk to Novices.

The studies were awesome. Dan was concentrating on Latin, since all of his studies after he left the Juniorate would be in Latin, both oral and written. He was also given weekly writing assignments. These were done on Sunday mornings at what was called "Scriptio" period.

Once every three months, the students were allowed to entertain their parents for one day. The Lyonses would drive the 175 miles from Seattle to Portland, then another 50 miles on a country road out to Sheridan, visit with Dan, and then return all the way back up the Coast to Seattle that night.

In a two-page, typewritten letter dated September 30, 1940, Patrick Lyons wrote variously of a recent trip down to see Dan, and of Jarlath's homecoming and other family and local news:

"Dear Dan:

> I am rather slow in writing to thank you and the good fathers there for the very nice meal you served us on our recent trip, not forgetting the dessert picked up under the trees. We had a very nice trip and enjoyed all of it, particularly the time we spent with you at the Novitiate. How very, very fortunate you are and how good God is to you. Peace and tranquility 'such as the world never saw' in your home and on the outside, wars and more wars. Before I start getting serious, maybe I had better close this part with the request that you convey to Father Moffatt our thanks for the bountiful repast served up to the Lyonses during our recent visit.
>
> Well, the 'mysterious man' Jarlath showed up Friday morning, and, of course, we were all glad to see him. I suppose you saw his writeup in the *Progress*. Jarlath got quite a kick out of it. It was a nice writeup, and the College, as well as the Prep, seemed to be pleased with it. Jarlath blew in about six o'clock and we spent all forenoon talking and listening to his many and varied experiences. He certainly has changed a lot—and all for the better. At last he has grown up, something I

thought he would never do. He is now taking life more seriously. He figured he might be able to stay home and draw 40-dollars a month extra but so far there is not much chance for that little scheme to work out.

Several of Jarlath's friends were at the house to see him. They really opened their eyes when they saw his sword—what an aviator needs a sword for is something I can't explain; it'd not even make a good bread knife, but it sure is handsome. When Herb Vallantine saw that sword his eyes stood out like a full moon in the fog. Jarlath is now set for about two months of hard work, although he said that his squadron was going to San Francisco in about a week to 'ferry' some planes there and then on another trip to Florida. I suppose he will have to return from the East Coast by train.

Incidentally, that alleged auto that Jarlath had sure did look tough when he got home. It looked as though the Navy had a stormy voyage and when they tried to 'dock' he sure must have knocked out some piling. It seems to me he should have a few old tires on the fenders like the towboats have.

I don't think there is much more to say, so I had better ring off for the present.

Love from all of us,
Dad"

On May 17, 1941, there is this brief report from Jarlath about his trip on the train from Florida to San Diego:

"Dear Folks:

Back in San Diego, with no planes, no money, no sunshine, and even less ambition. Right now we are just sitting around, looking for free rides while the Naval Acceptance Board is trying to find things wrong with our new planes. As soon as we get them we start back to Seattle. Probably within two weeks.

Our trip cross-country was entirely without mishap. I made one serious mistake, however. I came back by TRAIN. I'll never do that again. Sitting on that pitching, jouncing old train car is not my idea of traveling. There is absolutely nothing to see, nothing to do, and nowhere to go! I will forget about the train the next time. Ugh!

Thursday, I took one of the big Naval Douglas transports up to L.A., and nine of us flew some small scouting planes back on a ferry hop. It was a pleasant contrast from these slow sea-going 'cows' that we normally fly. They fly pretty fast, are very maneuverable. At one time, I hit 220 kts., roaring down the beach about 50 or 75 feet above the bathers. We flew formation, did stunts, and had a great time.

Did you read about the fellow who caught on the plane in a parachute jump? The whole show went on right here and was really a fine exhibition of flying. The victim's only casualty was a five-inch gash on his arm. I don't know about his mental condition.

That's all from here for now.

Toodle-do,
Jar"

Six months later—*Pearl Harbor!* Jarlath was suddenly deep in the war. He now wrote home of adventures which could cost him his life. He spoke of his danger, as he always did of any personal risk, with a tongue-in-cheek style. But make no bones about it, the risks were there, sharp and real. For six months, Lt.-Cmdr. Lyons flew a PBY, the Navy's slow, long-range patrol bomber, around the Solomons, suffering no more glamorous injuries than a wounded toe. The latter was sustained when a Jap bomber attacked his plane. Five of his crew were slightly hurt. Ensign Bill Hubbach, who came from Jarlath's neighborhood on Capitol Hill in

Seattle, was one of those shaken up. Bill was his second pilot.

Jarlath brushed off those risks with the shrug of a shoulder.

"There are no heroes in this war," he'd say. "There are only dead soldiers."

He then told the story of the Marine Commando who stood on the runway in the thick of the Battle of Midway, holding a submachine gun to his shoulder while bullets from a scudding Zero hammered him to shreds. The Zero got him, but he got the Zero, too.

Jarlath said, "Man, what a job of fighting fellows like that can do. A year ago, they were just filling-station attendants, store clerks, and insurance agents."

Of his own exploits, Jarlath seldom spoke. He was too full of the deeds of his fellow fliers. However, he was also battling Japs over the skies at Midway. At the height of the fighting, he was attacked by a twin-engine, land-based bomber, which was bad medicine. The resultant dogfight lasted for more than an hour. Jarlath had his starboard gun knocked out. The Jap knew he was helpless on that side, and kept trying to come in on it. Jarlath maneuvered like a wild man to keep out of reach. While he was skipping along 50 feet above the water the Jap tried to bomb him. Then Jarlath would climb furiously, twisting and dodging. He flew into some clouds and the Jap thought he had him. The Jap quickly swung around the clouds so as to nail him on the starboard side when he came out. Meanwhile, one of Jarlath's pals had heard the contact report and started for the trouble spot with throttle wide open.

Jarlath's pal hit the clouds, too, and came out on the far side first. The Jap thought he had a sitting duck to polish off, and came coasting up on the starboard side of the second plane, thinking it was Jarlath. What a reception he got. Jarlath's pal pumped enough firepower into the enemy aircraft to sink a destroyer.

"The Japs paid a terrible price at Midway," Jarlath said. "For every one of our planes they got, we got three or four of theirs."

While Jarlath intended to play down his combat experiences, the record showed that by mid-1943, he had been shot down and crash-landed no fewer than five times. Statistics also bore out the fact that from his original class of 80 cadets at Pensacola, only seven or eight still lived. Time was definitely working against him. "If I crash another plane," he wrote Dan, "I'll qualify for German Ace." He told his brother in another letter that he was giving small thought to ever getting married, "because I don't think I'll live through the war." Jarlath felt the war was going badly and would probably last for another four years. His squadron's slogan was: "The Golden Gate by '48."

Only a miracle saved Jarlath from serious injury in one crash. Both engines of his patrol plane went out, he managed to bring it down, but then it waterlooped. All fifteen men aboard were saved when the plane sank, and Jarlath, wearing a fiery-red beard, was greeted with most undignified language when a rescue boat fished him out of the ocean.

"JAR! JARLATH LYONS! WHY, YOU OLD RED-BEARDED SON OF A-GUN!"

The voice was that of Jack Green—a school chum from Seattle Prep days! Jack had the rank of Storekeeper First Class.

Jarlath flew missions in the South Seas for sixteen months before the Navy furloughed him. Back home for a rest, he told reporter Robert Heilman from *The Seattle Times* what it was like to take a Solomons native for a ride in a PBY Bomber. The native told Jarlath: "White man canoe him go too fast."

Jarlath respected the natives. Their judgment was impeccable, he discovered. There was a time ,he said, when one of his Navy friends rode in a canoe with a native. The native suddenly stopped paddling, and cupped his ear. "Plane coming," he warned the officer. The Navy flier saw nothing, heard nothing. He asked the native, "What kind of plane?" Quickly, the islander drew a star in the air with his finger, indicating it was a U.S. plane. (They drew a circle for a Japanese plane.) Then he indicated a straight line, meaning Flying Fortress. Five minutes later, a Flying Fortress flew overhead. When Jarlath heard the story, he wanted to hire the native for a spotter, but Navy regulations forbade it.

Jarlath told the *Times* correspondent: "The natives are excellent informal spotters. They'll paddle around an island and flush up Jap planes or subs for us. They're much like American Indians. They can be bad enemies. You'll be walking along a trail and suddenly there is one standing grinning at you. You give him a cigarette, turn for a second, and in a flash he's gone. You don't hear a sound. The Japs have learned of these traits the hard way. One native, with a bayonet he had stolen from a Jap in the first place, had killed 69 more Japs. The native did not know how to count that high, so he said, 'You write down, me tell.' When the count reached 69 the native nodded. Then he demonstrated how he did it—it consisted of sneaking up from behind and a stab in the throat. They are excellent navigators. I have seen them paddle as far as 180 miles from land. In their tiny canoes, hollowed from logs and handled very carefully by whites, they do not hesitate to stand up and wave to planes flying overheard. The natives learn fast. Now you see them running around with rolls of bills made from selling curios to service men. They even have cigarette lighters and alarm clocks. There was a time when a native sold everything he had for a mere three cigarettes. The other day, a friend of mine was out of cigarettes and bought some from the natives. It cost him 30 cents—for three!"

Jarlath was one of the youngest commanders in the Navy. He had his own PBY squadron, and was something of a local hero back in Seattle. He never took himself seriously, however. He smiled his way through the black clouds of war. In a letter to brother Dan, he typed: "There's a cartoon in Collier's magazine that strikes me as amusing. Shows a tow car with a flat tire. The driver has merely hooked the crane to that side and lifted it off the ground. While changing the tire, a passerby interrupts him. 'OK, OK,' the driver tells him. 'so maybe it is against all the laws of physics. But I'm a practical man.' So, now let me leave you with some advice: Go ahead and let all the book worms ponder and study and think things out. Then when they have it all settled, you can step in and spread it around where it'll do the most good."

Jarlath received orders to report to Corpus Christi, Texas, as an instructor in 1944. On May 14th, he hinted in a Mother's Day letter to his mother that rumors were going around that he soon would be going back to his squadron again.

"Dear Mom:

Happy Mother's Day.

We have a new batch of big boys on the base here and they claim too many pilots are stationed at A. & R. Most of us will move out and go back to the squadrons quite soon. They may even ship us to another base; no one knows yet or at least won't tell. In a way, I'll be sorry to leave. The work here has been very interesting and there is still much experience to be gained that'd be helpful after the war. However, it has been fine to be here this long, and time has passed quickly, with all its worries that seem so important at the time and are shortly forgotten in the press of new ones. My division now has around 750 personnel to be kicked into line by morning, bullying, or threatening, as the case may be.

The leave I put in for in May was disapproved, so I put in another slip for June. One Commander and two Full Captains turned it down, and the only one higher was Admiral Mason, but it seemed foolish to bother him with it. Especially since he'd undoubtedly throw me in the brig if it came in front of him. However, my new leave quota commences in July, and my request for 15 days has already been sent in. I am also asking for 8 days travel time. If it is granted, the best way to Seattle is to drive, but no one will give me any gas. There are plenty of gas coupons for me to get to

> Seattle. Could you find enough to get me back? It would take about 35 B or C coupons. Sure would be nicer than riding the train; as for flying, we have nothing down here that flies even close to Seattle.
>
> Danny also gets a letter today, so you can be quite proud of me. Thank you.
>
> Jar"

The most serious prank Jarlath was ever involved in as a teenager had to do with the time he and Hank Martin, a boyhood pal, threw two rocks through the front, fancy window of Mr. and Mrs. Parker, a childless couple who lived in the neighborhood on Capitol Hill and were forever nagging and complaining about the local children. Both boys were about 17, old enough to know better, and they pleaded guilty immediately when apprehended by the police. Their punishment was confined to paying for the window. Unwilling to cast any shame on Seattle Prep, Jarlath and Hank told the lawmen that they were "laborers, no fixed abode," and that's how the brief news item appeared in the papers. Naturally, both families of the boys were ashamed to death of the senseless incident, and they treated it most darkly. In time it was forgotten, and Jarlath and Hank went on to become Lieutenant Commanders within a few years.

Patrick Lyons had a long memory, however, and in a letter to Jarlath in late May, 1944, he chided our hero.

"Dear Jarlath:

> We had a lot of news yesterday from you. First, your letter to mother, then your box arrived, and finally an account of your 'hitch-hiking' experience when Green pulled alongside the PBY and was flabbergasted to discover the last man out of the ship was a long-

bearded VIKING. Oh, please don't tell me you have turned SWEDE!

Larry was in to visit and has his gold bars. Carl Auer was also in and came into the room where I was sleeping. It appears Tommy was drafted and sent to Fort Lewis. He was there only about six weeks when he was shipped to Africa. Carl sure wanted to hold my hand and weep but as I had just gone to bed I'm afraid he didn't get all the sympathy he was looking for.

Mother and I were to see Dan last week. Had quite a visit with him. He met us at the train and we spent the whole day together. We had to travel by train as automobiles are out of the question. Dan is looking forward to the time when he will be teaching at the Prep nearby. It will seem like old times to have you two back again, won't it though. He certainly looks good and for the life of me I cannot figure out how he finds time to do all the things he does, but as Jim Dougherty once said, when you want anything done ask a busy man to do it.

Was down to see Jack Martin this week. Hank is on his way West and you will probably see him in a month or two. Jack still has the two rocks you fellows shot at Parker, who, by the way, died a Catholic. Maybe the rocks through his window jolted him. . . . Always in our prayers,

Dad"

As a class, it is fair to say that the pilots were the gayest people in the Navy. When they came back from a mission they were usually full of high spirits. And when they sat around together of an evening, nine-tenths of their conversation was exuberant and full of howling jokes. There was very little grimness in their conduct to match that of, say, the infantrymen in the line.

For example, when Jarlath told his folk about being shot down in the Solomons and being picked up by his old school mate, Jack Green, he made his narrow escape sound funny, and meant it. He had an infectious grin and a perpetual sense of mimicry. In describing what it felt like to fly a high-powered PBY, he'd say, "You're just sitting there with hundreds of horses in your lap and a feather in your tail."

Jarlath added, "You laugh at some very sad things in wartime." He then told about the fate of a Japanese jeep. American planes were strafing an island road one day. They saw this Japanese jeep. The driver kept looking back over his shoulder in terror at the approaching planes, and consequently rode right off the dirt road and over the edge of a 300-foot cliff.

The war in Europe was almost over and done with by August of 1944. The end was inevitable. It could not be put off for long. The Germans were beaten and they knew it. Ernie Pyle, the most famous combat correspondent of the war, hastened to tell his readers, however, that while the end of the fighting would be a gigantic relief, it could not be a matter of hilarity for most Americans. "Somehow," he wrote, "it would be sacrilegious to sing and dance when the great day comes—there are so many who can never sing and dance again."

America was now moving into a confusing period. The end of one war was a great fetter broken from around the lives of this country, but there was yet another to be broken.

The Pacific war ranged on, long and bloody. It could not be approached with easy hopes. The next few months at home were going to be torn between the new spiritual freedom of half-peace and the old grinding blur of half-war. No one pretended to know the right answers.

In mid-Fall, 1944, Jarlath received orders to report to San Diego. From there he was given a furlough. Since attacking enemy planes had not been his job when flying combat, he said he was going back to Seattle without any enemy planes to his credit. He said the first things the kids in his neighborhood were going to ask him was how many planes he had shot down, and when he said "None at all" the kids were going to give him an awfully funny look.

Dan recalls asking Jarlath how much longer he felt the war in the Pacific would continue.

"About four more years," Jarlath said. "The Golden Gate by '48."

The A-Bomb was still the best-kept secret of the century. No one could foresee at that time how the devastation of Hiroshima months later would shorten the war.

Dan asked, "How many of your original class at Pensacola are still living?"

"Seven or eight."

"How many were in the class?"

"More than eighty."

At a dinner honoring Lt.-Cmdr. Jarlath Lyons, his father was asked to say a few words. Patrick rose, thoughtfully, and said, "I do not want to give a speech, but I will propose a toast." Then slowly, and with great passion, he lifted his wine glass and delivered the following lines:

"The wine cup, the wine cup bring hither,
And fill ye it up to the brim.
May the memory of Washington ne'er wither,
Nor the star of his glory grow dim.
May the Service united ne'er falter,
But e'er to its colors prove true—
MacArthur, MacArthur forever!
And three cheers for the Red, White and Blue!"

When he sat down, the banquet room burst in applause. There was not a dry eye to be found.

Jarlath, who had joined the Navy pilot program in 1939, was nearing the finish now. In the spring of 1945, he wrote home to say he was leaving San Diego for San Francisco. "From there I depart for duty on the *Bon Homme Richard*," he said in a brief note to his parents. "So the Good Man Lyons will call his home the Good Man Richard for his next tour of duty. She's a large CV class carrier. I'll be assistant in the air department in the ship's company. I probably won't know where she's located until I finally get aboard, but from my orders it is evidently 'way out West.' "

When Jarlath first joined the Navy, he thought the life of an aviator was going to be a dashing, romantic life. And it was, for the first few missions when everything was new and strange and he was just learning. But after that it was a job to do, just a job of "steaming, hard work." And all his fellow pilots agreed.

On July 10th, 1945, he wrote his last letter home.

"Dear Folks:

I thought I'd get a rest or so on the journey, but we came right through to this island, where I now sit and await my ship. They tell me it will arrive eventually but no one says *when*.

This afternoon, I went over to the airstrip and checked out one of the newer divebombers. I flew it for about an hour and decided it was enough. If you can imagine trying to steer our old Buick with a 100 pound dragline on each front wheel, you will get some idea of the way it handles. When I got back they asked me if I tried any stunts. Great Guppies! It took all of my power to hold it in level flight and to coax it into a few gentle turns. But tomorrow I'll try another one that really is a honey. If my ship stays away long enough, I'll fly every plane on the island out of sheer boredom.

A few beaten-up palm trees still stand on the island, though most are scarred and torn to remind us that a battle did go on here. Very few feathered folk are about—in fact, I have seen only one small crane—and, thank the Lord, few flies and no mosquitoes.

Mom, please stow all my uniforms before Pop, *Pat,* or the moths get them. I might need any of them at any time and will have to send for them. . . .

So long,
J."

Jarlath had entered the psychological phase of his combat career. That is, once he had completed his time on the *Bon Homme Richard* he would probably be sent back to America. For the pilot who had seen as much action as he had, it was customary to be given missions that were expected to be easy. But there were so many ironic cases of men "getting it" on their last flight that most squadron leaders were as nervous about it as the pilots.

The day after Jarlath wrote his last letter home, he checked out in a Hellcat-type plane for a routine flight. He was never seen again. On July 13th, at 5:51 p.m., the following telegram was delivered to the Lyonses:

I DEEPLY REGRET TO INFORM YOU THAT
YOUR SON LT.-CMDR. JARLATH JOSEPH
LYONS, USN, IS MISSING IN PLANE CRASH
AT SEA ON JULY 11, 1945, IN THE SERVICE
OF HIS COUNTRY. YOUR GREAT
ANXIETY IS APPRECIATED AND YOU WILL
BE FURNISHED DETAILS WHEN RECEIVED.
TO PREVENT POSSIBLE AID TO OUR
ENEMIES PLEASE DO NOT DIVULGE
THE NAME OF HIS SHIP OR STATION
UNLESS THE GENERAL CIRCUMSTANCES
ARE MADE PUBLIC IN NEWS STORIES.
VICE-ADMIRAL RANDALL JACOBS,
CHIEF OF NAVAL PERSONNEL

The first big heartbreak in brother Dan's life came to him when his parents phoned to tell him that Jarlath was missing at sea. It was an hour which he will remember with a degree of clarity all the rest of his life. The telegram his parents received spelled deep personal tragedy and he was certain that nowhere was there such dark sadness as filled his heart.

At first, the family held out hope that Jarlath, by some small miracle, was still alive. Patrick wired Admiral Jacobs for more information:

REFERENCE YOUR TELEGRAM JULY 13
CONCERNING LT.-CMDR. JARLATH
JOSEPH LYONS, USN, REPORTED MISSING
IN AIRPLANE CRASH. WAS LYONS PILOT OF
AIRCRAFT REPORTED MISSING OR PASSENGER? AT YOUR CONVENIENCE PLEASE
WIRE ANY FURTHER DETAILS YOU MAY
HAVE.
PATRICK LYONS

Patrick's wire was sent on July 15th. For four days he heard no word. Then, on July 19th, Admiral Jacobs replied:

> RE YOUR WIRE JULY 15, I REGRET THAT NO FURTHER DETAILS ARE PRESENTLY AVAILABLE CONCERNING LT.-CMDR. JARLATH JOSEPH LYONS, USN, REPORTED MISSING IN PLANE CRASH 11 JULY. WHEN ADDITIONAL INFORMATION IS RECEIVED YOU WILL BE PROMPTLY INFORMED. I AGAIN WISH TO EXTEND SINCEREST SYMPATHY TO YOU IN YOUR GREAT ANXIETY.

Jarlath's death was *officially* confirmed, on October 11, 1945, in a letter to his parents from Capt. Paul E. Gillespie, U.S.N.

"Dear Mr. and Mrs. Lyons:

In reply to your letter, dated September 13, 1945, addressed to the Commanding Officer, USS BON HOMME RICHARD, the following information regarding the loss of your son, Lieutenant Commander Jarlath J. Lyons, U.S. Navy, is furnished:

(a) On July 8, 1945, Lieutenant Commander Lyons reported aboard this station for further transportation to the USS BON HOMME RICHARD.

(b) On July 11, 1945, at approximately 12:00 p.m., Lieutenant Commander LYONS requested to be checked in a Hellcat-type aircraft to make a routine flight, for the purpose of obtaining the required flight time for that month.

(c) At approximately 12:27 p.m., Lieutenant Commander LYONS took off, alone, from Stickell Field, ENIWETOK and headed seaward.

(d) At 1:00 p.m., a plane, of the type Lieutenant Commander LYONS was flying, was observed to go into a spin and crash into the sea approximately two miles southwest of the field.

Rescue boats and personnel were immediately dispatched to the scene of the crash and a search was conducted in an attempt to locate the body of the pilot, but to no avail.

From the facts gathered by the Board of Investigation convened at this base, it must be presumed that Lieutenant Commander LYONS was killed, in the line of duty, as a result of this crash.

The findings of this Board of Investigation were that the accident was not a result of any violation of law or Naval Regulation and further that the accident was not caused by the intent, fault, negligence or inefficiency of any person in the Naval Service or connected therewith.

If it can be of any comfort to you at this time, it is my earnest opinion that your son died instantaneously and without pain.

Please accept my deepest sympathy and sincere regret in your great loss. The Navy has lost a fine officer and gentleman."

For Jarlath Lyons, there had been really two wars. There had been the war of maps and statistics. Then there had been the war of homesick, weary, funny, dedicated young fliers who washed their socks in tincans, complained about the food, whistled at native girls, or any girls for that matter, and stuffed themselves into cockpits day after day through as dirty a business as the world has ever seen, and did it with humor and dignity and courage.

Some of them—the lucky ones—came back the same

way they had gone to war. Some of them came back in coffins. Some of them didn't come back at all.

That was Jarlath Lyons' war.

On Tuesday, Oct. 2, 1945, a Requiem Memorial Mass was offered for Jarlath at St. Joseph's Church, where he had once served as altar boy. Rev. Harold O. Small, S.J., president of Seattle College, officiated. Subdeacon at the Mass was—Dan Lyons, S.J.

The Navy's file on Jarlath was officially closed two months later, December 15, 1945, with this letter to the parents from James Forrestal, Secretary of the Navy:

"My dear Mr. and Mrs. Lyons:

> I learned with deep regret that your son, Lt.-Cmdr. Jarlath Joseph Lyons, United States Navy, previously reported missing, is now known to have lost his life on 11 July 1945.
>
> I know what little solace the formal and written word can be to help meet the burden of your loss, but in spite of that knowledge I cannot refrain from writing to say very simply that I am sorry.
>
> I hope that you may find comfort in the thought that his sacrifice was made in order that the freedom of his country might be preserved.
>
> Sincerely yours,
> James Forrestal."

For one American family, the war had become a flat, black depression, a revulsion of the mind and an exhaustion of the spirit.

For their hero-son, the war, which was to end a month later, had gone on too long.

CHAPTER 9

The Search for Truth

It is ever difficult to see her clearly, if at all, that imperishable lady at one's elbow. Perhaps we do not wish to glimpse the inscrutable one who pounces upon us to exercise a last option. And although some poets sing of her as beautiful beyond lilacs and roses, and say of her that she is a refuge for the sick of heart, our personal opinion is that Death is a great prostitute.

The late Gene Fowler, author, used to say: "She sleeps with everyone, promiscuously and obscenely, and everyone must sleep with her without willing it. Why lie?"

An old newspaper boss of mine once told me, "We practice death a little bit every night when we go to sleep."

Death was a constant companion in the Lyons' home in 1945. First, there was the loss of Jarlath. Then there was Tom Lyons, the 55-year-old younger brother of Patrick. Uncle Tom was dying of cancer. Much of what Patrick thought about death and the life hereafter was contained in a letter he wrote to Tom on September 16, 1945. In it he stressed his strong convictions about God and Heaven. The teachings he had learned at his mother's knee wouldn't erase. He had a strong concomitant in the Catholic religion, and his letter to his brother showed just how intact his faith in God and the Church were. And yet he was never a blind believer. He was a questioner. When he grew up he studied all the great religions he could find books on before he decided that, as far as he was concerned, his parents had picked the right one in the Catholic Church.

The search for truth had gone on all his adult life. His feelings about life after death were devout; just how devout were brought out in this parting message to Tom:

"My Dear Brother:

We are all sorry that you are obliged to go to the hospital and that you are suffering so much—but going to the hospital is like going to the ticket office to get your ticket for going home. The more you suffer here the shorter will be your stay in Purgatory—and the shorter your stay in Purgatory the sooner will you be united with father and mother and Eddy and Norah and John and your little brother Matthew. (Editor's Note: Eddy and John were his brothers, Norah his sister.)

Do you remember baby Matthew? — I hardly think you do. He was, so far as I can remember, about nine months old when he died, and he died almost a month, to the day, before father did. That's a long time ago, 1892, and as he was there to welcome father home so also will he be there with all the other relatives to welcome you.

I often think when I see a ship pull out from the docks how like it is to a person dying—the passengers leave their friends behind and one sees them crying and waving their 'goodbyes' and the ship goes into and over the horizon and the friends left behind say 'there she goes' and they pray for the safe and quick arrival of the ship and the passengers—and in another land and on another dock the friends of those passengers are anxiously looking and waiting for the docking of the ship. Soon someone shouts as she comes out of the horizon, 'There she comes,' and soon all is joy and gladness and the people of the new land greet their friends with a joy and a gladness as great as was the grief and sadness of the friends left behind whence the ship came. 'In My Father's house there are many mansions' —Christ said so and added as though it were an afterthought, 'If it were not so I would have told you.'

So when you arrive in the new land of the 'many mansions' you will meet all your relatives there and you will meet John Higgins and his boys—and I wonder if John Higgins will have that Irish setter, you remember the one that was deaf and how we used to take him with us snipe hunting—and do you remember the day Kelly, the policeman, chased us and followed the dog home and almost stumbled on the bunch of snipe that we had hanging from the rafter? Well, I don't suppose John will have the dog, but he himself will be there—and there will be others there, too, that you will be glad to see, and it may be that some you will know and some you won't know. Why, you will get to know more people there than you do in this miserable old world, and when you visit the Irish Colony you will see a lot of the oldtimers. You will see Pearse, the both of them, and the others of 1916. And you will see those relatives of ours, those ancestors of ours, who fought and suffered and died to preserve the Faith for us down through the centuries, and when you see them, thank them for all of us for the sacrifices that they made for keeping the Faith, for that is the greatest possible legacy that they could have left us.

And as son Jarlath is still missing it may be that you will find him there—you will recognize him by his big, broad, boyish grin—smiling a welcome at you and bidding you a happy landing in the land of the Beatific Vision. And, finally, you will see there The Holy Family—Joseph and Mary. I remember when I was in Europe and I would get a tinge of homesickness; how I used to like to go into a church and sit down and look at Joseph and Mary. I always felt at home, and that Joseph must certainly have been a grand guy. I always liked to look at his statue and pretend it was real and talk with him. Sure, I knew he understood, and when things are tough with you just ask Joseph, who took such good care of the Baby Jesus and of His mother, to help you, and Joseph will, because he understands. And don't forget Mary, for, after all, she is our mother, isn't she? And, Dear Brother, remember that any sufferings that you may have to endure are as nothing to what she suffered. Ask her to offer to her Boy, Jesus, your sufferings for some poor soul, some poor soul in Purgatory that is forgotten by his friends. She, too, will help you.

We are all praying for you—praying that God will give you strength and patience, and when you arrive home please don't forget those of us you are leaving behind, as it is only a few years at most until, please God, we will be with you.

Affectionately,
Your Brother Pat."

Tom Lyons died a short time later. Few of us will ever be given a richer sendoff.

Alice Lyons shared her husband's faith in a life after death. This was clearly revealed only several days after she got the tragic telegram about Jarlath. One of his girl friends from Seattle dropped by the house and told Mrs. Lyons she was worried about him.

She said, "He hasn't written for weeks. I hope there's nothing wrong."

Mrs. Lyons opened her mouth to tell her the truth, but the words wouldn't come. Later, she confessed to Patrick, "I didn't have the heart to tell her that Jarlath was presumed dead. That look on her sweet face—well, I decided to wait and let Jarlath tell her himself what happened when they meet in Heaven."

In 1947, when he was 27 and teaching at Gonzaga Prep, Father Dan was giving a lot of thought to Death. She was coming dangerously close to taking away one of his father's closest friends for thirty years, Howard Irwin, a successful lumber mill owner at Coos Bay, Oregon. Ironically, only a few months before Howard's illness, he and Patrick had been deep in a philosophical discussion about the mystery and possibilities of life after death. So when Howard fell ill, Patrick asked Dan to put pen to paper and send his thoughts on the question along to Howard.

It was before Dan had started his theological studies. Yet the combined wisdom of faith and philosophy enabled him to write to his father's friend as follows:

"Dear Mr. Irwin:

The reason more people do not discuss the matter of

a future life is because it is generally taken on faith. Once a person admits there is a God, and that Christ was the Son of God, as He claimed to be in that most historical and trustworthy of all documents, the New Testament, then we find that there is nothing He testified to more conclusively than that there is a future life. In the New Testament we read that He was asked: 'What must I do to possess eternal life?' His disciples said to Him: 'For thou hast the words of eternal life.' St. Paul, Christ's greatest pupil, insisted: 'God hath given to us eternal life'; again, Paul urged Timothy to 'lay hold on eternal life.'

All the teachings of Christianity pivot around this one point. This was brought out forcibly when Christ said that if our eye scandalized us we should pluck it out and cast it from us, and that if our arm scandalized us we should cut if off and cast it from us, for 'it is better to enter lame into life eternal' than with all of our members to lose heaven. He told the Apostles that those who renounced their possessions for His sake would receive one hundred fold in this life and 'in the world to come life everlasting.' (I think all the possessions the Apostles gave up were a few leaky rowboats.) Again Christ testified that 'He that believeth in the Son hath life everlasting,' etc. The New Testament overflows with such statements. Also, by reading them in context it is clear that everyone is going to have life everlasting, and that 'life eternal' refers to the eternal habitat of the just, in contrast to the eternal abode prepared for the unjust.

Just as there are many proofs from Faith, so there are many proofs from reason attesting to the existence of a future life. Since some proofs tend to convince some people while other proofs have more force with other people, I will give seven or eight different reasons

Father Dan Lyons, S.J., author, newspaper columnist, lecturer, administrator, war correspondent, and freedom fighter. Age 51.

The summer of 1942. Last photo taken of the Lyons' clan together. Left to right, sitting: Father Dan, Sheila, "Pop," and Jarlath; standing, left, Patricia, Noreen, "Mom," and Eileen.

Photo taken in 1900 at Lake Whatcom, Washington, shows some of Father Lyons' mothe family. Rear, left, Villard, An (Mrs. Roscoe Tibbles), and H front, left, Sabin, Mathilde, John D. and Alice (Father D mother). They were strict Lutherans, but Alice joined Catholic faith after she marri Patrick Lyons. Henry, here pictured, is still living with his Clara at Van Zandt, Washing near John D.'s homestead, th home since they were married nearly 65 years ago. The only other from this photo who sti lives is Alice, who was 81 on Sept. 16, 1972.

Alice Linnell (Father Dan's mother) at the age of 20, three years before she married Patrick Lyons.

"Pop" Lyons, always a dapper dresser, was a successful exporter of lumber in Seattle for nearly a half-century.

"Mom" and "Pop" Lyons, parents of Father Dan Lyons.

Patricia Lyons, oldest of the Lyons' children, was athletic and won a number of skating competitions in Seattle as a teenager. She was student-body president at Holy Names Academy.

All-American Family—Father Lyons poses for family photo with parents and four sisters at wedding of youngest sister, Sheila, in 1957. Left, Pat (Mrs. Jim Matthiesen), Noreen (Mrs. Tom Gilkey), "Mom," Father Dan, "Pop," Eileen (Mrs. Bob Hume), and the new Mrs. Louis Leewens.

Danny Lyons' 8th grade graduation picture, at Seattle's O'Dea High School, in 1933.

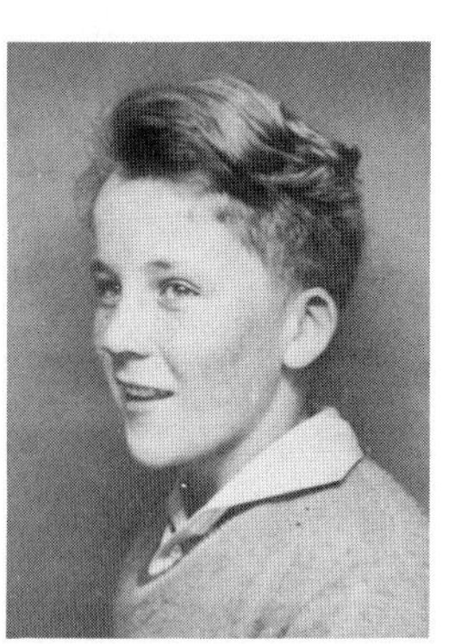

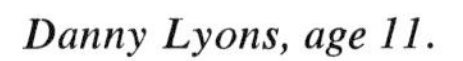

Danny Lyons, age 11.

Lt. Cmdr. Jarlath Lyons, skipper squadron 13C, at U.S. Naval Air Station, Corpus Christi, Texas, 1944. The older brother of Father Lyons, he died in a plane crash at sea in the South Pacific a year later.

The Jesuit Novitiate at Sheridan, Oregon, where Father Lyons received his early training. This was the way it was from 1933 to 1959. The picture below shows the Novitiate after Father Lyons raised half a million dollars to complete it and add on three new wings.

An interior shot of library at Mt. Saint Michaels, Spokane, Washington, where Father Dan studied, 1942-1945.

A shrine to St. Patrick that Father Lyons built at the Sheridan, Oregon, Novitiate, in 1941. He said, "I built it by cutting down a tree a mile away, hauling the log on a truck, then erecting it on its base and replacing bark around the niche. The statue was sent by my brother Jarlath from San Francisco."

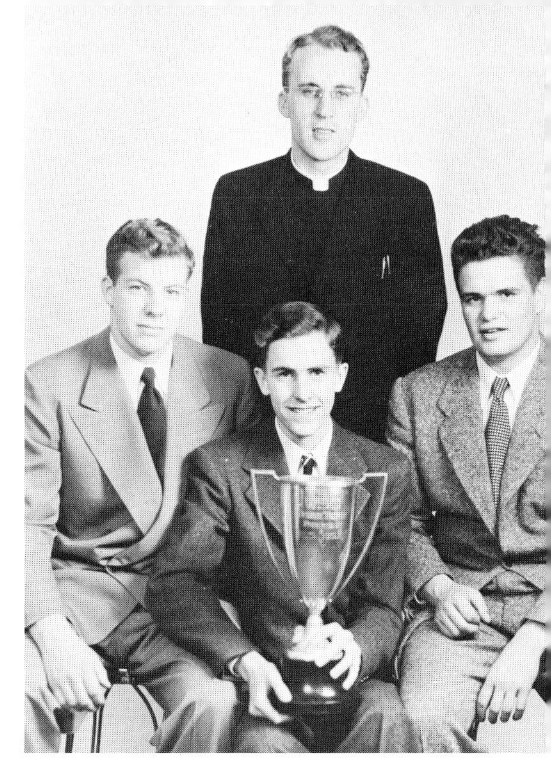

Coach Father Dan Lyons, S.J., and his 1946-47 Gonzaga Prep debaters, Washington State high school champions. Seated, left, Cul Smith, Ed Caffrey, and Henry Higgins. Caffrey is now a priest.

Father Lyons, Frank de Meyer, left, and O. McGowan are all smiles after winning the Pacific Northwest Debate Championship for Seattle University. Tournament was held at University of Montana, Missoula. McGowan has since become a Jesuit priest.

which lead us to believe in the existence of a future life, and you can choose those which most appeal to you. Although I fear this will make a long letter out of it, and I fully realize that you are a busy person; still, perhaps sometime at your convenience you will find time to read the rest of this over. My only excuse is that you have shown interest in the subject, and that the subject is certainly worth giving considerable thought to, if anything is.

One simple proof for the existence of a future life is the fact that the overwhelming majority of people, at all times and under all conditions, have been so sure that there was a life after death. Since most people have believed strongly in this, whether or not they ever heard of Christianity, it cannot be due to mere chance that man so believes. It must be according to his nature. If we believe that man's nature is not the result of mere chance but was designed by an intelligent Planner, then we must conclude that He who made us must have had a reason for putting in us the belief, and the longing, for eternal life. Else He would not be a God, but a monstrosity, since He would have acted unjustly if He so made us as to leave us frustrated. Such an act would imply injustice on the part of God, and as injustice is an imperfection, it could not exist in Him.

By studying an object we can find out what it was intended for. Even though we had never seen a clock, we could soon discover the purpose for which it was made. The dial, the face, the hands, the uniform rate, the inner works, all reveal to an intelligent mind that they were designed to indicate time. Similarly, by studying a bird, or a fish, we could tell that the former was intended to fly and the latter to swim.

Applying the same type of reasoning to man, we

see that in many ways he resembles animals: he is destined to eat, sleep, rear a family, etc. Yet nothing is clearer than that man possesses qualities and gifts that are *wholly* wanting in the brute creation. In particular, man has three abilities limited to him alone: 1) intelligence (as contrasted with innate instincts); 2) free will (which places man in the moral order); 3) rational affection or love. The possession of these marvelous gifts proves beyond all doubt that we were made, not for any finite, material creatures, but for the Creator of all creatures; that we were made, not for time but ultimately for eternity. Let me expand this a little.

Whether we believe in the existence of a Creator or not, we have to recognize as we look about us that every plant and animal which has a need or desire is capable of satisfying that desire, so that every creature beside man is capable of achieving what for it is perfect happiness. No animal's life is marred by chronic worrying. Put a cow in the pasture and you have a contented cow. But not so with man. Far from it.

Man's mind, for example, was made to acquire truth. As the philosopher would say, the proper object of the mind is truth. Yet the mind can never find satisfaction. I think I know something about that. In a few weeks I will finish courses for another Master's Degree, which will be my fifth college degree. Yet I am going to school for the next five years, and three more after that, if I possibly can. This year, more than ever before, I have realized deeply how little I know and how much there is to learn. Thirst of the body is satisfied by drinking; thirst of the mind becomes all the more intense as we attempt to satisfy it. The intellectual appetite, instead of diminishing grows stronger and stronger the more it is fed. How can we possibly explain this insatiable thirst for knowledge? There can be only one possible explanation: man was made to possess and enjoy eternal and uncreated Truth, which we call God. That will be one of the greatest joys of eternity, to go on learning continually. You have travelled a great deal. Yet I am sure you are more interested in seeing the rest of the world's wonders than you would have been had you never travelled. That, too, will be one of the great joys of eternity, for in an all-perfect Creator must lie all the beauties of ten thousand worlds which He could have created, each more beautiful than the last.

The learned Newton compared his vast hoard of information to one little shell, thrown up by the limitless ocean of truth. St. Thomas Aquinas, the greatest philosopher the world has ever known, was granted a foretaste of heaven in a vision. Afterwards he wanted to burn all of his works, not that they were wrong, but that they were 'like straw,' compared to the majesty of Truth Itself. St. Paul was trying to express a similar idea when he said, after he had been lifted up to the 'third' heaven' (whatever that means): 'Eye has not seen, nor ear heard, nor has it entered into the mind of man to conceive, what God has prepared for those that love Him.'

Man searches as eagerly as he searches in vain, in this life, for perfect happiness. The reason we can never reach it is because we are never without worries, or at least without fear of losing our happiness. Every action of every man is either in a positive search for happiness or in a negative effort to fend off unhappiness. This is true even of one who hangs himself. The world holds out fair promises, but they are delusive. Most people believe that happiness lies in great wealth, yet there is no reason for believing that even those few

Americans who became billionaires (before the days of income taxes) were especially happy. Disappointments, jealousies, mistrust of friends, all harassed them. Old J. D. Rockefeller was reported to have said that he would give all of his wealth for a new stomach. His fabulous riches may have distracted his mind for awhile, but they could never have contented his heart. Solomon, one of the wisest, most wealthy and influential of all men, wrote: 'Whatever my eyes desired I refused them not . . . . I saw in all things vanity and vexation of mind, and that nothing was lasting under the sun.' Napoleon, after conquering country after country, found his insatiable ambition forcing him still further, till he finally lost all, dying an exile in a foreign land. Alexander the Great, after conquering the entire known world in his time, wept because there were no more worlds to conquer. There can be no doubt that nothing can fill the void in man's heart. Why is it so utterly impossible for earthly things to fill that void? St. Augustine, who lived as a profligate for many years, gives us the answer: 'My heart was made for Thee, O Lord, and it can never rest until it rests in Thee.' If the heart of man were made for earth, then earth would satisfy it.

As I recall, I believe Dad used the argument that matter is never destroyed, and that since mind (the spiritual) is superior to matter (the material) then the mind can never be destroyed. (The mind here means the intellect and does not include the gray matter called the brain, upon which we depend in this life for the working of the mind.) It is true, as science affirms, that no matter has ever been destroyed (by that I mean, annihilated. We speak of a house being destroyed, in a certain sense, by fire, but all the materials merely undergo a change of form.) To change something into nothing takes infinite power, just as it takes infinite power to create something out of nothing. All the scientists in the world cannot *create* so much as a grain of sand or a drop of water. Nor will they ever be able to.

When a substance is changed into something else, e.g. water into hydrogen and oxygen gases, we say it undergoes a substantial change. Such changes are always brought about by separating a composite being into its constituent parts. Consequently a simple substance, for the very reason that it is simple (i.e. not made up of parts) is incapable of undergoing a substantial change. Not being made up of parts, it has no parts to be separated. But the soul, since it is a spiritual being, cannot be made up of parts. Yet no destruction or change is possible without a disintegration of parts. But the soul has no parts, therefore it cannot be destroyed. It is, therefore, by its very nature, indestructible.

How do we know that the soul is not made up of parts? Because of its nature, which we can come to know about from its operations. If the soul were made up of parts it would be material; yet the very idea of mere matter thinking in an abstract manner is repugnant to common sense. We see the infinite gap between animal and human intelligence when we realize that no animal has ever improved its manner of living. If you want a near perfect description of how bees build hives, for example, read Aristotle on the subject. He wrote 2200 years ago, and they have not made the slightest change since then.

The idea of conscience is repugnant to a material object. Yet man rejoices when he acts nobly, sorrows when he sins, repents when he reasonably reflects on what he has done. To suppose that the soul is made up of parts would be to identify it with the gross material substance of the body. Yet it is irrational to bestow on mere corporeal atoms the power of judgment, intelligence, and virtue. The fact that the human mind can know justice and truth, right and wrong, proves that it is a spiritual being.

Could God annihilate the soul, since He is all-powerful? No. There are certain things He cannot do, even though He is all-powerful. For example, He could not destroy Himself. Just as the mind works according to laws of reason, so, and much more, does God, Who is reason Itself, work reasonably. Since he has put into the human soul the desire for perfect happiness, the longing to live forever, He could not abort that desire, for to do so would be to act unreasonably. It would also be to act unjustly, and if God is not all Just, He is not all perfect, and could not have existed from all eternity. But if He did not exist from all eternity, He could never have come to exist at all, since nothing that comes into being can be the cause of its own existence. But this argument is getting off onto the subject of the existence of God, which we are not treating of here.

People are often confused into thinking that the soul and body are identified, simply because they influence each other in this life. Actually, the mind operates entirely independently of the body, except that it is dependent on the senses to inform it. (After death, the medium of the senses will no longer be necessary.) A marksman is dependent on the accuracy of his gun for manifesting his skill, yet his skill is entirely independent of the good, or bad, gun he may be using.

To touch briefly on another proof of a future life, we look at the testimony of conscience. The strongest urge in man is to do good and avoid evil. So much so, that even the hardened 'lifers' in a penitentiary almost all try to justify their actions in one way or another, since they cannot bear to face the fact that they deliberately acted wrongly. When slavery was in vogue in the South, a thousand theories were concocted by Southern whites to try to justify their actions to themselves. When New England factory operators a century ago were running their plants 14 and 16 hours a day, even for small children, they tried to convince themselves that for their employees to work less would lead to immorality, since they needed the 'wholesome discipline of factory life' for at least 64 hours a week. Even 'Babyface' Nelson, a notorious murderer, rationalized that he never shot, except in self-defense.

There is nothing that so outrages a human being as injustice. There is a whole rash of articles in leading industrial and sociological journals at the present time about the fact that more discontent is caused by petty injustices on the part of foremen than by anything else. I taught at Gonzaga, in Spokane, the last two years, and soon found out that boys have a natural sense of justice that is extremely keen.

To what purpose have we been given this thirst for justice? Whence comes this strange but powerful monitor of conscience to be stationed at the door of our hearts? Surely it has been placed there by the Author of our being. And why? It must have been placed there for a purpose, and that purpose must be that He intends to reward obedience and to punish disobedience. There can be no other explanation. If there is any justice in God, there must be a future state where the good will be recompensed and the evil punished. If not, then all of Christianity, upon which our entire civilization, from our calendar to our code of ethics and our form of government, is based, is folly. So also would our very human nature, which supplies us with the motives for our actions, be folly if there were no hereafter. Either we must deny the very existence of God, whose existence the whole universe proclaims, or we must postulate a future life.

Some people hesitate to admit the idea of a future life because they think it will take the joy out of this life. This is not true at all. Many think that they will have to accuse themselves of wasting their time if they do not live like hermits in a cave or monks in a monastery, once they admit that there is a future life. Such people make God out to be quite unreasonable. What He mainly asks of anyone is that he fulfill the duties of his state of life. For most people that means raising and supporting a family, and keeping the Commandments, (the first one of which, though, does insist that we give some thought to Him, and find out about Him). I like to think of St. Joseph, who spent most of his life at his job. He was a breadwinner and a family man, yet he is rated above all the saints who have succeeded him.

Cordially,
DANIEL LYONS, S.J."

Howard Irwin had a stubborn loyalty to life, and it was actually several more years before he died. Remembering the incident, Dan later wrote in a note to me: "Mr. Irwin died a few years after I wrote him. He soon knew a lot more about the hereafter than any of us still around."

Recently, Father Dan wrote an essay for the *National Catholic Register* in which he frowned on those persons who take religion for granted; so much so, he said, that they do not practice it.

"They think they can put the blame on the Church when they *lose their faith,* when they have simply let it starve," he wrote. "Many of us who do practice our religion also take it for granted. It seldom occurs to us what it would be like to be without our religion: as an individual, as a family, as a nation."

Father Dan once visited with an Irish family in Birkenhead, England. The woman's husband was dead. He had been a dedicated physician until life suddenly ended for him in his early 40s. His wife, a widow now with three children to raise, had obviously been deeply in love with him. Yet she remained so cheerful. Why? "I don't know what we'd do without our faith," she told Father Dan. It was a refrain he would hear over and over again during the next four years he lived in Ireland. "God knows best," they'd say.

Father Dan can recall times without number when this Irish philosophy served people of his acquaintance. "Remember," he said, "when President John Kennedy was gunned down and his mother remarked, 'If God had not wanted Jack, He would not have taken him?' And then there was the young nurse at the New York hospital named Brigid Reid who had just returned from evening Mass, which she frequently attended after work. On joining her friends for coffee at the nurses' quarters, a psychiatrist remarked that her attending Church so much was a *crutch*. 'Oh, yes,' she replied, 'and what have *you* got?' 'I've got myself,' he answered bravely. And she said, 'Well, I've got myself *and* my religion.'

"What does religion mean to us? It gives meaning to our lives. It teaches us to look to the next life. This the atheist cannot do, though he has to face the fact with bewildered sorrow that this life will soon be over. It will end, though we crave for eternal life and cannot be satisfied in this one. Religion also gives emotional stability to our lives. It enables us and helps us get along with others. It helps us win the most important battle there is: that struggle between the good we want to do and the evil we are dragged into by our wretched inclinations. The key to a happy family life is winning this struggle within ourselves —never completely, but day-to-day, gradually."

Father Dan often thinks what it would be like for an entire nation to be without religion. He recalls how the great Russian writer, Alexander Solzhenitsyn, talked about the sadness in the Soviet Union without it. Though Solzhenitsyn was only a child when the Communists took over, he still notices the churches today as he walks along the country roads.

"You begin to understand," Solzhenitsyn said, "the key to the Russian landscape. Wherever you might have been in the fields, you were never alone. Above the trees, the stacks of hay, the surrounding earth, there was the church tower beckoning. People have always been mercenary and often evil. But there was a time when the evening bells tolled out, drifting over the village, over the fields, over the woods. They reminded everyone that it was necessary to cast off petty earthly matters, to devote time and thoughts—to eternity. This tolling of the church bell aroused the people from what they were doing in order that they might sink down—in prayer. But now the churches are no longer living. The crosses have been knocked over or bent down, the ragged cupolas gape with skeletons of rusting ribs. There are weeds on the roofs. . . . On the church porch—barrels of oil. A tractor swings around them. Or a truck enters, backing its body into the nave to pick up sacks. A banner proclaims, 'Let's strive for higher yields! A great feat!' In these stones, in these bell towers, our ancestors put all that was best in them, all of their understanding of life."

Thinking about those words from Alexander Solzhenitsyn, Father Dan said, "We should pray every day for the people behind the Iron Curtains of the world, deprived of their priests, their churches, their heritage. Deprived of the meaning of life. Praying for them should remind us not to take religion, our most precious possession, for granted."

Recently, Father Lyons received a tape recording in the mail in which the man spoke of his conversion to Catholicism. It was his feeling, he related to Father Lyons, that a lot of priests seem to know God intellectually but not personally.

Father Lyons elaborated:

"It's pretty hard to distinguish between the two," he told me. "We have been at this business of what we hope is spiritual growth for a long, long time and are not very much given over to one personal experience. On the other hand our faith has always been the deepest thing in our lives. Most of us, certainly myself, have never had any doubt about our Catholic faith. It has been so much a part of me that I could not operate without it. A common example in more recent years of a priest getting married and in some cases leaving the Church and in other cases staying in the Church but giving up the priesthood—this, to me, would be impossible. The idea that a priest would fall in romantic love is the culmination of the fact that his faith must have, somehow, left him. It would simply be impossible for me to do something like that.

"I would much sooner die tomorrow than deny my faith because it's so much a part of me. No, I couldn't do it.

"It has always been a part of Catholic tradition that we do not wear our religion on our sleeve. We take it for granted. It is between ourselves and God, and it is a personal thing. Any day that I might miss Mass because I'm hospitalized or because I'm traveling to Vietnam on a plane or something, there's something very big missing for me in that particular day. But otherwise I simply do not miss offering Mass.

"With some of the younger generation, the aspect of concelebrating with other priests takes on great importance. The main thing is that one says his prayers, or as a priest offers Mass, or as a layman attends Mass according to his own conscience, his own inner convictions. Whether or not it's done with others is secondary. There has been too much emphasis on this business of group participation. This is what is lacking today. At Mass, for example, people do not pray as individuals as much as they should. They are more taken up in the social side of it.

"The great men of the past, men like St. Vincent DePaul who did so much to care for the sick and the poor—such men did this out of their own personal inner-spiritual lives and not because they prayed in conjunction with others. There's room for both, of course, but I think group participation, even at Mass, has been greatly over-emphasized. Catholic spirituality always has been something personal between the individual and God; at least, that's the way I see it. Naturally, in the seminary we did a great deal together; still, we also did a lot as individuals—an hour's morning prayer, as novice's we had a half-hour meditation in the afternoon—this was never done in a group, it was done individually. I find this superior still as a way of praying . . . as the best way to get in touch with God.

"To summarize, I never have had any doubt about my faith. I find it very hard to understand what it would be like without religion. I'm most grateful to God for the fact that I have an abiding faith . . . a *constant* faith . . . and at the same time I realize that one's faith can be lost. Perhaps it is lost because one does not nourish it, and in other cases sometimes God allows people to be tried by losing it.

"We must accept the truism in religion that we are dealing with a lot of mysteries. I really believe that a man could lose his mental equilibrium if he tried to solve the problem of eternal punishment, for example. How can this be? We cannot possibly understand it. We can only say that God is just, God tells us there is a life of eternal punishment, life of eternal reward . . . we have to take this for granted, there's no use trying to understand that which we cannot understand.

"In regard to the work I'm trying to do, there seems to be a race against time. My work is never finished. There's so much that can be done. As one faces life from his early 50s he realizes he has to do more than he's doing. He has to do it better, he has to do it more efficiently, and he has to do it more effectively.

"Never before has the United States faced an enemy that could virtually destroy us. This is a spiritual problem as well as a national problem, because if this enemy is successful, it will be the end of the Catholic Church and religion as we know it. It seems to take a hundred to a hundred and fifty years to outlive movements. If, for instance, Hitler had succeeded in ruling all Europe, it would have probably taken several generations to overcome that. Surely, there has not been a movement in world history quite like Communism, and it came at a time when it threatens to take over the world. Only the United States is standing in the way. Everything depends upon the propaganda war, the Cold War people like to deny is the real war. The very fact that the Administration had so much trouble in getting a very limited defensive missiles program passed through the U.S. Senate by one vote shows in what a serious condition we are.

"The founder of the Jesuit Order, St. Ignatius, used to say we should act as though everything depends on us and pray as though everything depended upon God. God works in powerful ways. He works through men. I, as one man, have been very fortunate in many ways. I have been able to spread ideas and reach millions of people the past ten years because this is the way God works. I feel He has been working through me. I don't believe God will allow the Western world to be conquered, unless somehow or other in His Divine plan he permits this. If we pray hard and if we work hard, then we can be confident that God will stay the hand of the Kremlin.

"You can't talk like this to a lot of people, I know,

because half of them don't want to face it, and half of them aren't well enough informed to realize that it is the most serious problem that has faced the world in the last thousand years."

The Jesuit Order always has believed in the value of a well-rounded education. Therefore, a lot of attention is given to the classics in their schools—English, Latin, history, philosophy, theology, and skills in writing and public speaking. The Jesuits maintain that if a person acquires this learning he will be aptly prepared to adapt himself to virtually any sort of work later on.

Father Dan, who went through it himself, says, "A good education, training of the mind to a high degree, provides the tools and sharpens them. Jesuits call this ability to adapt oneself to whatever task comes along as 'transfer of training.' Even such specialists as the lawyer, the doctor or the engineer should get a liberal education before he specializes. You are first a person before you are a specialist, and a man should be bigger than his specialty. Otherwise he is not an educated man but merely a technician.

"We see this in the type of work most Jesuits do. They teach high school as part of their training. They then may teach in college, give Retreats, run a parish, go on foreign missions, work as an administrator, or do several of these jobs in succession. St. Ignatius saw his men as an army. But every man had to be trained to serve as a private or an officer, even serving as a private after being a top officer. The head of the Province or president of a college, for example, may be assigned to the classroom or assistant pastor in a parish the day he steps out of office."

In the life of Father Dan, as in the lives of so many Jesuits, we have seen this "transfer of training" in practice. He was taught to think, he was trained to work, he was motivated, and then assigned to teach a variety of subjects. He was told to raise $500,000 on one project, and $1,200,000 on another. He was assigned to write, he was asked to lecture, he became a Federal labor arbitrator, he was told to serve as Dean of Students, he was encouraged to run radio and TV programs, he started a speakers' bureau, he wrote books, magazine and newspaper columns —and on none of these assignments was he ever given special training. The Society educated him and encouraged him to develop. It was thorough training, with more depth than broadness. The emphasis was on flexibility and adaptability.

Father Dan's intellectual versatility has served him well. When he was still a scholastic, his Provincial superior, Father Leo Robinson, asked him to co-author a book with him about the social problems of the day. Father Robinson had been head of the sociology department at Gonzaga, followed by a stint as president of the university. He also served as president of the American Catholic Sociological Association. With Father Van Francis Christoph at Gonzaga, he had already written a text book on introductory sociology. Together, Father Robinson and Lyons outlined the proposed book, dividing up the chapter assignments to fit each man's preference.

That was in 1947, when Dan, not yet a priest, had finished his second year of teaching at Gonzaga Prep.

His third year of teaching—or "regency" as it was known —was spent in special studies in sociology at St. Louis University, and by early December of that year he had completed his half of the book. Unfortunately, Father Robinson's health was failing, and his doctor advised him to stop work on the manuscript. Dan, meanwhile, kept up his studies in graduate school at St. Louis U., with a 3.5 grade average, and at the same time went to work and finished writing Father Robinson's share of the text. With two secretaries in St. Louis and his own mother in Seattle typing up the final draft for him, the manuscript was completed in May, and in June he submitted it to the Provincial for censoring. According to Jesuit habit, the Provincial assigned it to two priests who were working full-time in the colleges.

Six months passed. In the meantime, a new Provincial was named. The censors, unknown even to each other, recommended numerous changes in the text, and in some cases contradicted themselves. But Dan went along with their suggested changes, and continued to return the manuscript for censors' approval.

Then, in 1949, Dan left America to study theology in Ireland for four years. The censors kept the manuscript for another six months. The upshot was that the book never was published. The project seemed doomed from the start. The *coupe de grace* was when Dan's seminary in Dublin caught fire, and all the pictures he had gathered in government bureaus in Washington, D.C., and elsewhere went up in flames.

He told me, "By that time, my enthusiasm for the project

had dimmed, and I let it drop. I figured the book was probably premature anyway, but all was not wasted. I was able to use much of the material in articles I wrote for *Studies,* the Irish quarterly, and the *Irish Monthly.* Any way you look at it, my first attempt at writing a book was valuable experience. One cannot organize and write a 400-page manuscript without learning something. It taught me a lot about writing. And the ability to write is the most important skill we can have. The ability to speak I place second. I have always felt that one can learn to speak rather quickly, but the ability to write constantly and well requires both discipline and skill that is not easily acquired. The ability to write, like the ability to type or swim or ride a bike, is never lost."

Backpedaling, Father Dan's first teaching assignment was in 1945. Now that he was what the Jesuits call a "scholastic," he and his fellow seminarians were formally addressed as "Mister." It was somehow a step up from being called "Brother" at the Novitiate. At Mount St. Michael's, punsters demonstrated what killed vaudeville with gags like this: "If a place where nuns live is called a *nunnery,* then a place where Misters stay should be called a *Mistery*!"

There were five high schools in the Oregon Province: Seattle Prep, Gonzaga Prep (Spokane), Bellarmine Prep (Tacoma), Loyola High (Missoula, Mont.), and Marquette High (Yakima). The one school that Dan didn't want to be assigned to was Gonzaga Prep.

He said, "It was located just a few miles from Mount St. Michael's, and while the scholastics stopped by Gonzaga from time to time, they were considered outsiders and not a real part of the place. But no one asked me for my preference. I was in the army of Ignatius and was expected to go where I was needed. So fresh from my philosophical studies, I was sent to Gonzaga Prep. I had received my M.A. in philosophy, and had received my B.A. in sociology, and I came back to Gonzaga from St. Louis University in August and took up a full load of teaching at the high school. I also taught evening classes for adults as Associate Director of the Gonzaga University Industrial Relations Institute. Added to all this were three more assignments: (1) Prefect of resident students, (2) debate coach, and (3) coach of the boarders' athletic teams."

Those two years at Gonzaga Prep still rank among Father Dan's happiest memories. Spokane is a fine city, the weather is ideal, the people friendly, and Father Dan enjoyed his classroom teaching. It was a big improvement over a summer in St. Louis, hot and humid.

One day, Father Jack Taylor, who had spent three years in St. Louis, met Father Dan on the Gonzaga campus and said, "How could you stand all that heat back in St. Louis?"

Cheerfully, Dan replied, "It was under 100 degrees most of the time I was there."

"Yes," Father Taylor said, "but it is so muggy there when it gets that hot."

"Oh, I don't know," Father Dan said. "The people back in St. Louis said it was a comparatively cool summer."

"But don't you see?" Father Taylor said. "When they say comparatively, they are comparing it to *Hell!*"

It was a question, Father Taylor said, whether St. Louis

was hotter than Yuma, Arizona. It is said of Yuma that there is a greyhound there who, because of the heat, has been chasing rabbits at a walk for years. "Very little is said of St. Louis," Father Taylor said, "for it is too hot to talk about."

"I did not enjoy speculative courses," Dan told me. "The courses in sociology and economics interested me much more than had metaphysics three years earlier. Nor did foreign languages appeal to me. Sociology, economics, and political science were much more in my line. While Greek roots were unappealing to me, I was fascinated with world affairs and current events, with a penchant for social problems. Communism, too, had always held my attention."

In Spokane, Father Dan became one of the most successful debate coaches in the history of Gonzaga Prep. In his very first year his team won the state championship.

One of his star debaters was a high school senior named Tom Foley. Tom used to tell Father Dan that his big ambition in life was to be a U.S. senator some day. He went on to law school, worked as deputy prosecutor, served as Assistant State Attorney General, established a private law practice, spent three years working for Senator "Scoop" Jackson, and then ran for Congress. It was thus 15 years after being on Father Dan's debate team that Tom Foley was elected to the U.S. Congress on his very first try. He was the first Catholic ever elected to Congress from the State of Washington. Father Dan had sent him students from Gonzaga to help with his campaign. Congressman

Foley is now serving a third term, and to this day he and Father Dan remain good friends.

Gonzaga Prep was located in Gonzaga University's main building, and Father Dan spent the summer of 1946 teaching social psychology at the college level. He also continued to coach the debate team.

When I asked him what he looked for in a prospective debater, he said, "An orator did not have to be especially bright. Debating was something else again, however. I looked for boys with a sharp intellect. That was a must. I asked a sophomore high school teacher at Gonzaga, Father Louis Gaffney, S.J., now president of Seattle University, to give me the names of some particularly bright kids. I felt it was easier to teach them to speak well enough to debate than it was to teach a dull person to think well enough to debate. He gave me the names of some very shy sophomores. But they turned out well. One of them, Father Ed Caffrey, became a high school principal and is now chaplain at Washington State University. Another, Bob Egan, went on to become a Jesuit and recently received his Ph.D. from Fordham. Then there is Don Manson, a Ph.D. in physics; and Tim Cronin, who also became a Jesuit and vice-president of Seattle University. All of them were shy at the outset, but they picked up debating quickly, and we won a lot of tournaments. We used to say, 'We'll win our share—and Gonzaga's share is the Lyons' share.' "

Time marched on for Father Dan at Gonzaga Prep. He never got more than five hours of sleep on school nights, but his constitution was such that he thrived on hard work and long hours. He was never one to be idle. After two years at Gonzaga Prep, Father Dan had been sent to St. Louis University for special studies in sociology. Normally they continue with their teaching assignment in their third year as a "regent," as they are called during those few years of teaching before theology, but Father Dan was sent to St. Louis U. to earn his M.A. degree. His spare time was absorbed in reading and attending lectures. His minor was in economics.

After finishing his studies in St. Louis, Dan was sent to Ireland for four years of theology.

Next stop: Dublin!

CHAPTER 10

An Innocent in Ireland

Ireland is a very small part of the world where two gentlemen may sit cross-legged upon the tops of two huge wardrobes in a hotel room and discuss Grotius and Polybius, summoning the floor waiter ever and anon by ringing his bell with the ferrules of their walking sticks, and have absolutely nothing said or even thought about it. It is a country wherein three gentlemen may sit on the North Wall above the Liffey conversing in the moonlight while one of them removes an artificial foot and holds it across his lap for greater stump comfort, until dawn, whereupon a most decently mannered policeman will call a cab, close the door for you, and wish you a pleasant good night.

In the country areas like Kerry, you can still see children on a spring day, in their Sunday best, walking barefoot to Mass, carrying their shoes to be put on when they get there. And when they stub their toe on a stone, they remark: "Wasn't I lucky I wasn't wearing my shoes!"

They go to Mass, even though when they are at home, God is nearer than the door, and you can see Him in every turn of the road.

There are flocks of black sheep in Connemara—so many that when you see a white sheep you wonder what it has done. And the kelp sloops off the Aran Islands have black sails. On the fourteenth of June the Stations of the Cross are performed in the tomb of St. Kevin in the cemetery in Inisheer and after the missioner blesses the fishing curraghs, twenty or thirty of them put off the beach after him and escort him halfway to Inishmaan in the horizon mists. At the Shelbourne Hotel in Dublin the page boys have six-pointed gold crowns embroidered on their collars and there are coal fires in the rooms. In the washrooms the fittings are of polished copper and there is a sheafed board in the foyer marked "Hunting Notices." The shrimp at the former Jammet's in Nassau Street is the best shrimp in the world, and there used to be an old judge at Bray who once knew Parnell.

Father Dan has known Ireland personally since 1948, when he set sail for Dublin to begin four years of theological graduate studies at Milltown Park seminary. By then the Emerald Isle had changed somewhat since the days when his father was growing up there. The beggars had gone and there were motor roads and a tire factory and a motorcar assembly plant and an Irish cigarette, and the signs by the roads now gave you your last town and the mileage, your next town and the mileage, and your present town. Withal some claimed the southern beaches still echoed with the ghost keening of mothers whose sons died in

Dillon's Regiment fighting the English for the King of France.

Today, it still faintly irritates Father Dan to hear New York policemen give way to maudlin Irish sentiment, for it is not a country to weep over for joy or sadness.

Can I tell it all the way it really happened inside for him? There was the homespun philosophy that rubbed off on him: "There's a wisdom in the Irish wit—and a wit in the Irish wisdom—that has a strong appeal and provides buoyance and a sense of balance." And the little old Irishman who told him, "I don't know if it's a wake or a wedding, but it's a grand success!"

Perhaps it was the inn clerk at Carrickfergus who looked at a name upon the register and said it aloud with the slight aspirate trace of a letter missing these several generations by American law, because it was a silent letter to all but Celts—and therefore dishonest to the strait-laced mind that had it cast out.

"You know that name? Even this way it is written?"

"Ah yes—but it is not spelled the way it should be spelled."

"It is strange you should notice such a small thing as that. Are there people hereabout who spell it in the old way?"

"No—they have gone these many years."

"Almost three hundred, by the even count."

"That could be."

"And none have returned in that time?"

"None but you. It is a long time. You must not wait so long again."

On his long walks around the west of Ireland, Father

Dan noticed that the fields were fenced with slabs of stone set upright in the turf. There was no regularlity of outline, and where one opening broke into the next field and went on to break again, the whole became a labyrinth when the fog rolled in and hid the lighthouse and the ruins of O'Brien's Castle. Then he could wander until the night came down upon him and hung heavy to his shoulders with Atlantic damp. But there was no fear of wandering, for there were no deeds to the fields and no law courts to argue ownership. That was remembered from mind to mouth, in primitive justice of thought that was old when Aristotle wrote of it. And if that be sentiment, take a coin and hold it out to the little boys the next time you visit Inisheer, snap it quickly up your sleeve, and hear their soft voices whisper, "*Magi.*"

Father Dan's pride was in the lilt of the words and invention that he marked as being Irish. When he first arrived he asked an oldtimer what Ireland was like. The answer he got was a philosophy of life: "There are some things here you'll like, and some things you won't, but the best thing is to make up your mind you're going to like it, whether you like it or not."

Father Dan spent the next four years trying to adjust to that basic fact of Irish life. He was in Ireland only a few weeks when he asked an 80-year-old gentleman how he could find College Green. The old man walked several blocks to show him. Dan told him, "Thank you very much."

"Don't mention it," the old man said.

"But you walked half a mile to show me."

"Father, if it were twenty miles, I'd show you better."

Those four years at the seminary in Dublin served as a golden opportunity for Father Dan to get acquainted with his Irish side of the family. The only kin he had known back home were Protestant, his mother's folk; but through his father, the Ould Sod had long ago become something deeply personal, religious and sentimental. He remembered still that day in 1930 when the family helped his father pack for his first visit to Ireland in 25 years. Patrick's own father had long been gone, but his 90-year-old mother was still chipper and so were his sisters. The journey had been a grand success, and the daily picture postcards he mailed back to Seattle, the scores of camera shots, the long letters, had instilled in Dan's breast a yearning to some day see Ireland for himself. Thanks to their father's strong influence, Irish blood ran thick in all the Lyons children.

The seminary where Dan did his graduate work hired a number of lads from surrounding farms to work around the grounds and attend to janitorial chores. They were not used to telephones. The result was they often garbled phone messages. One day, Dan heard one of the farm lads tell Father Paul O'Dea he was wanted on the phone. Father O'Dea, a professor, had a deep and abstract mind. In calling him to the phone, the boy said, "I think it's your mother."

"Well, it must be long distance then," Father O'Dea said, half to himself, "because she died in 1939."

Dan met an Irishman who had visited the States as a delegate to the I.L.O. convention in Seattle.

"What is your impression of the United States?" Dan asked him.

"I am amazed at the number of gadgets," the Irishman

replied, "and even more amazed that they all seem to work!"

Dan found that the country trains were anything but powerful, and it was not unknown for passengers to have to get out and walk up a hill. Veteran passengers had a saying: "The First Class passengers *ride* up the hill. The Second Class get out and *walk*—and the Third Class get out and *push*!"

Dan and his fellow priests at the seminary used to take Thursday off, instead of the customary Saturday. They usually went for a picnic in the Dublin hills. On one occasion, Charlie O'Connor, another Jesuit, and Dan stepped into the back entrance of a bus and climbed to the upper level. They did not notice that the bus was going off-duty and was headed for the garage. When they got there, they asked the driver, "How can we get a bus?"

"Where are you going?"

"To Howth."

Howth was about 10 miles from the garage.

"Sure," the driver said, "I'll run you over in the bus."

And he did!

"On the country roads," Dan said, "it was not unknown for a housewife to see the bus coming and run out to stop it, then go back and pack her bag. One time I watched the bus driver deliver a package. It looked very much like a cake. In fact, the lady of the house made him sit down inside and have a piece, with 'a spot of tea.' Then she cut a larger piece, wrapped it up, and asked him to drop it off at her friend's house, down the road a bit.

"The Irish will never tell you how far it is to a place. It is 'just a little ways' unless it is several miles. Then it is 'a mile and a bit.' But as they say among themselves: 'The bit is longer than the mile.' "

Dan once asked a farmer, when he was cycling, how far it was to the next village. "A mile and a bit," he said.

"Is it two miles?" Dan asked

"It is," he said.

"Would it be three miles?" Dan asked.

"It would," he said.

"Would it be four miles?"

"It would be all of that."

"Would it be five miles?"

"Ah, no."

So Dan figured he finally knew how far it was. He cycled on for half a mile, when he saw the sign: *It was eight miles*!

Dan later told a group of farmers standing in the road that the good folk of England didn't do that to him.

"They don't say it's only a mile and a bit when it's really eight miles," he said.

And the farmers replied, "They don't think enough of you to encourage you."

After living in Ireland (1948-1952), and returning for visits many more times, Dan Lyons testifies that the Irish-American is apt to feel more at home in Ireland than he ever did in America, even though it was his father, and not he, who had left the Emerald Isle. As a boy growing up in Seattle, Patrick Lyons had told Dan: "Never ask a man where he's from; if he's from Ireland, he'll tell you, and if he's not, there's no need to embarrass him."

The approach to St. Patrick's Day each year always

brings back a thousand memories to Dan. After his first four years in Ireland, it has since seemed odd to him that the 17th isn't a declared Holyday, on which Catholics are obliged to attend Mass. It is the day when the whole world goes Irish, he points out, a national feast that has become an international festival, the day of the patron saint of one nation that is remembered among all nations, as Irishmen from Ireland and Irishmen from Scotland and Irishmen from Sweden and Irishmen from Wales, all turn to the wearing of the green. It recalls the remark of Pope Pius XI: "The Irish, like the presence of God, are to be found everywhere."

The box Dan received from Dublin on St. Patrick's Day, 1972, contained enough shamrock to graze a goat, and he laughed at the lavish hand that sent it. But in the fury of distribution and the claims from all sides, he had a hand-to-hand struggle keeping a sprig for himself.

Dan adds, "There is nothing better than the shamrock for unlocking those songs, and for opening the hearts of the poets. The shamrock, unlike the thistle of Scotland, never wounds, and, unlike the rose of England, it wears no thorn."

Ireland is host to more than a million visitors a year, and, as Dan will tell you, she never tires of any of them, least of all her relatives and friends from America.

"Fortified with Irish surnames," Dan says, "you fall in love with Ireland the moment you land. She is as green as a pool table, as pretty as a park, and as interesting as the Land of Oz. The people are delightful. Never do you feel less like foreigners. When you first arrive, you think that even the cows moo with a brogue. But you soon learn that the brogue is the one thing never to be spoken of. Like the presence of God, it is taken for granted. I was amused at the brogues, even when they used to tell me: 'Ah, shure, I love to hear your accent.'

"If it is a sign of nobility to oblige, then the people all seemed descendants of kings. I couldn't ask directions without being led down the street. Even in Dublin, one of the oldest capitals of Europe, there is the cheerful ease of a country town. Somewhat larger than Seattle, Dublin is an easy-going city, with unfailing optimism and constant courtesy. Even their complaints have a fresh approach. Of high prices, they remark: 'Nothing comes down but the rain.' When the fifth graders were told in geography class that Dublin is the driest part of Ireland—32 inches of rainfall annually—they wanted to know, 'What's it loike in the rest of the country?' "

At the seminary, Dan's house of studies had students from eight different countries living there. The bus conductors called it the League of Nations. Dan was boarding a train in County Wicklow with a Hungarian Jesuit one day, when the stationmaster asked them where they were from.

"Budapest," said the Hungarian.

"The States," said Dan.

He then asked, in a strong Cork accent that betrayed his County, "Where do the smartest people in Ireland come from?"

"County Cork," said the Hungarian.

"County Cork," said Dan.

Delighted, the stationmaster took them, with their third-class tickets, by the arm and insisted: "Ride in the first class!"

And they did.

"The wit of the Irish is hard to overrate," Dan said. "Their irrepressible habit of embellishing a fact with an anecdote makes conversation in Ireland longer than elsewhere, but more pleasant. The word 'police' is never used there. They had enough of them under English rule. Instead, they have Civil Guards, huge men for the most part, right off the farms. I remember seeing an English car make a U-turn in the middle of O'Connell Street, and the Guard whistling it down. The Englishman looked worried sick until the uniformed patrolman leaned down and said, with a powerful Kerry accent: 'You're not used to this Irish whiskey over here, put a little water in it,' and he smiled as he strode away.

"When I asked my cousin, Vincent McGovern, a Guard in Ballyvary, if he arrested many people, he replied seriously, 'Ah, no. I know most of them!' It is said of the people from County Kerry that they never answer your question, but reply with another. I was in Kerry one summer, and bet my Dublin companion I could make a Kerryman answer my question. He bet me I could not. I went up to a farmer leaning against the postoffice in Tralee and asked: 'Could you tell me where I could find the postoffice?' He replied, 'Is it a letter you want to post?' I lost my bet."

A professor at the National University of Ireland was speaking of Irish humor, and what is known as an "Irish bull." An American student asked about the difference between an Irish bull and a similar figure of speech in another country. He was told the difference is that an Irish bull is pregnant. For example, when an old Irish woman described to her neighbor a sermon that she had heard on hell, she added: "To hear that priest talk on hell, you'd think he was born and raised in it."

An Irish politician who had successfully lectured all around the country, aroused the ire of his native village when he spoke to them: "My dear friends: I won't call you ladies and gentlemen, I know you too well."

And the farmer's wife who was told by her neighbor not to be beating her donkey because Christ had ridden to Jerusalem on a donkey, replied in a flash: "If He'd had this beast, He wouldn't be there yet!"

Dan told us, "They have a philosophy of life that brings true enjoyment. When it comes to the essentials they are more serious than any other nation. Concerning their Creator, they are the most religious people in the world, with an enormous spiritual empire of foreign missionary priests and nuns. The Irish take the time to enjoy living; to take the less important things in stride. When a business man from New York criticized a Dublin shopkeeper for the easy-going attitude of Irish business people, he was told: 'We get just as much out of life, and we take just as much with us when we die.'

"Ireland," continued Dan, "is a poor country as to money,

but as the citizens will tell you, they have purple heather and mountains golden with gorse; and they have rivers, great-bosomed and friendly, where men may dream. Irishmen successful in America like to think of revisiting their native land, and of doing something to help it, of returning some token of what they brought away in their youth. After such a visit, however, they will invariably tell you that it is they who have become the richer, that where they dropped silver, they picked up gold.

"The visitor to Ireland finds kindness on all sides, kindness that is genuine and so overwhelming. I met two girls from Tacoma who had been cycling around Europe. On the Continent, they said, they used to ask at the farmhouses if they could sleep in the hay, and they were seldom refused. In Ireland they asked the same question, but were always put up in the guest room."

Dan found that the people still know how to entertain each other. They excel at conversation, and they like meeting strangers. Their speech is motivated, not by mere courtesy, but by a friendly interest in one's neighbor, a genuine refinement of communal feeling. A beggar's thanks are always "God bless you!" or, "I certainly will remember you in my prayers." It is not a matter of a superior and an inferior person, but of two Christians, equal in the sight of God, both realizing that we are born naked into this world, and leave the same way.

The spirit of Ireland was expressed in fine poetic fashion by the Rev. Francis P. Donnelly, S.J. Answering the query of an American boy who had asked what his father meant by "Machree," Father Donnelly wrote:

" 'Tis the white of the day and the warmth of the sun;
The ripple of waters that laughingly run;
The sweet bloom of youth, the harvest of years;
The gold of all smiles and the salt of all tears;
'Tis the thrill of the hand, the light of the eye;
The glow of the cheek and lip's parting cry;
'Tis mother! 'tis father! 'tis children and wife;
The music of woman's—the wine of man's life;
'Tis an Irishman hearing a voice from Above;
'Tis an Irishman's heart making vocal his love;
The whole of creation and one isle in the sea;—
That's what an Irishman means by 'Machree.' "

One of the best story-tellers in Ireland was the late Capt. Jack O'Neill, manager of Irish Shipping, Ltd. A veteran of the seas, he had a language all his own. One day, as his 17-year-old son, Jack, and Dan Lyons, were getting into their car, the boy asked: "Dad, shall I drive?"

"Of course!" replied the captain gruffly, but with a twinkle in his eye. "Of course! When you keep a dog, you don't bark yourself, do you?"

"On the subject of Irish humor," Dan Lyons said, "two stories that should go down as all-time classics I heard from Father Tim Healy, whose illustrious father was leader of the Irish Party in the English Parliament. On one occasion the elder Tim was denounced by another member of the House for having made threats, when actually, said the English M.P., 'he hasn't the courage to say boo to a goose.' Tim rose to a point of order, was recognized, and said to his opponent: 'BOO!'

"Another time, when word reached the House of Commons that one of its members had just passed away, various expressions of sorrow were made by different members in the House. The deceased had been very hostile to the Irish cause, and they were all afraid of what Tim Healy might say. But he stood up in a very solemn manner and expressed his deepest regrets that the deceased member had gone 'where Cromwell has gone.' His reference to Oliver Cromwell was taken as an insult, and Tim was called on to apologize.

" 'Gentlemen,' Tim replied, with feigned surprise, 'I see you all realize where Cromwell has gone!' "

At the end of Dan's second year in Dublin, his youngest sister, Sheila, went to spend a year there at University College, a branch of the National University. She was only five years old when her brother had left home to join the Order, twelve years before. So the year in Dublin gave Dan his first real chance to get to know her.

While Sheila was in Dublin, their mother came to spend two months with her. One evening, Dan drove them to a dance in Killarney, and that night his sister met a young man from Holland. He was on vacation. Two of his uncles were priests, one a Jesuit. Sheila and the young man became good friends. The friendship blossomed into love. Six years later, in Seattle, Dan officiated at their wedding. Today, they have six children and live in Holland, where he manages a plant for a California company. Dan baptized their sixth child there, in 1971.

"Their getting engaged was not as simple as it sounds," Dan remembers. "Louis Leewens was working in Johannesburg, South Africa. After Sheila returned to Seattle, she corresponded with him. My father said he was not going to buy her a ticket to Johannesburg just because she met someone from there. So she decided to become a stewardess. It had to be Pan Am, she said, as it is the only U.S. airline that flies to Johannesburg. She flew for Pan Am for several years, getting to South Africa on numerous occasions. Meanwhile, Louis managed to visit Seattle a few times. It turned out to be a very happy marriage. They love to sail with the children. I joined them once. When I asked them why the boat was named 'Maria Lecina' they hemmed and hawed. They said they had thought of changing the name, but were told it was bad luck to do so.

"I asked them, 'Who was Maria Lecina? She certainly wasn't Dutch.'

"My brother-in-law said, 'She was a character in an Italian novel.'

"Finally, Sheila admitted that Maria was 'a woman of pleasure—but it isn't a bad name for a boat!' "

The summer of Dan's Ordination, 1951, was filled with happy expectation. He drove his mother and Sheila around Ireland, and rowed them around Killarney. Their father and sister, Noreen, joined them in mid-July. Their first cousins, Father Tom Higgins and Father John Lyons, natives of Ireland but pastors in Ohio, also arrived in Dublin for the Ordination. Father Higgins had served for 15 years as a chaplain in the U.S. Air Force. Father John Lyons is still a pastor in Youngstown.

"I was offering Sunday Mass in Father John's parish a few years ago," Father Dan recalled. "While I was seated with the altar boys, he ascended into the pulpit and told the congregation about me, his cousin. In the middle of his remarks he turned to me and loudly said: 'WILL THE REAL FATHER LYONS PLEASE STAND UP?'

"Father John's rectory is a great gathering place for priests in the Youngstown area. He is a terrific entertainer, with his Irish songs and stories. Were he not a priest, he could have made a good living on the stage.

"When he was asked to start a new parish a few years ago he said to the bishop: 'You've got to be kidding!'

" 'No, I'm not, Father John,' the bishop said.

" 'Do I have a choice?'

" 'Yes. But think about it for a week.'

"Father John went to an older priest and told him what the bishop said. The older priest said, 'Well, what were you ordained for?' So Father John accepted the parish, starting Mass in a theater. Before holding the first Sunday Mass, he drove over and checked out the building. Workmen were busy posting the name of a new movie on the marquee: 'THE RUSSIANS ARE COMING, THE RUSSIANS ARE COMING.' Father John walked up to the theater manager and said, 'Can't you change that to read, 'THE CATHOLICS ARE COMING, THE CATHOLICS ARE COMING?'

"It was a young parish, and when Father John tabulated the collection that first Sunday, he told the parishioners from the pulpit, 'I didn't know we were a depressed area. I think I'll apply for Federal aid.' He made his point, and the next time the plate was passed they dug deeper into their pockets. But later, when interest payments were greater than income, his assistant,

Father Tim Healy, preached about it. The January snows were piled deep on the ground outside, and Father Healy said in his sermon, 'If our collections don't improve, Father John and I are going to have to shovel snow for some added income—*and we don't have any mittens*!' The money rolled in.

"Ireland is a grand place for gathering stories. Did I tell you about the bishop who couldn't remember names very well? He was consecrating a church one Sunday, and as he praised the pastor who had served there for so many years, his old friend, he looked at the slip in his hand and read, 'Father Murphy, whom we all know so well, and his wonderful assistant . . .' (looking again at the slip) . . . 'Father Martin, so dear to all of us.' Finally, he concluded, 'Lastly, we must give thanks above all to Our Lord and Savior . . .' (looking at the slip for a moment) . . . 'Jesus Christ.'

"We took a trip north of Dublin, in County Cavan. A farmer there had taken out a rather large loan for his little farm. Not only that, but he started to default. So when the bank examiner came along, he asked the farmer if he had any business besides the farm.

" 'Yes,' replied the farmer. 'I'm in the manure business.'

"The banker waited for an explanation, but he waited in silence. Finally, the farmer asked, 'Have you ever been in the manure business?'

" 'No, of course not.'

" 'Well,' the farmer said, 'you are now.' "

Ordination for Dan meant the culmination of 13 years in the Society. It was a highlight in his young life. His family was very proud of him. Being in the Order to Dan meant living with God's special friends, and Dan always felt it to be a singular privilege.

"I have never met a Jesuit, or any other priest, I did not like," he said. "The training leaves a person such as myself feeling very humble, surrounded by such wonderful men—God's very own."

It was heart-warming for Dan to be able to share the joys of Ordination with his own family, and he knew that a year later he would offer his first home Mass in St. Joseph's parish in Seattle, where he had first attended Mass, and had often served as an altar boy.

Dan Lyons, S.J., was ordained on July 31, 1951, the Feast of St. Ignatius of Loyola, founder of the Society. He had been waiting for that day since he first entered the Novitiate.

"During our fourth year in theology we helped out in a parish every week end, a different parish nearly every week," Dan said. "It gave us ample opportunity to use our precious powers, offering Mass for thousands, and hearing the Confession of thousands, week after week. They were very happy days for us, and time moved quickly."

After his first year of theology, in 1949, Dan studied at Oxford for a while, and toured England and Scotland. The following summer he spent six weeks in France, learning to speak the language, and visiting such coveted shrines as Lourdes and other historic places. He also went to see the famous Passion Play at Oberammergau, in Bavaria, in '50—staged every ten years.

Details of how Dan spent part of his life in Dublin

are contained in letters he wrote back to his friends at Gonzaga. Excerpts from letters of 1949 and 1950 reveal his interests at age thirty:

> "When I went to preach a sermon in the Refectory (dining room) two months ago, there was the beaming face of Oregon itself: Pat O'Reilly! He had come out by accident on that day. He is barnstorming on the Mission Band in England. No doubt they will put up plaques in the churches: 'Fr. O'Reilly spoke here—and nobody slept!'
>
> "We hope to arrange to meet DeValera and Costello, (the President and Prime Minister) and also to visit dear old Mand Gonne McBride, the revolutionist of '16, whose son is now Minister of External Affairs. There are others, too, we plan to see. No one can call us pikers!
>
> "On the 26th, Fr. Bill Costello and I took the train to Belfast. It is a city about the size of Seattle. Not much to see there, but nice country on the way, along the coast and in the mountains of Mourne, and old County Down. It is about 220 miles round trip, two hours and fifteen minutes each way by train. Incidentally, I covered about 1,000 miles during the vacation, which is hard to do without splashing into the sea, but I managed it. Two years ago, when I spent Christmas with Dick Bradley at St. Mary's, Kansas, I covered only 500 miles, so according to my typically American way of measuring everything by size and distance, I figure this vacation was *twice* as good as that one!
>
> "Father Bill Costello had grown up around so many Irish Americans in Spokane, he had heard about Ireland all his life. How thrilled he was to be in Ireland for the first time! He asked me so many questions, but the 50th question was typical, and his reply:

'What is the population of Ireland?' About three million, I said. 'You mean there are only three million people in Ireland?' Then he thought about all the Irish in his life, and all the Irish he had ever read about, and added: 'They sure throw their weight around!' Indeed they do!

"Father Bill had been studying in England, the first Catholic ever to attend his college at Oxford for 400 years. They were signing up the students, being very formal and stuffy, in the English manner. 'Sign your name legibly, your grandchildren will be reading it some day,' said the Provost. They took for granted Bill was stuffy, too, until he replied: 'If any grandchildren of mine ever read this, it is going to be highly irregular.' It was not the first solemn occasion an Irishman livened up.

"Next day, we had dinner with the Jack O'Neills, and heard all about his latest trip to New York and Montreal. He said he heard a Cork accent in the Waldorf Astoria dining room, as the waiter served hot water and tea bags. O'Neill asked the waiter where he was from.

" 'County Cork,' the waiter said.

" 'Well,' O'Neill said, 'is that the way they make tea in Cork!'

"The waiter was offended, and he protested that they made very good tea in Cork. 'But,' he countered, 'that's the way they make tea in New York!'

"I told Captain O'Neill we had just spent a week in his native County of Wexford. 'We know all about the Wexford people now,' I said confidently. 'You mean you think you do!' he laughed. One never gets ahead of the native Irish in conversation. The struggle is to keep up. When I asked a farmer in Cork how come there were no Jesuits there, he replied quickly: 'We attribute that to the power of prayer.' "

Dan's father was right at home in Dublin. When he visited Dan, he had a grand old time. He also made good newspaper copy. MacAlla, a reporter for *The Irish Press,* caught up with him and wrote the following:

"The most charming American you could meet in a day's march is Patrick Lyons of Seattle. As well as being an American, he is, of course, an Irishman. When he left Ballyhaunis for the States, Ireland was still in the doldrums with the Union Jack hanging limply at the mast.

"Patrick Lyons as a young man had been educated at St. Jarlath's, Tuam, and when he came to Dublin he tried to make his fortune selling sewing machines. When he looked for his first job in America, selling books in Philadelphia, the boss said: 'So you sold sewing machines in Ireland. That means you can sell anything. You're hired.'

"The Lyons story is the story of a success. Business colleagues respect him for straight dealing, and being two jumps ahead. But I think the merry twinkle in his eye was his biggest asset. Today he owns the United States Trading Co., Inc., which does a multi-million dollar export trade.

"I asked him what he considered the most progressive business step we had made since we shook off the shackles. Like a shot he answered: 'Irish shipping.' A translation of his speech on the social-political-economic magnificence of our ship founding reads, 'It's great.'

"Mr. and Mrs. Lyons, and daughter, Noreen, travelled over for the Ordination of son Danny. A Jesuit, with us for the last three years, he said his first Mass a few days ago in Trinity Church, Dublin Castle. Father Dan Lyons, S.J., you will hear more about. He is a brilliant sociologist, and has contributed much to Ireland's knowledge of the state of society beyond her shores.

"Patrick Lyons is hotly 'anti' two evils, humbug and the stage Irishman. Greater than all his business achievements he values his acquaintance made with an American newspaperman, Robert Heilman in Seattle, who every year on St. Patrick's Day prints for him a piece that smokes all the pigs in that land from under the bed, and raises blisters on shillelaghs.

"On his travels around Ireland he made an 8 mm. film of the best things in Ireland, and he will show it to convents and Irish clubs back in Seattle. 'More than anything else,' he said, 'that is the job the Irish tourist people should do. It would roll in the tourists.'

"Most remarkable thing about this man. After nearly forty years in America, he still carries the grand rich accent of Ballyhaunis."

For years it was customary for Cyril J. Fairhurst, who had worked for him in the late Twenties, and then went out and co-founded Fairhurst Lumber Co., with operations in the Western states, to send Patrick a telegram on St. Patrick's Day. This one was sent in 1956 and was typical: "THE TOP O' THE MORNING TO IRELAND'S RARE GIFT TO AMERICA."

The elder Lyons' pride in the Ould Sod ran deep. When

Holiday magazine published an article about Ireland by Frank O'Connor, Patrick took offense at what he felt were blatant potshots at his people. He did some investigating and discovered through friends in the Department of External Affairs in Dublin that the editors had insisted that O'Connor use such terms as "benighted" and "priest-ridden" to describe the country. That was no excuse, Patrick said, and he shot off a letter to the editor of the magazine.

"Dear Sir:

> The Bible tells us of the time when Balaam was riding along on his donkey, intent on doing evil, and the donkey miraculously spoke and rebuked him. History does not tell us what happened to the talking donkey. But now I see he has finally found a place on your staff, where at long last the *ass* has found a home.
>
> Sincerely yours,
> Patrick Lyons."

The point in this chapter is quite simple. You must take Ireland or leave it. You cannot change it unless you have centuries to spend on the job.

PART II

CHAPTER 11

A New Life Begins

In 1953 Father Dan completed his final year of training at Port Townsend, Washington, a third year of spiritual studies called tertianship. He was then assigned to Portland as assistant director of the Seminary Association and assistant editor of *The Oregon-Jesuit.* His prime project for the next two years was raising funds for bricking the novitiate at Sheridan and adding two new wings. The whole Pacific Northwest was his territory now, and a large segment of *The Oregon-Jesuit* readership responded generously to his articles, letters and personal appeals. Total raised: $350,000-plus!

Two years later, Archbishop Edward D. Howard asked Father Henry Schultheis, the Provincial, to start a new high school in Portland, and the latter sent Father Dan out to search for the most suitable location. He hired an airplane and photographed several prospective locations. Then he contacted the owner of the best site—a former dairy pasture—and convinced him that the 57 acres could be used for nothing better than the future campus of Jesuit High School.

The land was purchased in August, 1955. The school doors swung open in September, 1956. Father Dan proved he was a man of action. All told, while spearheading Jesuit High's drive for funds over a seven-year period, he raised more than $800,000 in cash and another $250,000 in pledges.

One Jesuit at Sheridan recently recalled those days. He told me, "Father Lyons was a miracle man. He got us as extra gifts from his friends, the furniture in our parlors, the chairs in the auditorium, the beautiful statue of Our Lady in the dining room, the large cross above the center building, complete sets of vestments for six chapels, and many other things."

Father Erwin Toner, S.J., who was director of the Jesuit Seminary Association for the Oregon Province, and editor of *The Oregon-Jesuit* while Father Dan was there, told of the conversation he had with a Jewish gentleman named Frank Malina, who had given Father Lyons more than $50,000 for the school.

Frank said to Father Toner, "You know what really got me interested in Father Dan's work? Well, there he was, a priest, in his work clothes, loading the lumber we had given him to help build the school—and driving that big truck, himself! When you see a priest working for the kids that way—well, it gets you. You then pile in and do all you can, too." In recent years, Frank Malina and Father have worked very closely together in New York. No one is more dedicated to Father Dan and his work.

Others who helped a great deal in those days included Tektronix, with $25,000 for science equipment; the Franz Bakery, with $30,000, and above all, the thousands of little people who helped Father Dan by pledging between $5 and $10 a month for a period of three years. The biggest single benefactor was Al Sauvie, who had immigrated from France as a boy, lived modestly, and kept helping until he had given $100,000.

When he gave an initial $35,000 for a Jesuit residence, Father Dan had half of the building materials donated, and Jesuit Brothers do the labor. Another friend did the architectural work free. They got a $90,000 building for the $35,000. When Mr. Sauvie saw the finished building, he said to Father Lyons: "I spent that much on my nephew, and have nothing to show for it." He kept on helping. Where is he now, I asked Father Dan? "He is up there in the land of the many mansions, something he never had on earth."

Jesuit High in Portland continues to thrive. The property Father Dan picked out in 1955 for $152,000 turned out to be more than was needed. The worst half of the 57 acres was later sold for $610,000.

In December, 1959, Father Lyons was on the move again. His work at Jesuit High was finished. Orders had come down from the Provincial assigning him to teach at Seattle University. Since the spring quarter did not begin for five weeks yet, he was asked to go to the Jesuit parish at Havre, Montana, and help out.

A Montana winter is not precisely Palm Springs. The

temperature was 40 degrees below zero when Father Dan stepped off the train. A fierce North wind howled. Dan turned to the young priest who had been sent to meet his train and said, "Does the wind always blow this way in Havre?"

"No," the priest replied thoughtfully. "Sometimes it blows the other way." While in Havre, Father Dan joined the Knights of Columbus. The pastor of the Havre parish was Father John O'Hara. He had been Father Dan's teacher in high school, 26 years before. He told Dan, "You'll be replacing Father Maurice Meagher, S.J., who's in the hospital recovering from surgery." Father Meagher, a lawyer before he entered the priesthood, was a descendant of Thomas Francis Meagher, the Irish-born first territorial governor of Montana. Father Dan remembered Father Meagher well. He remembered his first meeting with him, 22 years before. Dan had been riding with his father to school and they saw Father Meagher walking toward the Seattle University campus to give a lecture. Patrick Lyons stopped the car and told him to get in. On the way to the university, Father Meagher turned to Dan, a senior at Seattle Prep, and asked him if he planned to go to college.

"No," Dan said, "I'm going to the Novitiate at Sheridan."

"You are going to college," Father Meagher said.

January 15th, 1960—and Father Dan took up his duties as a teacher of freshmen speech and composition at Seattle University. Father Arbie Lemieux, the president, also encouraged him to revive the debate teams, and within a year Seattle U. was winning more tournaments and trophies for debate and public speaking than the Chieftains had won in many years.

Father Dan enjoyed his teaching duties at S.U. But he was on a collision course with the population explosion. The freshmen enrollment had been steadily increasing, and the college, facing shortages of funds, succumbed to financial pressures and decided to do away with "Frosh Comp," since it required small classes and many teachers. At a department meeting, the academic dean announced, "We can only afford to keep 17 composition teachers, and we need at least 30. So we're going to abolish the course."

Father Dan asked to be heard. He told the dean, not too tactfully, "Granted we can exempt the better students from taking Frosh Comp, but why abolish the requirement for those who need it most? Why do away with it altogether? Give us the 17 teachers you still have and we'll do the best we can with the lower 50 or 60 per cent of the students who need so badly to learn how to write effectively. Otherwise, they will never do well in college."

The dean felt challenged. Father Dan had obviously perturbed him.

He snapped, "The decision has been made. Frosh Comp is being abolished!"

Father Dan reddened. He said, "Then why did you call this meeting to discuss it?" It was the tone he used when he felt strongly, and though it served debate teams well, it also caused harsh feelings when he took a stiff position. There never has been anything indecisive about him.

Diplomacy under pressure is not his forte. He cannot hold back his intense emotions. He must speak his mind.

Father Lyons was not asked to leave Seattle University. That should be understood here and now. The president, Father Lemieux, was very appreciative of his work, both in the classroom and with the debaters. He also expressed his gratitude to Father Dan for a number of talks he gave to groups off campus. But when the Dean of Men at Gonzaga, Father Frank Harrington, suffered a heart attack, Father Lyons wrote to his old classmate of Sheridan days, Father John Leary, who was now president of Gonzaga University, and told him he would be pleased to serve as temporary Dean of Men "until you can find a good one." The upshot was that Father Leary arranged with the Oregon Provincial, Father John Kelley, to have Father Lyons assigned to him for that purpose.

Only three months earlier his sister, Mrs. Eileen Hume, had been named Dean of Women at Gonzaga. Eileen was a graduate of Seattle University, had a Master's degree in education psychology, and for several years was girl's counsellor at Issaquah high school near Seattle. At the time of her appointment, she told a Spokane reporter, "I believe that, as the advancement of education and technology makes most aspects of living more complicated, the need for college women increases. I also feel that a good college education contributes greatly to success in marriage and raising a family, and leaves a woman more capable of performing the volunteer organization work she undertakes."

Before Father Dan took the post, his sister had asked

him, "Who do you think the new Dean of Men is going to be?"

"You can never tell," he said. "It might be me."

"I'll resign," she said, in mock protest.

As deans, Father Dan and his sister, Eileen, worked together closely. They were chairman and co-chairman, respectively, of the Disciplinary Board, and ran a tight ship.

"It is much easier to have law and order than to have half-order and half-chaos," he was often heard to say.

Both Father Dan and Eileen were well liked, but, more important, they were highly respected. They were considerably stricter than any of their predecessors—at least for many years—or their successors.

One day the school chaplain, Father Dave Freitag, S.J., was in Father Dan's outer office talking to Eileen. On the wall was the coat of arms of the Lyons family. Father Freitag, a mild, friendly and much-liked person on campus, read the motto on the coat of arms: *"Noli irritare leones,"* or "Do not irritate the Lyons."

"You know," he said to Eileen, "that's really true, isn't it?"

She replied, "You're darn right it is!"

Father Dan and Eileen had just the right family name to go along with their strict thinking, some students felt. One of them hung a sign on Father Dan's office door with the letters: "THE LYONS DEN." And when a student got in trouble, it was said on campus that he was being "tossed to the Lyons."

Basic discipline at Gonzaga had always been stiff. What Father Dan and Eileen did was to make the rules standard and consistent. A resident student was not to be out overnight without permission, for example. The curfew on Friday and Saturday nights was 1 a.m. The deans expected it to be strictly observed, unless prior permission had been granted for any special reason. Drinking was not tolerated, and no boy was ever to go beyond the parlor of a girls' dorm, and vice-versa.

Father Lyons told me, "It was easy to enforce the rules. What was not easy was only half-enforcing them. Someone might break a rule and not get caught, though even that was relatively rare. But when someone did get caught, I figured the whole campus wanted to see if Eileen and I meant what we said about the rules being enforced. If, for instance, a student stayed out all night and was brought before the Board, if that student were not suspended for the semester, there would be no way of ever enforcing the rule, and it would be honored more in the breach than in the observance. But if a boy or girl resident stayed out overnight and were summarily dismissed, as happened two or three times each fall, the rule was never threatened, and the campus was in better disciplinary order than almost any other campus in the nation. The purpose of rules is to make it easy to be good."

His sister agreed. Both relied on Pete Baaken, a detective for the City of Spokane, to help them find out whether or not the college rules were being observed. Pete worked under their direction on certain nights. He was an expert at searching out a thief, if one showed up among the students. One did show up. He was a boy from Portland who had forged a $5.00 check belonging to his roommate.

Pete caught him, turned him over to Father Dan, and he was kicked out of school. "I told him he could come back in September and try again," Father Dan said. "I knew his family well, but I felt he had to be taught a lesson. When such cases were sent home they forfeited all paid tuition. That boy simply had to learn now that you don't forge checks. I don't care if it's five dollars or one dollar."

Fortunately, that particular case had a happy ending. The boy returned to Gonzaga the next term and was a model of propriety. Father Dan had no more trouble with him.

Neither deans, nor both together, could dismiss a student from the university. Protocol called for a hearing in front of the Faculty Disciplinary Board, which in turn made a recommendation to the president. Father Dan, as Dean of Students, was in the role of prosecutor. He was the only one who could bring a case before the Board. His job was to present the evidence and recommend what should be done.

As dean in charge of student activities, he was responsible for student government. This included student publications, extra-curricular programs, social events, and the housing and conduct of resident students. His big job each summer was arranging housing for nearly 1250 boarders who would be coming back in September. Once they arrived, his main job then was keeping order. He was responsible for all student life outside the classroom. He took his obligations very seriously. His interpretation of the position went like this: "Rules are made for those one-third of the students who are not mature enough to live without them. My task is to make the student do what he ought to want to do."

Father Dan left the conduct of the Gonzaga coeds entirely up to his sister. They saw eye to eye on almost everything. There was no way for students to drive a wedge between them, not because of family ties, but because they agreed on what was good for Gonzaga and Gonzagans as a whole. Their job, they felt, was to protect the school. Their offices were right next to one another and the line of communications was always open.

Father Lyons lived in a student dormitory as a prefect. This was not a new experience for him. He had done it as a scholastic. Some of the prefects he had to work with were not only highly capable, but old friends as well. There was Father Tim O'Leary, and Father Joe O'Connell. They required no more than a little cooperation and support, and were always on the job. Others were student prefects, young fellows like Roger Miller, a senior boarder and today a medical surgeon.

Eileen Lyons Hume was a widow. She had two teenage children, Robin and Jarlath. The boy was born shortly after Uncle Jarlath Lyons lost his life in the South Pacific in World War II. Father Dan made it a practice to join Eileen, Robin and Jarlath for dinner at least once a week. The rest of the time he rarely left the campus. His sister often came back to campus activities and burned the midnight oil.

As Dean of Students, Father Dan encouraged student government and student publications. He put his foot down only when he felt something was in danger of hurting the school's reputation. He attended the three-hour student council meetings every week, seldom raising a voice. It was their meeting and he let them run it as long as they adhered to the rules of good taste. But he required his signature on any student checks.

Despite the heavy load, Father Dan still found time to coach the university debate team and develop some of the finest debaters in Gonzaga's history. In checking the records at Gonzaga, I ran across a list of debate awards that his 1963-64 team compiled. Some of the highlights were:

Columbia Valley Tournament (32 colleges): First place, Senior Women's debate (Kathryn Auvil, Joe Anne Keopple). Second place, Senior Men's debate (Chris Ledwidge, John Dugger).

Western Speech Association (61 colleges, 539 contestants): First place, After Dinner Speaking (John Dugger).

Linfield College Tournament of Champions (39 colleges, 410 contestants): First place, Senior Men's Lincoln-Douglas style debate (Joe Verovsek). Second place, Senior Men's Oxford style debate (John Dugger, Joe Verovsek). Second place, Over-all Senior Sweepstakes. All named were Gonzaga students.

At the end of the year, Father Dan's team was selected as one of the three top college debate teams in the Pacific Northwest and qualified for the National Debate Tournament, sponsored by the Air Force Academy, at Colorado Springs, and also at the West Point Tournament.

Father Dan's interest in competition did not end with the debate team. He also followed the Gonzaga basketball and hockey teams, frequently going with them on their road games. The hockey players called him their "honorary captain," and insisted he sit with them on the bench. He seldom saw a game to the finish, however, because times without number he would have to rush one of the hockey players off to the emergency ward of a hospital to patch up cuts and bruises.

"One thing about debating," he said. "It's a lot safer."

The years 1961-1964 left Father Lyons with some very definite ideas about law and order in the colleges. He told me, "I will never be convinced that our campuses had to give up so much control as they did in the sixties. After I was gone, Gonzaga was hit very hard. They had a young priest come in as student dean with all kinds of wild ideas. He completely demoralized the school's discipline. And as so often happens with these people, he then left the priesthood, leaving nothing but shambles behind him for others to clean up. Thank God, Gonzaga has since returned to fairly sane policies. I found it no real problem to run the student life well.

"No one was ever out at night late that I did not know about—and we had 1,250 boarders. I had one of our priests assigned to each men's dormitory, and I stayed in one myself. At the time, there were only two dorms for girls. In a sense we had three. One of them was almost a double dormitory. But we had very good control. Mature women ran the women's dorms.

"I got pretty fed up with our colleges in the mid-sixties. They used to be our main source of patriotic leadership, but at the height of the campus riots they were mostly the source for sabateurs. There was a time when more than fifty of our colleges were playing a rather deadly game in regard to Vietnam. As long as we were losing they remained quiet, but when we started to win, the demonstrations perked up. Where were the campus protests and student marches when North Vietnam was succeeding in its savage efforts to conquer the South? Where were the marchers when our embassy was bombed and 121 civilians injured? Where were they when American families were grenaded in their apartments? Nothing gave Hanoi and Peking so much solace as the remarks of some of our college professors. My experience in debating left-wing professors taught me that they are impossible to convince but easy to refute."

Tranquility seems to have returned to most campuses in the 1970s. Indications of the "good old days" a la panty-raid escapades, etc., are popping up all the time. At Gonzaga, a couple of students broke into the Crosby Memorial Library last spring in the dark of night, snuck up to the second floor and into the Bing Crosby Room, where all the famous crooner's treasured trophies and photographs and original mementos were on permanent display. Among the priceless keepsakes locked up in the tightly-sealed glass display cases was Bing's coveted Academy Award "Oscar," which he had won for his performance as a priest in "Going My Way." It was one of the library's most glamorous possessions. Heavy security measures had been taken to protect it.

In as imaginative a heist as any ever perpetrated in an Alfred Hitchcock movie, when Father Clifford Carroll, S.J., the head librarian, made his routine inspection rounds the next morning, lo and behold Bing's golden statuette had vanished. In its place stood a toy replica of MICKEY MOUSE!

Just as mysteriously, "Oscar" returned to its display case one morning a week later.

"It's good," Father Carroll said, "to see boys being boys again."

In late 1963, it was time for Father Lyons to move on again. When he was asked by the University of the Seven Seas to serve as professor and Catholic chaplain on its first around-the-world cruise, he jumped at the opportunity. It was to be his first chance to visit the Orient. Gonzaga authorities quickly cut through the red tape.

A new life was about to open for him.

When Father Lyons set sail from the Holland-America pier on Manhattan's lower west side on October 11, 1963, he could not possibly have realized how much that 110-day cruise was going to change the lives of 285 students. None would ever be quite the same again, least of all himself.

One of the first persons he met on board was Dr. Stephan Pan, head of Asian studies on ship, and with whom he has been collaborating ever since. Through Dr. Pan, Father Lyons also met Archbishop (later Cardinal) Paul Yu Pin in Rome, and again in Taiwan on the same trip. He and Dr. Pan, who is a Knight Commander of St. Gregory, also had a personal meeting with Pope Paul, and they met with Cardinal Antoniutti, the head of the Sacred Congregation for Religious, in his apartment.

President Diem of Vietnam, who had often stayed with Dr. Pan at Cardinal Yu Pin's residence at 86 Riverside Drive in New York City before becoming president in Saigon, had been assassinated on November 2, a few weeks after the ship had set sail from New York. While the ship was docked in Beirut, and Father Lyons had taken a side trip by car to Damascus, Syria, President Kennedy was assassinated.

Six weeks later, as they headed up the river to Saigon, Father met another important figure in Asian circles, Father Raymond de Jaegher. From Archbishop Paul Yu Pin and Father de Jaegher, Father Lyons learned the inside story of the propaganda in the United States that had provoked the cruel assassination of Diem. Through Father de Jaegher he met "Big Minh," then Chief of State in South Vietnam. Minh was the first of many heads of state that Father Lyons would meet over the next 10 years in Vietnam and throughout the Orient.

The S. S. Seven Seas circled the world in three and a half months, and when the cruise ended Father Lyons arranged for Dr. Pan to give a lecture at Gonzaga. Father Lyons had presented a convocation at a junior college near Spokane only the week before, and he told Dr. Pan, "The students at the junior college complained to me that all they were getting were left wing speakers, and couldn't something be done about it. We ought to form a lecture bureau of our own and cut through all this Red propaganda."

Dr. Pan said, "I agree. When I get back to New York I will talk to Archbishop Yu Pin about it."

A week later, Dr. Pan wrote to Father Lyons and said that the Archbishop strongly favored the idea. "He will put up the first thousand dollars to get the bureau started," Dr. Pan wrote. "I'll keep you advised."

Father Lyons heard from Dr. Pan again, two weeks

later. "His Excellency will be passing through Seattle next week en route to Taiwan," he wrote. "Be over at Sea-Tac to meet his plane." Then Dr. Pan added this postscript: "Great men often pay little heed to small details. Be sure to ask him for the thousand."

Father Lyons got the thousand dollars, which he later paid back. The Archbishop also offered to place him under his supervision on loan from the Jesuits, and to supply offices and living quarters for him at his New York residence on 86 Riverside Drive. It was no idle gesture. The Archbishop meant every word. He wrote to Father Dan's Provincial in Oregon and explained that he had had Jesuits loaned to him before, and now he would very much like to borrow the services of the priest from Gonzaga. After an exchange of letters back and forth, permission was finally granted.

Now it was New York City, gangway for Father Lyons.

New York . . . here was a place where real things were going on.

Here was the scene of vital action.

Here was a place where anything might happen.

Here was a place where something would certainly happen.

Here he might even leave his bones.

A whole new career was opening up for Father Lyons. "If you can make it in New York," he said on his arrival, "you can make it anywhere." For the next eight years and more his work bench was going to be the podium—the microphone—the TV cameras—and his typewriter; most of all, the latter.

Priest and students in front of Liberal Arts Building at Seattle University, where Father Lyons taught for one year, before going to Gonzaga.

As honorary captain of the 1963 Gonzaga University hockey team, where he was Dean of Students, Father Lyons, front row far right, rarely saw the end of a game. He nearly always had to leave early to take a player or two to the emergency ward at Sacred Heart Hospital, Spokane, for patching up. All the Gonzaga players were from Canada.

Father Dan offers Mass at Chapel Royal, Dublin Castle. He explained, "The chapel was built for the English King and his Lord Lieutenant. Dublin Castle was the seat of English rule. In 1946, the chapel was turned into a Catholic chapel. The Irish used to be imprisoned in Dublin Castle, and when my father heard that I was to be the first priest to offer his first Mass there, he said, 'Now we're getting places!' "

After his Ordination, Father Dan is shown here giving his first blessing to his parents. Later in the day, the Prime Minister of Ireland, Eamon de Valera (now President), knelt for Father Dan's blessing in his office. He was an old friend of Patrick Lyons.

Ordination Day for Father Lyons, July 31, 1951, at Dublin, Ireland, was reason for a gathering of some of the clan. Seated, left to right: Father Tom Higgins (Dan's 1st cousin), Noreen Lyons Gilkey, father Patrick Lyons, Father Dan, mother Alice Lyons, Sheila Lyons Leewens, and Father John Lyons (1st cousin). Back row: Mrs. Kathryn Brons (Seattle), Jim McCready (now Jesuit at Gonzaga), Jack O'Neill (Dublin), Vincent McGovern, John Higgins, Ed Egan (all 1st cousins from County Mayo), Mrs. Jack O'Neill (mother of young Jack).

Dan's sister, Eileen, in a photo taken while she was Dean of Women at Gonzaga University, 1963.

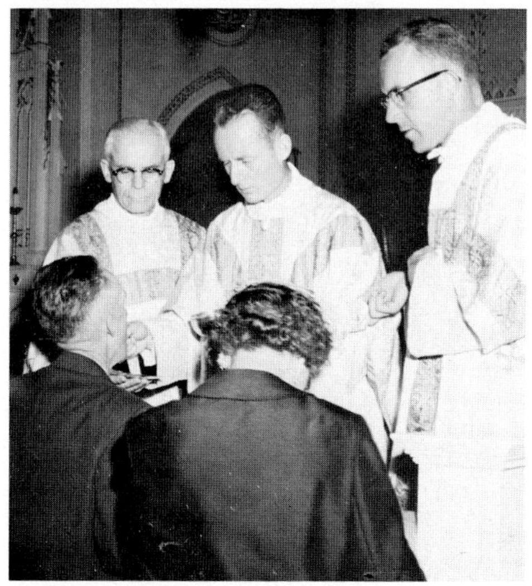

Father Lyons helps his former Gonzaga student, Father Joe Ringwood, S.J., give communion to the young priest's parents. The event was held at Sprague, Washington, and was Father Ringwood's first public Mass.

DeSmet Hall, below, the men's dorm at Gonzaga University, where Father Dan lived. Photo, above, is a broader view of the famous old Spokane, Washington, Catholic institution, established in 1887.

Father Lyons, who performed the ceremony, congratulates newly-weds Marty and Sabine Manning at Tacoma, Washington. Marty, a State Patrolman today, is Dan's nephew.

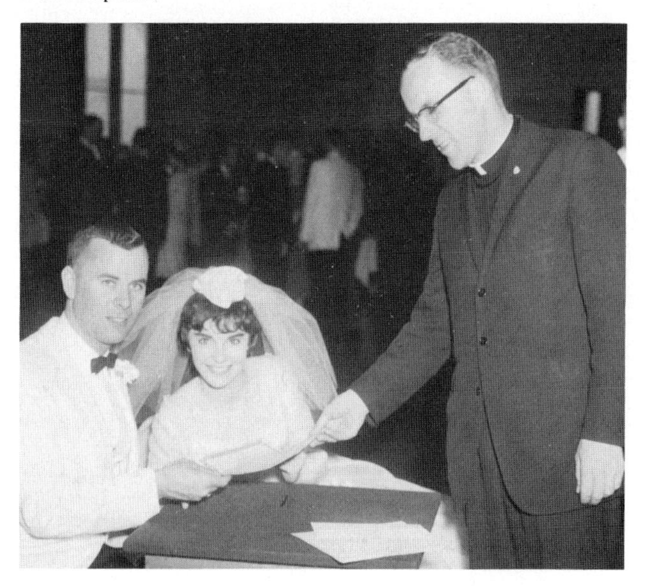

Father Dan and "Mom" Lyons share cake at recent family reunion in Seattle.

Sheila Lyons Leewens, Dan's youngest sister, with her husband, Louis, pose for photo just after their wedding on Christmas Day, 1957. They live in Holland.

Father Dan's little niece, Shannon Gilkey, hangs on to the Irish wolfhound that her mother, Noreen, brought from Ireland.

Father Dan's sister, Noreen (Mrs. Thomas Gilkey), and her five daughters prepare to take off from Seattle-Tacoma Airport, 1957, for move to Peru.

Gail Matthiesen, at about the age of 4, was one of her granddad Lyons' favorites. She has since graduated from University of Washington, and is taking graduate work at Seattle University today. She is the daughter of Father Dan's sister, Pat.

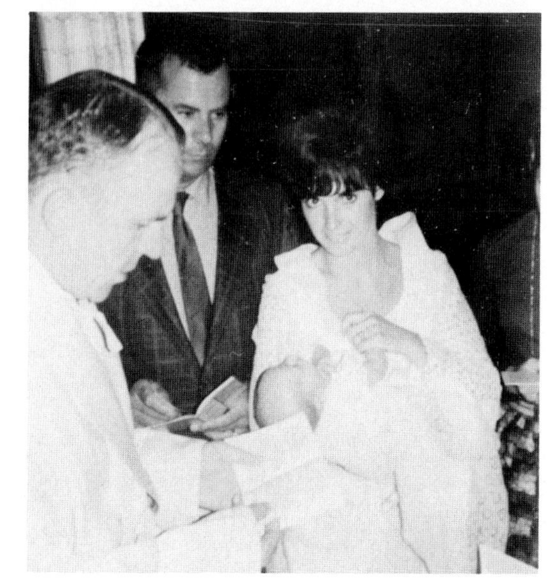

July 31, 1971, Father Lyons officiated at the Christening of his sister's baby, Lisa Marie Leewens, in Holland. Pictured also are Marty and Sabine Manning, godparents, from Tacoma, Washington.

86 Riverside Drive, above, has served as the offices and residence of Father Lyons since 1964. Located at 81st Street on Manhattan's West side, the building is the former home of movie star Douglas Fairbanks, Sr., and is also now the U.S. residence of Cardinal Paul Yu Pin.

Father Dan and sister Sheila study a rare copy of Book of Kells, donated to Seattle University by their late father, Patrick Lyons.

CHAPTER 12

The News Beat

Father Dan first wrote for the *Inland Register*, the Catholic paper in Spokane, in 1940. He was still just a young scholastic fresh out of the Novitiate. He wrote every chance he got, learning his trade, writing against deadlines, writing to make stuff timely rather than permanent. As a reporter, he soaked up persons and places and life like a sponge. No matter what he wrote or why he was writing, or for whom, the search for the facts went on.

In his hard-hitting articles, he showed himself to be a good reporter, with a grasp of politics and economics. He was an amazing observer, and knew how to dig for information. His craft was the craft of non-fiction, factual reporting, and he wrote as he saw things. If the details were sometimes slighted, the picture as a whole—full of the emotional impact of the events on the people—was clear, lucid and full. For the picture as a whole was what Dan Lyons the reporter cared about.

Father Dan's literary apprenticeship displayed a youthful enthusiasm, compassion, and imagination for the human interest story. His maturity as a journalist grew with experience, and by 1964 he was contributing serious articles to national and international periodicals. Locally, he urged Gonzaga University to let him revive *The Quarterly*, the Gonzaga magazine which had been defunct for many years, but he was told instead to supervise *Charter*, a new student publication.

Here was his chance. In one of the first issues he wrote the shocking story of the overthrow of President Diem in November 2, 1963. In it he attacked the U.S. press, charging them with being the victims of the Communist propaganda machine. His account was immediately picked up and reprinted by *The Spokane Chronicle* on page 1. An anonymous reader in Spokane sent the clipping on to Dean Clarence Manion, erstwhile head of the Law School at Notre Dame, who had started what was known as The Manion Forum, with headquarters in South Bend, Indiana. Dean Manion wrote to Father Lyons and asked him to appear on his syndicated radio and television programs.

Dean Manion, in his letter, said, "Suzanne Labin, the French writer, was on the Forum recently. She had just returned from South Vietnam and her account of the situation over there is similar to yours. Her remarks on the Forum have provoked a lot of comments. I'd like to hear what you have to say. Make a tape and send it on."

It sounded complicated. Father Lyons wrote back and offered to fly to South Bend and do the interview in person. Dean Manion was pleased. "Come right ahead," he said.

"We have more than 300 radio and TV stations carrying our programs."

Some of the lay faculty at Gonzaga were against Father Dan's appearance on a Right Wing program. After all, he was their Dean of Students. They argued that it would reflect upon the school's reputation. Father Dan's rebuttal was typical: "Those who listen to the Manion Forum like it—and those who don't like it, don't listen. For every enemy I'll make a thousand friends."

He did more than that. He made a whole new career. It marked his very first appearance on national radio-TV, serving as a harbinger of things to come. After his success on the Manion Forum, Father Dan returned to Spokane and wrote a 4500-word pamphlet entitled, "Accepting Defeat in Vietnam." He financed its publication himself and had it printed on the Gonzaga Press. "The point of that title was that until we stopped granting sanctuary to North Vietnam," he explained, "we were going to be defeated in the South." The first 5,000 copies were sold within three months and meanwhile the U.S. had started hitting Hanoi's bases in the North. Father Dan then changed the title of the booklet to "The Future of Vietnam" and ordered a second printing of 20,000 copies. This was later replaced by "Vietnam Crisis," a paperback he co-authored with Dr. Stephen Pan, and which enjoyed a run of 140,000 in the English edition, and 20,000 copies in a full Chinese issue.

Father Lyons had the literary bug now. "Vietnam Crisis" was followed by "The New Morality," first released by the Gonzaga Press and later reprinted by *Our Sunday Visitor.*

This second handbook quickly became a best-seller, and seven years later it is still in print.

The Lyons reputation spread. His booklets found their way into the hands of the Schlaflys, Fred, Eleanor and Phyllis. Eleanor Schlafly was Executive Secretary of The Mindszenty Foundation, in St. Louis. Dean Manion had often spoken to Father Lyons about the Foundation. It had been a prime target of *Look* magazine.

Father Lyons told me, "There is an old story about the two Irishmen who saw a fist-fight in full throttle, and they walked in on it and said, 'Give us a side, boys.' I suppose I'm like that. I've never been shy about taking sides."

The Mindszenty Foundation was holding its annual conference in St. Louis, and the Schlaflys ordered 300 copies each of "Vietnam Crisis" and "The New Morality." They also invited Father Lyons to attend the convention. "We cannot afford to pay your fare," they told him, "but if you can get here we'll be happy to have you give a talk."

The conference was held in the Fall of 1964. It served as another turning point in Father Dan's career. There he met Patrick Frawley, a man who was to have more influence on his career than any other single person since he left home in 1938. It is a curious habit of most men to stay silent in regard to benefactors who gave them a leg up in the days of their becoming. A successful man, whether he owns a tungsten mine or writes a nationally-syndicated newspaper column, seldom volunteers a word of thanksgiving for the generosity of an ancient grubstaker or some friendly piano tuner of long ago. Perhaps it is to safeguard one's ego, this forgetfulness of Good Samaritans. Possibly an outspoken memorial for past favors would demolish a treasured American religion, that of the self-made man. It is therefore a satisfaction to record that Father Lyons proves an exception to the rule of professional ingratitude. He may be self-sufficient in many respects; he inherited strong family ties, together with a keen mind and bodily endowments that earmarked him for success; yet he has often ackhowledged to me that his writing career has been prominently accommodated by timely help.

On his way, perhaps it would come as a word cast by some teacher into the swift current of his mind, or as a talent-rousing direction by someone of cool discernment. Then again, it might be simply the respect and devotion of a superior that uplifted him.

One of these early monitors of Father Dan's life course was Father John E. Moffatt, who often had offered Mass at the Carmelite convent, where Dan went to Mass daily as a boy. Father Moffatt gave him his first two years of training at Sheridan.

In Father Dan's files is a letter from Father Moffatt, dated August 4, 1967. The handwriting is shaky, barely legible, but the words and the tone are inspiring and filled with conviction. The penmanship was that of a dying man, a stroke victim. From the Little Sisters of the Poor home in Cleveland, the old gentleman wrote:

"My Very Dear Father:

> I am sending this brief word from my deathbed where, in perfect peace and happiness, I am awaiting the Master's coming to take me Home. . . .
>
> Father, you have done, and are doing, magnificent work for God, for the Church, the Society, and the

world. I am proud of you, not indeed as if I were taking any credit for your enviable success, but comfort in the thought that during those two years of our intimate relations as Novice and Master, at least I did not interfere too greatly with God's grace as He was forming within you the spirit of another Peter Canisius which now is so beautifully manifest. God love you, Father.

Most Gratefully and Devotedly
in Corde Jesu,
John E. Moffatt, S.J."

In more recent years, Patrick Frawley, the former chairman of Eversharp, Inc., and supporter of conservative causes, has been Father Dan's most reliable patron saint. Their views of Catholic faith and American freedom are attuned.

At the Mindszenty conference, Father Lyons also talked at length to the Schlaflys. They and Pat Frawley and his wife were urging Father Lyons to talk to *Our Sunday Visitor,* the nation's largest Catholic weekly, about writing its famous "Right or Wrong" column. Father Lyons agreed to try.

The next day, he rented a car and drove the 200 miles to Huntington, Indiana, for a meeting with Monsignor Joseph Crowley, the editor of *Our Sunday Visitor.* With him rode Monsignor John Cleary, a pastor from Staten Island, New York. Father Lyons felt that since he himself was relatively unknown, a fellow Monsignor would lend his cause respectability and help him get a chance to write "Right or Wrong."

Spokane's *Inland Register* had become part of OSV's

chain of newspapers the previous year, and Father Dan's best calling card was the columns he had written for Bishop Topel's paper. Monsignor Crowley reasoned that if Bishop Topel's *Inland Register* carried them, they must be pretty sound. He read a few, and liked them.

"You're a good writer," Monsignor Crowley told him. "But what is it you want from me?"

Father Dan said, "I'd like to write your Right or Wrong column. I know Father Coogan is sick and can't do the job."

The Monsignor rubbed his chin, thoughtfully.

"There's a slight hitch," he said. "The column always has appeared on page two, the best spot in the paper. But Dale Francis now has taken over that space. I have a suggestion, though. Why don't you write articles for us instead of a column?"

"I had my mind set on that column," he confessed. "I don't want to settle for anything less."

The Monsignor said, "I'll compromise with you. We don't have room on page two for the longer Right or Wrong column, but we can make room for a shorter column of about 500 words. You can give it a name."

"What about Keeping Posted?"

"Fine," the Monsignor said. "We've just hired ourselves a new columnist."

Father Lyons went back to Gonzaga and began mailing the column to *Our Sunday Visitor* regularly. His mail picked up noticeably. The readers began to respond, most of them favorably. Soon the by-line Daniel Lyons, S.J., was a hot item. Newspapers were quoting him now. Within a month after he started, Father Lyons received a phone call from Monsignor Crowley.

The Monsignor told him, "Father, your columns are too *short*. Can't you make them longer?"

It was Monsignor Crowley's way of saying he had decided to make Father Lyons the new proprietor of "Right or Wrong."

Father Lyons wrote the column for two years. Then he and Patrick Frawley launched their own ambitious venture, *Twin Circle*, the new national weekly. That was in 1967. Two years later, after Father Dan's first year as editor, the paper was voted the best national Catholic newspaper in America, in a poll of all U.S. bishops.

No. 2 was *National Catholic Register.*

And third? *Our Sunday Visitor.*

Three of the U.S. bishops had voted for the leftist-oriented *National Catholic Reporter,* explained Archbishop Hannan of New Orleans when announcing the results. "Because of the nature of the poll," he commented, "their names are known only to the Almighty."

CHAPTER 13
Pop Lyons Passes On

Knowing his weakness for the homeless of South Vietnam, friends of Father Lyons weren't surprised to learn in July of 1966 that he was on his way back to the combat zone once more. During the long flight over, he had a vague feeling that something was going to happen. Something in the form of bad news. It wasn't exactly a premonition, and he really didn't worry about it. Yet a slight tension was there. So when at last his plane came over Saigon, after eight thousand miles of probably the most perfect trip he ever had, he thought to himself, "Well, we crack up when we land here, I suppose. It's our last chance for anything to happen."

He was pretty jumpy when they skimmed down the runway. It seemed as if the pilot would never get the wheels on the ground. But finally they did touch, light as a feather; the big plane ran smooth and straight. And nothing happened at all.

For the next three days, Father Lyons moved among the damned. His special domain this time was the highlands of Vietnam. He talked to the Montagnards. He spoke with the refugees. He visited with American G.I.'s. The front-line soldiers he talked to had been living like animals for weeks. They were veterans in the cruel, fierce world of death. Everything was abnormal and unstable in their lives. They were filthy dirty. They ate if and when, slept on hard ground without cover. Their combat clothes were tattered and they lived in a constant haze of dust, pestered by flies and heat, moving constantly, deprived of all the things that once meant stability.

In one of his dispatches to his home paper, Father Lyons wrote how the front-line soldier had to harden his inside as well as his outside or crack under the strain. Vietnam was no place for sissies.

On the afternoon of the third day, the bad news caught up with Father Lyons. It was a telegram that had originated in Seattle, gone to his office in New York, was then picked up by the State Department and relayed to military headquarters in Saigon. Finally it reached him through a chaplain. His heart sank as he read the message:

"FATHER PASSED AWAY TODAY.
PLEASE CONTACT HOME.
LOVE, MOTHER."

At 84, after a long and active life, the old ticker of Patrick Lyons had given out. A lot of thoughts went through Father Dan's mind. He remembered the time he went with his dad to visit the home of an elderly, wealthy lumberman in southern Oregon, and on their way back to Seattle,

Patrick had said, "Poor old John. He's got all that money—and no one to say a prayer for him when he dies."

It was very Irish. It was Patrick Lyons.

Father Dan also recalled earlier days in Seattle, when he was 16 and served with his dad on the parish council of the St. Vincent de Paul Society. He recollected, too, the letter his father wrote him several years later while he was attending St. Louis University: "We finally bought another house. It is just four blocks from church, all on one level—and in my old age I can go to church in a wheelbarrow." The last time Patrick had been to church, Father Dan and his sister Pat had taken him. He had gone in a wheelchair, not a wheelbarrow. His health had been failing gradually for about a year, and he had spent the past few months in a convalescent home, where he regularly received Communion, and had been anointed.

On his way over to Vietnam, Father Dan had considered the possibilities of his father dying while he was away, and yet the doctor had assured him that Patrick's condition was not critical. "There's just no way of knowing for sure," the doctor had said. And then a couple of days before his death, the old man started having trouble with his breathing and was taken to the hospital. His breathing came like the sound made by a knife-blade being ground on a stone wheel. His wife, at his bedside, was worried, but Patrick gripped her hand and assured her he was going to be all right. "Just a little indigestion," he said. For a while, he seemed to rally. He was showing surprising, quick strength in his battle to stay alive. He was trying, it seemed, to rise with the instinct of a knocked-down champion, his senses beaten, but his spirits never. He fought as only the young fight against this last antagonist, for the old seldom come to grips with the final aggressor. They slip away, as if on some quiet journey into the night.

Alice Lyons said goodbye to her husband early the night before and promised to return to him at mid-morning the next day. Patrick had been sharing a room with another patient, and when she came back only one of the two beds was occupied. Her husband was not there.

"Where's Mr. Lyons?" she asked the nurse, who had just come on duty.

"Didn't anyone tell you?"

"Tell me what?"

"Your — your husband —died."

"DIED?"

"Yes. At five o'clock this morning."

Alice Lyons blinked. She dabbed at her eyes, holding back the tears.

The nurse said, quietly, "I'm terribly sorry, Mrs. Lyons. I was sure you had been phoned."

"No—no one called me. There must have been a mix-up."

Indeed, there had been a breakdown in communications between shifts. The hospital was very apologetic and kind to Mrs. Lyons over the unfortunate incident, but that didn't lessen the shock any. It was still a hard way for her to learn about her husband's death, even though she had been expecting it.

They were strong, brave, determined people, those old country mothers. No matter what the circumstances, they could take a blow, and maintain their poise. Alice Lyons, who was all alone, went to work and made arrangements for the funeral. As soon as Father Dan received her wire, he telegraphed her that he was coming straight home.

When the news reached General Westmoreland, he personally arranged for his friend to be on the earliest flight possible going to Seattle, via Tokyo and Anchorage. Father Dan was anxious to get home in time for the funeral. At 4:30 the next afternoon his plane touched down at Seattle-Tacoma Airport with time to spare. When he got to the terminal he phoned his mother from a phone booth, and when she heard his voice she said, "Oh, Danny! Are you still in Saigon?" He had beaten his own telegram home.

Father Dan's arrival was a big comfort to his mother. She had resigned herself to believing that none of her children would be able to come home for the funeral. They were spread all over the world. The prospect of none of them being with her in her grief was a dark situation for such a closely-knit family. Patricia had just left Seattle for Greece. Eileen's last letter indicated she would be tied up for a month at Moorehead State College, in Minnesota, where she was the Dean of Women. Noreen was living in Peru, and Sheila, the youngest, had been home to visit her parents only a few weeks before, but had since returned to her husband and six children in Holland.

Noreen was unable to make it in time, but Eileen arranged some emergency leave and flew in from the Midwest. Meanwhile, Patricia had stopped off in New York before catching her plane for Athens, and phoned Father Dan's office. Jerry Farmer answered the call and told her that her father had died, so she quickly turned around and returned to Seattle.

Brian Matthiesen, Pat's 16-year-old son, also got back for his grandfather's burial. Instead of going with his family to Greece that summer, he got a job on the Ambrose McAuliffe ranch in southern Oregon at Fort Klamath. It was a cattle ranch and, besides the sun-up to sun-down hours, he learned to ride well enough to enter the rodeos. When he heard that his granddad had died, he paid his own way to Seattle so that he could serve the Mass along with his cousin, Jarlath Hume.

Even Patrick's last living brother, Mike, came up from Florida—and he was over 90. When Pat Matthiesen picked him up at Sea-Tac Airport, it was raining, and he said, "No wonder he died. With weather like this in July, he froze to death!"

Father Dan was limping badly when he walked off the plane at Sea-Tac. He had somehow infected his knee while traipsing around the highlands in Vietnam, and he was in pain. From the airport he phoned an old family friend, Dr. Matthew Evoy, and made an appointment to stop by his office on the way home. Dr. Evoy, whose brothers Jack and Gerard were also Jesuit priests, gave Father Dan's knee a shot to kill the pain. Father Dan then went home, shaved, and took his mother over to St. Joseph's Church, where he conducted the Rosary services at 7:30 p.m.

Next morning, he personally offered the funeral Mass, assisted by his nephews Brian and Jarlath. The strain and fatigue told on his face, yet Father Dan's poise did not abandon him. Later, when a friend of the family congratulated him for his calmness, he was somewhat surprised, and said simply, "You do what you have to do."

St. Joseph's Church was full to overflowing with Patrick's friends and relatives. "It was wonderful," Pat Lyons Matthiesen told me. "Almost the only flowers were a green and white spray for the beautiful wooden coffin that Mom picked out. She said she picked wood because Pop lived with lumber all his life. The green flowers were for the Irish. Everyone knew that Pop thought flowers were a waste—but the Mass cards were unbelievable!"

In life, Patrick Lyons had often said, "I gave one son to God, and one son to country." Now he had gone to join the one in Heaven.

On the flight crossing the Pacific between Tokyo and Alaska, Father Dan wrote a column for *Our Sunday Visitor*. All that he felt for his father flowed from his pen:

"My father immigrated from Ireland in 1905. He had the strongest faith I have ever seen. Every morning for many years he took the six of us to early Mass. It was to this that I owe my vocation. He often remarked that the best thing about America is the free night school, which enabled him to educate himself over a ten-year period, after working all day on the docks. From 1920 until 1960 he exported lumber all over the world, and he was known throughout the world for his integrity. The world is a better place for his having lived in it. Even Heaven will gain by his arrival. He used to say that we all gather a little dust as we walk along life's path, and he had great devotion to the souls in Purgatory. Kindly say a prayer for him."

So many memories of his father—so long ago—when six

children were all so young, and knew and expected so little —and it didn't matter.

Now, only the memories remained.

No, we'll take that back. Father Dan put it differently in a letter to his mother later: "We will all be reunited again, never to be separated, in the land that God has prepared for those who love Him."

Later, in a conversation with me, he elaborated on this theme: "While the glory of this world ends in the tomb, it is in the tomb that the glory of the Son of God begins. If we were not to rise again we would be the most wretched of men. Without a future life there would be nothing to look for, nothing to work for, nothing to hope for, nothing to pray for. It is in the final resurrection which Christ has promised us that all our hopes are laid, and the resurrection of our Divine Lord is the surest pledge of our own future life. For if Christ could raise Himself to life, why can He not raise others? If He could raise Himself from the dead, why cannot we, by that same omnipotent Hand, be restored to life? As St. Paul tells us, 'We shall all, indeed, rise again.' Yes, some day our body shall be laid in the grave. But we too shall rise again, as the recording angel pronounces over our tomb that beautiful epitaph of the first Easter Sunday: 'He is risen; He is not here.' "

Though it was inevitable that Alice Lyons could not go on living alone in her house forever, she managed it for a few more years. She loved having her grandchildren around her, sometimes for months at a time while they attended college. She knew, however, that time was not on her side. She had read about apartments in Long Beach, California, for Gold Star Mothers, and told her children that was where she wanted to live out her life.

Dan drove her from Seattle to southern California finally, taking along only what they could pile into her car. They left the house and everything in it for her four daughters to dispose of. As they shut the door for a final time, Dan said to his mother, "That was really a good idea. You did the right thing to just walk out of the house and leave everything behind."

She flung one last glance over her shoulder.

She said, "I just beat it!"

Alice Lyons, in her eighties, lives today with those wonderful Irish nuns at Mary Crest Manor in Culver City, a few miles north of the Los Angeles International Airport. She had lived for a year in Denver at the Sacred Heart Home, run by the Little Sisters of the Poor. She was very fond of them, but preferred California, with the ocean nearby, beautiful flowers, a warm climate, daily Mass, equally charming Sisters, and her daughter Noreen and her five children to pick her up and take her for rides in the car.

Whenever Father Dan goes to Los Angeles on business at *Twin Circle* headquarters, he sees his mother often. He said, "If I could find the time, she would ride with me up the Coast to Seattle and back again. She loves sightseeing in a car. One of these days I will have to fly her up to Seattle for a visit with the old hometown. But I know what will happen. I always travel coach, but when I take her I have to buy first-class tickets. Not that she's fussy. She simply sees those seats when she walks onto the plane, and says, 'Let's sit right here.' Life has never been complicated for her. She just takes it for granted she can sit wherever she wants."

I asked him, "How has she adjusted to the new Liturgy in the Church?"

Father Dan grinned.

He said, "It's given her no trouble at all. I watched her one day when it came time for the kiss of peace. As the lady next to her turned to take her hand, mother said as she shook hands, 'I'm from Seattle.' Mom's a gem. The only time such parents cause their children any grief is when they die. But they have to die sometime if ever they are going to get to Heaven. They put in some good words for us, too, when they get there. And it's always nice to have a friend in court. With a little luck I hope to get to Heaven some day, and when I do I can just hear Our Lady say, 'We thought you'd never get here. Your mother always speaks of you.' When I get there, I hope they won't be disappointed. You know how parents are, talking about their kids."

One of the grandchildren who spent a lot of time around her grandparents was Gail Matthiesen, an Art History major who graduated from the University of Washington, in 1969. A student with a near 4-point grade average, she is now taking graduate courses at Seattle University, and plans to specialize in working with emotionally disturbed students. I recently sat down with her and asked her to talk to me about her grandfather Lyons. What influence, I wanted to know, did he have on her? Her answer was refreshing. It totally refuted all we had been hearing in the 1960s about the so-called generation gap.

"When granddad came over from Ireland," she began,

"he brought some of the ancient folklore with him. I was probably an imaginative child anyway, but this quality was encouraged and fed by a large, close family. I learned to read over an older brother's shoulder, and we were always put to bed with a story. There were nights when granddad would act out, rather than read, the familiar fairy tales. He would have us screaming with delight or fear until Mama would have to put an end to it and calm us down so we would sleep.

"We all learned to read quite well, long before we went to school. When my little sister, Molly, was only in the first grade and her classmates were reading such lines as 'Run, John, run,' and 'Jane, see John,' she turned to the nun and said, 'Sister, this is *stupid*. Can't we read something more *adult*?'

"I still treasure the memory of those special evenings when grandfather Lyons would tell us 'real' stories of his boyhood in Ireland. And many an evening I fell asleep on the living room floor, listening to the good talk of the grownups as they laughed over family stories everybody knew.

"It is a tradition in our family to 'talk about it' in times of trouble, and somehow in the telling we have learned to recall the good and funny, and through the tears comes laughter. All this is commonplace for us and I am always amazed to learn by talking to friends that stories and imagination were not part of everyone's childhood. This is strange to me, and I cannot come away feeling that I am the one who is the worse for it. It is a special way of looking at life.

"I have carried these experiences to everything I've done,

from learning about and dealing with people, to work and school, and while traveling. And I am the richer for it. Our family has traveled a great deal. I have stood on the Acropolis on the night of the full moon and watched the shadows reconstruct the ruins, and heard the words of the ancients in the whisper of the wind.

"I have driven in New England on a moonless October night down a dark and twisting road overhung by bare branches, expecting to meet the Headless Horseman round the next bend. I was welcomed home in Denmark when my interest in a statue, and the tale behind it, proved to the people I had met that I was a true Dane come home.

"I have heard the tales, seen the belief, or felt the superstition of fishermen and farmers from Greece and southern France to Ireland, Puerto Rico and Alaska, and among our Pacific Northwest Indians. I have talked to old people and seen my grandfather in the wrinkles of their weathered, leathered faces and especially the twinkle in their eye. And I have known that, though some of them had never read a page or written a word, they know more than I can ever hope to know.

"And everywhere I heard the stories and the songs, I would become a little girl again sitting by my grandfather's knee. And there would be things in the shadows cast by the fire and words in the wind, and I knew what the ring around the moon meant.

"Do I believe in leprechauns? Well, I have never seen one, not for sure, so I can't say I do. But I won't say I don't. In many parts of the world, I have found people wise in many ways who do believe, or say they do, and I believe in the power of that belief.

"Somehow I cannot forget something grandfather Lyons once told me when I was very small; small enough still to be riding on his knee. He stopped bouncing me and said, 'Now I want you to listen, *really* listen, because you might not understand what I have to say. But I want you to remember it.' I didn't understand, but I remember twisting my face into what I thought must be a serious expression to let him know I was listening, and that I would remember. Then he told me:

" '*You have something very special.*
I have often seen a leprechaun,
But I have never been *one.*
You can be *one.*' "

Good old Patrick Lyons.
A credit to his Maker.
Sweet dreams.

CHAPTER 14

Father Dan on Blacks

The neighborhood where Father Lyons grew up was a neighborly neighborhood. It had a heart. It was neighborly in the old-times sense that everyone knew everyone else's business and most of the women were on sugar-borrowing terms.

The area on Seattle's northeast side was middle-class. Nobody had much of anything in the early thirties, but they shared what they had and they had an enormous amount of fun. Some of the men were loafers and sentimentalists; the ladies were dreamers. Practically everyone attended nearby St. Joseph's Church and school, then Seattle Prep, the Jesuit high school. The girls attended Holy Names Academy, which the boys irreverently called "homely dames."

In almost every direction there were two-story private homes, broken, here and there, with four-story apartments.

It was an earthy neighborhood, but clean and well-kept, the lawns well-manicured. It was a place where snobs were quarantined.

In this neighborhood, the best job for a young boy to have was delivering the *Seattle P-I*, or *The Seattle Times*. Dan did both, at different times. His subscribers ranged from 123 to 128, and about half of them were black. His paper route stretched from near his home to down around 23rd and Madison, the Negro section. It was one of a score of villages inside Seattle where loyalties were jingoistic; where a black boy had to fight to belong; where short Anglo-Saxon words were used, not so much in blasphemy but as a means of punctuation; a place where the dumb-waiter and a code ring of the downstairs bell were part of the daily life; where petty theft was not regarded as real stealing; a place where, at sixteen, a girl could become known to one and all as a lady or as a tramp; at the same age, a boy who was well dressed, had a dollar in his pocket and no job was quite a guy. A man, almost.

In this neighborhood, the gang to belong to was the Zulus. It was composed of teen-age boys. They had sweaters and they fielded a baseball team, and, now and then, they met in a guy's house on Madison. Here they argued, made plans, paid dues, plotted against their rivals, indulged in horseplay, voted secretly on the admission of new members, told stories about grownups in the neighborhood, and talked about "broads."

Dan's mother was apprehensive about her son venturing down into the 23rd and Madison section after dark. She feared for his safety. It had the reputation of being a tough district. But in the year and a half that he delivered papers there, he did not suffer a single incident.

He said, "I was cheated a couple times—by *whites*—but there was never a case where a Negro family didn't pay me. Call it a small boy's naivete, trust, or whatever, but I never worried about trouble in the black neighborhood. And I made most of my collections at night. In those days, I got 90 cents from each house subscribing to the daily paper, and $1.25 from those taking both the daily and Sunday editions. I'd start out on my collections with about $10 in change, which I kept in a canvas bag, and before I finished my rounds I'd have more than $80. Though I was only 12, no black ever even threatened to rob me. I've never forgotten that."

Father Lyons, a trained sociologist, always had a very real concern for the black man. While he was at Gonzaga, he gave much time and energy to the problem.

It began for him at Mount St. Michael's. There he spent three years studying philosophy and sociology. The curriculum was heavy. All of Father Dan's classes were in Latin. Even the lectures, textbooks and the written and oral exams were in Latin.

At the end of each year, he was given an hour-long oral examination before a board of four professors. All in Latin!

And at the end of the third and final year at Mount St. Michael's, he had to pass an oral exam covering the entire three years. It was no place for a dolt.

You hear a lot of talk today about more and more schools eliminating the conventional grade-system. To Father Lyons, that is nothing new.

He said, "The Jesuits have been playing down grades for years. It is traditional. Though grades were kept, we never knew what they were. We were not supposed to be working for grades, except when we went to an outside university. Our course was based on the teachings of St. Thomas Aquinas. He had drawn much of his teachings from Aristotle, the greatest of the ancients. At the Mount we said he baptized Aristotle. Aquinas had the revealed truths of Christianity to superimpose on the classic writings of Aristotle. Certainly his mind matched Aristotle's. They are still the two greatest minds in history.

"We hiked a lot at the Mount. Thursday was our day without classes, instead of Saturday, and was known as Villa Day. The 'Villa' was various cabins some miles away from Spokane. For additional recreation, we played handball and baseball. I am a lefthander and did some pitching on the baseball team at the seminary. I am lefthanded in everything but writing. The Sisters switched me to the right hand in the first grade, for which I have always been grateful, as classrooms are geared for righthanders.

"We also played ice hockey quite a lot. There was no artificial ice, but we managed to get a lot of natural ice. We took turns volunteering to put down a spray of water on the ice at 10:30 p.m., followed by another group at 4 a.m. We used old fire hoses the city gave us. They let us have them because they were worn out and full of holes. So we looked like human icicles when we finished the job. We also flooded the four tennis courts for ice skating, and at night almost the entire community of 110 Jesuits came out to skate, complete with hot chocolate, doughnuts, and Strauss waltzes.

"At the Mount, we studied with Jesuit scholastics (seminarians) from the California Province. They had spent their first four years at Los Gatos, California. The rest of us came from Seattle, Spokane, Portland, and from other towns throughout Washington, Oregon, Idaho, Montana, Alaska, and several from Eastern states.

"In my first year at the Mount I worked with the Negro Mission: teaching catechism and visiting Negro families around Spokane. I was director of the Mount St. Michael's Negro Missionary Society in my second and third years. There were only about 1500 Negroes in Spokane, and we knew all of them. During World War II, there was an Assistant General of the Jesuits for America, since Rome was cut off, and he, Father Zacheus Maher, asked for volunteers from the rest of the Provinces to spend our lives after Ordination helping the southern Province work with Negroes. I wrote to my Provincial, volunteering for the work. But the project was never launched. Since then, most of the blacks have moved to the North."

A few years ago, while he was still assigned to Gonzaga University, Father Lyons explored the Negro problem in America, and what he found shocked him.

"Americans seem to know amazingly little about Negroes," he told his audiences later. "Yet because we have a certain familiarity with it, we are oblivious of all that we do not know. This whole question of race in America is so complex that no one fully comprehends it. It varies from state to state, from neighborhood to neighborhood, and from block to block. Furthermore, it is changing constantly. There is room for optimism, yet reason for pessimism; grounds for hope, yet cause for despair. People who think they have the answer do not really understand the problem at all. Even where it is 'simply a matter of rights,' we soon realize that rights overlap.

"To think that the racial problem exists only in the South is a sad mistake. It exists wherever there are colored people. No group was ever more indelibly marked or more easily identified. No segregated minority was ever involved in such a vicious circle. Shaw described it well when he said: 'The haughty American nation forces the Negro to shine its shoes, and then condemns him for being a bootblack.'

"The slaves were freed, but were never prepared for their freedom. The reform brought about by the Civil War was only political; there was no economic or social reform. Freedom implies a certain independence. A slave can be liberated by education, even if he is still a slave; but a slave who is freed remains a slave, if left in ignorance.

"The job of freeing the Negro was not finished by the Civil War. He was still victimized by a policy of prejudice that made it difficult for him to get a good education, to earn a decent salary, to occupy suitable housing, or, in the South, even to vote. This situation has persisted, in more or less degree, right down to our own day, and to some extent it still exists. It is the unfinished business of American democracy. It offers a special challenge to the Catholic Church.

"To say that the Negro has been content with his lot all along is false. To declare that the racial demonstrations in recent years have been the work of outside agitators is largely fallacious. The more the lid of oppression is lifted, the more oppressed people react. The Irish, the Italians, the Polish, the Jews, and other oppressed minorities fought for their rights, and were proud they did. The Negroes, too, are fighting for justice and equality. For the most part, they are proud of their leaders, proud of their progress, and proud of their victories.

"For sixty years the progress seemed microscopically small. But it was there, and finally the results were manifest everywhere. During the past twenty years the Negro has made more progress than in the previous fifty. In the next ten years his progress will double that of the past twenty. It started during World War II, when President Roosevelt established a Fair Employment Practices Commission, forbidding any discrimination in hiring by the government, or by firms doing business with the government. This was established only after the noted Negro leader, A. Philip Randolph, threatened a march on Washington with 10,000 Negroes. Now an elderly man, it was the same Mr. Randolph who led the celebrated march of 200,000 Negroes in 1963, in favor of civil rights legislation.

"Every step forward made the next step easier. The FEPC conditioned whites to working with Negroes, and to working with them in higher occupations. It educated the Negro to working with whites. In 1948, President Truman integrated the armed forces. This made whites come to know the Negro, while the added responsibilities brought out the best in the black soldier, as only responsibilities can. Negroes became secure in the CIO, and the A. F. of L. broke down many of its traditional barriers. In 1954, the

Supreme Court outlawed segregated schools, declaring that in practice separate meant unequal, and was therefore unconstitutional.

"A full 40 percent of the Negroes today still live in substandard housing, contrasted with only 10 percent of the whites. Yet the worst disadvantage the Negro faces is in a lack of preparation for suitable employment. Most whites are high school graduates; most Negroes have never finished high school. Unemployment with Negroes is twice as high as with whites. The traditional kind of Negro job is rapidly disappearing. Being unskilled, they are the hardest hit of all by automation. This presents an enormous problem. It also presents an unprecedented opportunity for him to raise his status permanently, with better types of work.

"A new era is dawning for the Negro. People have never been less prejudiced. In thousands of cases, employers are going out of their way to put Negroes on the payroll. The conscience of America has been deeply stirred, and the Negro need never again feel there is no outlet for his ambition. Those who can qualify find a variety of desirable positions. This is especially true with the federal government, where Negroes hold about 15 percent of the jobs.

"Some Americans resent this, since Negroes constitute only 10 percent of the population. But we must realize that opportunity has been denied the Negro all along; that he has been bred on slums, nursed on discouragement, and fed on anti-social attitudes that only a black man can feel in a white man's world.

"Most of the decisive battles have been won. The majority of Americans, and the full force of federal law, favor civil rights. The racial demonstrations have served their purpose. While Negroes must prove that whites have very little to lose from mixed association, whites must show the Negro that he is no longer to remain a second-class citizen, neither politically, economically, nor socially. A combination of new leaders is needed, leadership that itself is integrated. Interracial citizens' councils should be formed at the highest levels, and at every level.

"Both sides have a great deal to learn about each other. The Negro organizations have broken down much of the hard core of resistance. Now we need leadership from both sides, working together to analyze the problems remaining, and to help society work out the best possible solutions. We especially need to stress personal responsibility, reform of the individual as the basis for reforming society, personal integrity as the key to racial justice and the price of peace and interracial progress. Above all, we need to realize that 'they labor in vain, who seek to work without Almighty God.'

"In 1950, the Sacred Congregation of Propaganda in Rome warned the Catholic Church in the United States that, if it wanted to make any progress with the Negro in America, it must rid itself completely of any approval of segregation, not only in education, but in housing and employment. Have we been doing our share as Catholics to help solve the race problem? Or have we been seeking the easy way out, the way of not getting involved?"

As a Jesuit seminarian and teacher, Dan Lyons was a forerunner of the supreme court's first great decision for the Negro when it declared, in 1954, that segregation in schooling was unconstitutional. Writing in *Studies,* the scholarly Irish Quarterly, while he was studying in Dublin in 1950, he pointed out, as he had many times in America, that the solution to the problem was threefold: religion, education, and legislation.

The race question, he said, was historical and economic, cultural and educational, "but its solution must be based fundamentally on religion." Education and legislation, he insisted, will not affect a lasting moral change "unless they are reinforced by religious motives." Morality cannot be legislated, he pointed out. Besides, he said, "the race question is primarily a moral issue. If America's Catholics would correct their attitude, Catholics would revolutionize America's race relations." He quoted the words of Pope Pius XII, addressed to the U.S. Catholic clergy:

> *"We confess that we feel a special paternal affection, which is certainly inspired of Heaven, for the Negro people dwelling among you; for in the field of religion and education we know that they need special care and comfort and are very deserving of it. We therefore invoke an abundance of heavenly blessings and we pray fruitful success for those whose generous zeal is devoted to their welfare."*

Second only to religion for solving the race question, said Lyons, is education, the handmaid of religion. "Ignorance and prejudice commonly go hand in hand. Nothing will dissipate prejudice like a Christian education. Prejudice is a rash judgment. An untrained mind is open to prejudice because, by jumping to conclusions, it is quick to generalize."

He quoted his long-time friend, Father John LaFarge, S.J.: "The first step toward combating wrong emotions and distorted habits is to clarify one's own ideas." The second step toward the elimination of prejudice, wrote Lyons, "is to stop breeding children on it."

Negroes, he asserted, need education also. "Poor housing and poverty produce, not just in Negroes but in everyone, inferior bodies and weakened wills. A person cannot be judged because of his race. He must be given the opportunity to prove himself. Color of skin is no more signficant than color of hair, as far as individual worth is concerned."

Writing in 1950, he spoke prophetically of the need for federal legislation: "Those who declare that the race question will never be solved until everyone is filled with the spirit of Christianity may sound pious enough, but they could hardly be less practical. Such an attitude in politicians simply means that they are shirking the difficulties of setting up a social order adapted to man as he is. To wait until everybody loses his prejudice before passing laws against discrimination is like waiting until every thief stops stealing before hiring policemen. Where selfishness enters in —and much of prejudice is financially profitable—we cannot rely solely on the moral integrity of everyone.

"Should the legislation be by the separate states, or by the federal government? Much of it will have to be federal: firstly, for uniformity; secondly, because the states in the deep South have proven themselves over-reluctant to take any steps at all. The problem involves federal responsibility. Since the American Constitution guarantees to every citizen the exercise of his natural and civil rights, it should be uniformly enforced for everyone, no matter in what state he lives.

"At long last the federal government is realizing that the race crisis in America is a national problem which depends for its solution on federal action. After prolonged indifference, the United States supreme court is now aware that to uphold the Constitution, to guarantee to those reasonably qualified a chance to vote in national elections, and to safeguard even the Negro's constitutional rights, is the obligation of the federal government. Every state should guarantee to all the impartial use of such public services as parks, schools, police protection, libraries, and the right of buying a home where they are able to and where they choose. But the federal government must be prepared to step in where the states wantonly fail to do this."

Like the rest of his writings, these views have stood the acid test of time.

Arguing from the standpoint of science and logic, Dan Lyons wrote:

"The color chemical which causes a brown or black pigmentation in one's appearance is called melanin. There is, of course, no connection of any kind between any cultural or moral quality and the amount of melanin in the body. Yellow pigmentation is caused by another chemical, carotene, while a pinkish tinge is due, not to one's political affiliations, but to the blood vessels showing through the skin. Everyone but an albino has some degree of these color chemicals in his body, and albinos occur in every race."

Fifteen years later, in 1965, he wrote in his weekly

"Right or Wrong" column on page two of *Our Sunday Visitor*: "Catholics who discriminate against the colored cannot plead ignorance as an excuse. Apart from the many strong pronouncements by the hierarchy everywhere, Christ Himself made charity the supreme test of our sincerity: 'As long as you did it to the least of these, you did it to me.' Love is the greatest commandment, the true measure of our faith. It is by our love that we are to be recognized, and it is by our love that we are to be judged."

He quoted Archbishop Denis Hurley, O.M.I., of South Africa, who had recently declared that Christianity's greatest enemies are hypocrisy, short-sightedness, and moral cowardice. "Can we really reproach the Communist," asked the Archbishop, "when they enter the field of social reform left wide open for them by Christians, with a crusading zeal and sense of conquest that makes Christians look like flabby and ineffectual windbags, if not downright supporters of an evil system?"

The teachings of the Church are inspiring, wrote Father Dan, "but many of our practices are not. White Catholics often flee from their parishes and head for the suburbs when they spot Negroes on the horizon. The percentage of blacks in Catholic schools is extremely low. As areas become predominantly Negro, Catholic schools sometimes shut down. Yet here are mission fields that are ready-made, and ripe for the harvest. Often coming from unstable homes, the Negro children need Catholic schooling and are very deserving of it. The level of achievement with Negro children may not average out the same, but the progress is just as real, and even more important.

"Most of us do not realize the subtle effects of 'caste' in America which hinder the development of the Negro. We do not comprehend their cultural isolation, the disheartening treatment they receive, their being denied an outlet for anything more than bread-and-butter ambition. Nor are we aware of the injustice and frustration they encounter, and which tend to produce a withered and thwarted personality.

"Race prejudice is a heresy that denies the basic truths of our faith, the doctrine of the Mystical Body, the fact that we are all children of a common Father, mutually sharing in the redemption of Christ. Yet parishioners remark that they rarely hear a sermon on interracial justice.

"Much of prejudice is traditional. We are not aware of our false impressions about the Negro, impressions that we absorb as imperceptibly as the blood pulsing into our fingers. While the Church on the foreign missions has concerned itself with native problems by founding cooperatives and credit unions, we have failed to concern ourselves with the problems of the Negro here at home.

"The only way to testify to our beliefs is by our actions. The Church has often led reforms in the past, but in the field of racial justice we seem to be lagging far behind. Monsignor John Cooper of Catholic University declared that by our inaction in the face of unjust discrimination 'we are taking most deadly means to stifle whatever sympathy the non-Catholic Negro may still have for the Catholic Church. Perhaps there is yet time, but we shall have to act quickly.'

"Catholics have so adjusted to the society in which we live that we are in grave danger of being absorbed by it.

By 'not getting involved' we fail to stand up for what is right. For example, how did you feel about the civil rights bill, the most important bill of the century for minority groups? It represents an honest and a reasonable effort to extend to the Negro some of the rights to which he is entitled by the Constitution, rights that God intends for him to have. It is not an encroachment on anyone's rights, or even on states' rights. All it does is prevent certain states from denying human decency to our Negro brethren. Did you really care if they got their rights? If not, can you profess as a Christian to being either hot or cold? Aren't you just lukewarm?

"We cannot ignore the fight for the rights of all men, nor can we afford to be slackers or draft-dodgers in the struggle. The biggest barrier to the Negro is the wall of isolation surrounding him. We have to help him make a breach in it. We have to do whatever we reasonably can to help him progress.

"First of all, our own attitude has to be enlightened. To accomplish this we should try to get to know some Negroes. For some of us this will mean joining interracial groups, such as the Urban League or the N.A.A.C.P.; for some it will mean going out of your way to know Negroes personally, at work, at recreation, or in your own neighborhood; for some it will mean making friends with Negroes, inviting them to your home, and going to theirs. For some it will mean looking after a colored foster-child, realizing that no one is more homeless than a Negro or an Indian child who has been orphaned or abandoned, and that no child is dearer to Almighty God.

"For each person it may mean something different. But for all of us it means praying for the Negro, speaking well of him, and loving him with that same love with which Christ first loved us. This love of our neighbor was the great concern of Pope John, who urged us to 'expand the areas of love.'

"We all know that the Negro is discriminated against, and that barriers of custom and tradition keep many doors of opportunity closed to him. But in what does this discrimination consist, and where are these barriers in our own locality? We should: 1) be interested enough to find out; 2) help to see that they are eliminated.

"The hunger in the heart of the Negro is not for some heroic act on our part; it is not even for alms. His hunger is for everyday recognition of his human dignity. Negroes are still kept out of nicer neighborhoods and many of the more desirable clubs. Yet they are not prisoners of war, nor odd inhabitants from another planet. They are loyal Americans who have no allegiance to any other country. Their ancestors have been here twice as long as our own. They are our fellow citizens in peace as well as in war, our equals in Christ, our brothers under our very thin skin."

The decisive legal battles have been won, Dan Lyons pointed out nearly ten years ago. The majority of Americans, and the full force of federal law now favor civil rights for the Negro. He went on:

"The problem now is one of personal responsibility. The need today is not for people to go to Selma or somewhere else, but for people who will help motivate Negro youth, so that the forthcoming generation will be prepared for the opportunities opening up for them. We need groups of whites and Negroes who will meet for the common good of both. The first thing to integrate is the leadership.

"We especially need to stress personal responsibility, reform of the individual as the basis for reforming society. Personal integrity is the price of peace and interracial progress. Leaders who condone violence and preach contempt for the law are the enemy of the Negro, not his friend. The Negro must assume full responsibility for his actions, and so must the white man.

"It is not enough just to put the Negro on perpetual welfare. We hurt him as much as we help him with our welfare programs. Nor can we solve the problem merely by passing laws. Passing all our problems onto the government is the surest way to lose our freedom."

After living seven years in New York City, Father Lyons is painfully aware of the evil of putting people on welfare, particularly if they belong to a racial minority, rather than trying to provide jobs for them. "It alienates them from our whole society," he laments. "It makes them irresponsible, causing their homes and families to break up, when what they most need is to be taught responsibility." Politicians like Mayor John Lindsay, with their elaborate welfare programs, he asserted, "are merely buying votes, taking the easy way out."

Nor was Father Dan impressed with Martin Luther King's views on Vietnam. He felt Dr. King was either misinformed or deliberately following the Communist line: "I went to hear this famous Christian leader when he spoke at Riverside Church on April 4, 1967, in New York City. I was never more shocked in my life. He preached the straight Communist line. In elaborating on 'the madness of Vietnam,' Dr. King praised Ho Chi Minh as the only true leader of the Vietnamese people. He condemned the United States as 'the greatest purveyor of violence in the world today.' He called Ho Chi Minh an independent democratic leader, and condemned the late President Diem as 'one of the most vicious modern dictators.' We may have killed a million, mostly children, he said.

"I wondered where he dug up those strange statistics. He obviously crossed the line between responsible dissent and irresponsible divisiveness. Everyone wanted to see the war ended, but Dr. King's five-point proposal simply amounted to surrender. Of course we could have given up, but that would not have solved anything. It would merely lead to more and bigger wars, as did our peace treaty over Laos in 1962, when we trusted Ho Chi Minh and his promises.

"Dr. King praised the Viet Cong as 'the only party in real touch with the peasants.' He charged that 'none of the things we claim to be fighting for are really involved . . . We have no honorable intentions in Vietnam . . . Our minimal expectation is to occupy it as an American colony . . . We are on the side of the wealthy . . . Our war is against the people of Vietnam . . . We must all protest . . . only Marxism has the revolutionary spirit . . . If we are to get on the right side of the world revolution, we as a nation must undergo a radical revolution of values.'

"Dr. King condemned our defense of South Vietnam as a 'tragic attempt at re-colonization.' He urged that strong protests should be made about the governments of Guatemala and Peru, Thailand and Cambodia, Mozambique and South Africa. He urged that committees should be formed to cooperate with revolutionaries in those six countries. Anyone familiar with Communist designs knows that he could not have picked countries that the Communists are more anxious to take over."

Father Dan took up the subject of forced busing of school children when done entirely for purposes of integration. "A judge who rules that the quality of education in an entire school system should be made to suffer substantially for the purpose of racial integration," he pointed out, "is showing disdain for education himself.

"When a federal judge in Los Angeles ruled in 1970 that every school within that enormous district should have at least 10 percent blacks and never more than 60 percent, he was ignoring such problems as Spanish-speaking students who have Spanish-speaking teachers assigned to their schools.

"The judge was also ignoring the serious side-effects of keeping small children on buses for several hours every day during the Los Angeles rush hours. He was saying that areas like Watts and Harlem should have tens of thousands of white children bused into them in order to provide a very arbitrary percentage of racial mix.

"To what extent judicial rulings affect the learning process obviously does not matter to such judges. They are not qualified to know, and they make no attempt to find out. They do not consult the school boards, the teachers, the pupils or their parents.

"Should white children be bused into such areas as Watts or Harlem in order to have integrated schools in such areas? Should all the schools be closed in predominantly Negro areas like Washington, D.C.? Surely the consent of parents should be obtained before children are bused all over town. Parents and taxpayers who make the schools possible do not agree that the bureaucrats know best.

"To show how far we have strayed from a reasonable position, Chief Justice Burger assured the nation that 'the racial mixture of each school in a community does not necessarily have to be the same as the racial mixture of the community as a whole.' Gee, thanks! Anyone who thought it did should have his head examined.

"It is one thing to advocate integration for a city like Washington, D.C., which has been all but abandoned by our congressmen and other government officials, white and black. It is another thing to say you must bus 100,000 children from other areas into the city in order to have racially balanced schools.

"Since Washington is the only large city in the area, you would have to bus the children from 50 or 100 miles away. Our congressmen and judges will never allow that to happen to their children and grandchildren. Washington is the only city run by the federal bureaucracy. With its low level of schools and its high crime rate, no wonder the general population mistrusts our federal planners.

"The very fact that our judges feel free to order the destruction of our traditional neighborhood system by changing school districts completely, without either knowing or caring about the harmful effects involved, shows how far this nonsense has progressed.

"Why," asked Father Lyons, "should we put all the burden of this enormous social problem on the backs of little children? Why waste their time and risk their lives every day on the highways at rush hour? Why not spend the money on better classrooms, better texts and better teachers?

"Open housing and more integrated neighborhoods with neighborhood schools is a much more sensible solution. Perhaps we could start by requiring all of our federal officials to move back into Washington, D.C., whence they fled."

Father Lyons has little sympathy for those teachers who insist that children be allowed to speak incorrect English all their lives, as long as they are black. He has attacked *The New York Times, Newsweek,* and other publications, as well as the Washington, D.C., school district and other school systems for trying to perpetuate "Black English" when such students will be forever held back in the business and professional world for speaking and writing improperly.

When *The New York Times* reviewed a book by J. L. Dillard entitled, "Black English," Professor Toni Cade Bambara of Rutgers insisted that to say Black English is a deviant of English is "ignorant." Admitting it relates to pidgin English and to Creole, Bambara yet insists the teacher should not correct the child speaking it. "John run" is all right for "John runs," and "Is they gone there?" is fine for "Have they gone there?" as long as a black is talking, says Bambara. The question Father Lyons asks: "How far is a black student going to get in college with such poor English? Won't he be looked down on when he goes to Rutgers and elsewhere when he tries to write term papers?

"The real test," said Father Lyons, "is whether *Newsweek* and *The New York Times* will hire such a person to write for them. If not, aren't they being hypocritical when they condone such English? For teachers to condone and even encourage bad English because one's skin is black makes no more sense than to encourage bad grammar by any other immigrant or minority group."

The biggest mistake about the black problem, writes Father Lyons, is to think it can easily be solved. Yet since he first started working with the Negro, in 1942, much progress has been made. The percentage of the national income being received by blacks has increased from three percent to almost eight percent. Progress has been made, he insists. Progress *is* being made. But there are no quick solutions or fancy shortcuts.

Education and family stability, he claims, are still the key to progress. "If a family holds together and provides a better home life than its forebears, the children will be better. If the opposite is true, the children will have been set back. Even to appreciate one's schooling, there has to be interest and cooperation in the home. There is no other way."

To show how much progress has been made in the last 25 years, we are concluding this chapter with a talk given in May, 1947, by a Negro boy in Spokane, Washington.

The talk was given by John Hopkins, then a senior at Gonzaga Preparatory School, where Dan Lyons, then 27 and a Jesuit scholastic, was teaching.

Dan had coached John for debating and public speaking the year before, and Hopkins was now student body president at Gonzaga Prep. John was asked to address the downtown Kiwanis Club in Spokane, at the city's leading Davenport Hotel. John was a handsome boy, well mannered, and a fine speaker. But he was shy, and would have never chosen to speak on the Negro question.

As often happened, Dan Lyons' thinking was ahead of the times. He picked the subject for John: "What It Is Like To Be A Negro." Lyons also wrote the talk, word for word. Hopkins memorized it and gave it well, with his mentor, the young Jesuit, in the audience. The talk, which was received with much enthusiasm, has historical value, portraying conditions that were considerably different then, but at that time they were taken for granted. The talk follows:

"First of all, I wish to thank you for the invitation to come here and speak to you. I appreciate the opportunity, and consider it both a privilege and a pleasure. I only hope that I can find something to say which will interest you.

"Of all the people in this room, the least qualified to speak is myself. I wonder just exactly why I was asked. The fact that I happen to be the President of the Student Body at Gonzaga isn't reason enough. In the first place, I did not campaign for the job, and in the second place Student Body Presidents come and go almost with the frequency of leaves on the calendar, as the years roll by.

"Nor was I invited here because I happen to be valedictorian of my class. After all, there has to be one in every class, and it just happens this time to be me. Valedictorians, too, are rather numerous, over a period of years.

"I wondered just why I was invited down here. What possible reason was there for you to single me out? It must have been because I am a colored student body president and valedictorian.

"The second question in my mind was, just what could I say that would be of interest to you. On what subject would I dare address business and professional men. I, who have yet to commence my higher studies.

"Again things pointed to this puzzling question of color. Only in this field do I feel qualified. And only in this field am I confident that you are not qualified. You cannot understand the race problem. You do not know what it is like to be of my race. And I do. I have been colored for a long, long time. In fact, I have been colored for as long as I have been.

"You know, this so-called 'Negro problem' is not a Negro problem. It is a white problem: it exists in the white man's imagination. I am not going to speak to you of race hate. That is rare in our day, and only exists in the mind of the ignorant, anyway. Even in the Deep South, my people are seldom hated. We are the family servants, preparing the meals and dressing the children. We are hated only when we 'forget our place.' But our place is a menial one.

"But what about up North? There isn't any discrimination up North, and especially out West, is there? Well, let's face the facts. You have asked me to speak to you. Supposing I were to apply, later on, to join such an organization as this. Would I be allowed to, no matter how much I might have proven my qualifications? I doubt it very much. The odds would be 90 to 1 against me.

"I can't even get served in the cafeteria of this hotel. In fact, there is hardly a decent restaurant that will serve me. Roland Hayes, one of the greatest singers America has ever produced, came to Spokane several years ago. He had just been singing for the nobility in Europe, including a special program for the King and Queen of England, from all of whom he received magnificent applause.

"But out here in this little town of Spokane, the hotels felt he was not good enough for them. Finally this hotel, by way of exception, let him have some kind of a room, but he was forced to use the freight elevator going to and from. If this dinner today were held on a higher floor, I would have not been allowed to use the passenger elevator.

"I do not say these things with any tinge of bitterness or hatred. I will never lower myself to hate anyone. I am merely setting a problem before you—it is the problem of your race, since it was you who created it.

"For generations America has been ridiculed by the rest of the world because of her bungling of the race issue. That is why, today, we have not the confidence of other minorities throughout the world, and that is one big reason why the United Nations may never succeed, and more wars may come.

"Europe says of America in derision: 'The haughty American nation makes the Negro shine its shoes, and then condemns him for being a bootblack.' My people are forced to go to third class hotels, cafes, and dance halls, places where you do not dare to let your children go. No other places are open to us, yet you come by and condemn us for going there.

"What opportunities are open to me as a Negro? I cannot become a teacher, as no public school in town will let me cadet. I could not get a job as a clerk if I had an armload of college degrees. There are no opportunities in business for a colored boy. Should I enter the professions? I might. I could become a lawyer, like Paul Robeson did, but would probably find, like he did, that, again, no opportunity to practice my profession would be open.

"There are no superior races. We fought Hitler over that. But there are superior opportunities. My people constitute 10 percent of the population. Yet we receive only 3 percent of the national income.

"Why is it we are denied opportunity? It is not that we are lazy, for we do most of the hard work in this country. But the undesirable jobs and the lowest paying jobs are the only ones left open to us. It is amusing to hear a white person come home after an unusually hard day at work, and say: 'I worked like a Negro today.' Yet if you ask him about us, he will say we are lazy!

"It is not that we are not clean, for if that were true you would hardly have us cooking your meals and making your berths.

"It is not that we are more criminal. Here in Spokane, for example, we constitute one percent of the population, yet the police department has shown that we commit less than one percent of the crimes.

"It is not that we are ignorant, for every year hundreds of our people are graduating from such universities as Harvard, Fordham, Columbia, and Cornell. In the South, it is true, the Negroes are less educated. But you pay the Southern Negro too high a compliment if you expect him to learn in four or five months what the white children have trouble learning in nine. For every $1 spent per pupil up North, the South spends 13 cents per colored pupil.

"Lastly, it is not that we must be kept down for fear of intermarriage. We do not desire that any more than you do, and since marriage is a matter of choice between two individuals, it does not follow that by giving us opportunities to get jobs on the basis of ability, that this must happen.

"We are faced with two problems. No desirable jobs in business or the professions or government service are open to us. Secondly, most decent neighborhoods are closed to us. This, of course, is due mostly to unscrupulous real-estate men. If they can get us jammed into one section, our rents are raised. And if they can make you think your section is 'protected' from our moving in, then they charge you more, too. We are sometimes asked to look at a house for sale. Then the real estate man tells the neighbors that he may sell to us, and in this way he hopes to get the exorbitant price asked. This is an old game, and the white population is often victimized by it—victims of your own prejudice.

"It is not that we are bothersome. Or that we will not keep our yards up. In fact, we frequently find cause to com-

Benedict A. Howath

plain about the way our white neighbors neglect their yard. All of these objections are not the cause of prejudice. For we do not all have these faults. Yet we are all discriminated against.

"May, as you know, is the month when the Church pays special honor to Mary, the Mother of God. I have often thought of that scene in the cave at Bethlehem when the three wise men, one of them colored, came from the East to visit the Holy Family. They came in good faith, and Mary and Joseph welcomed them, regardless of race or color. Yet in America today, the color of a man's skin makes all the difference in the world, when it comes to getting a job or finding a house. Is white America better than Mary, the Mother of God? The poet has called her, 'Our tainted nature's solitary boast.'

"I do not want you to think that it is for myself I speak. Unlike the rest of my people, I will never have to seek employment, or a residence. For I have already been accepted to study for the priesthood in the Oregon Province of the Society of Jesus, the Jesuit Order—for 400 years the greatest educators in the world.

"But remember this: If you discriminate against my people because they are uncouth, they can become mannerly. If you ostracize them because they are unclean, they can cleanse themselves. If you segregate them because they lack knowledge, they can become educated—and they will. But if you discriminate against them because of their color, they can do nothing. God gave us our color."

CHAPTER 15

How He Saw the Struggle in Vietnam

In 1965, Father Dan and *Our Sunday Visitor* decided it was time he went back out to Vietnam again to check up on the fighting. It had been more than a year since he last visited the battle ground, and he looked forward to seeing it first-hand again. Not that the sight of war was something to anticipate, but as a journalist he felt compelled to return and learn whatever he could.

The trip, by commercial airline, was sponsored by the Department of Defense. Four writers were selected to go along: Ben Hartley, of the *Presbyterian Survey* magazine; David White, of the *Jewish Digest*; Calvin Thielman, chaplain at Montreat-Anderson College; and Dan, whose *Right or Wrong* column had been attracting a tremendous Catholic readership throughout America.

Leaving Honolulu they took the long hop to Guam, in the Mariana Islands, stepping across the International Date

Line and dropping a day off the calendar, to be mysteriously restored on their return. From Guam they flew to Manila, and then to Saigon. There were unfriendly people around the Saigon airport the last time Dan was there. The Viet Cong had a nasty habit of firing at foreign planes when they tried to land. Bullet holes in the fuselage were not a very nice reception. This time, however, the airport was guarded by U.S. Marines, who seemed to have things well in hand.

What Father Dan set out to do on this particular mission was tell the story of the war in terms of men who were fighting it. He wasn't going to deal with strategy, ideology or campaigns. He was just going to try to tell an ordinary reader back home what it might be like for some of the people involved in the fighting.

Little of Father's anguish at what he saw actually got into his newspaper columns. He wrote very personal copy, but he knew that few readers were interested in what was happening to him. They wanted to know what was happening to the soldiers and officers and civilians that he saw and spoke to.

Excerpts from his dispatches read like a diary:

> "Sept. 5: Saigon is different, even before you land. Your 707 makes an S turn or two as it approaches the airport from 8,000 feet, dropping down to the huge Tan Son Nhut airport at a very sharp angle. Your pilot may head for Bangkok when he notices groundfire, but otherwise you will land, with a little bit of luck . . . The fact that there is no front to the war is realized immediately. A hundred windows in the airport terminal are still broken from a suitcase bombing by

the Viet Cong . . . Col. Dean, the Chief of Chaplains, met our plane. He had just finished presiding at a memorial service for five American soldiers near the airport. . . . We landed just an hour after the office of the Saigon chief of police had been blown up. Six Vietnamese police officials were killed and 17 wounded. One American was injured slightly. This is not a war between Asians and white men, as the Communist would have you believe. It is a war of Communist aggression against a free country, pure and simple. When the Viet Cong bombed the *My Canh* restaurant, June 25, for example, the Viet Cong-Hanoi radio called it 'a great victory against U.S. aggressors,' but most of those killed were native women and children . . . Those who say that the war against the South is a nationalist movement overlook the fact that Ho Chi Minh got rid of all the nationalist leaders he possibly could . . .

"Sept. 12: We flew to the *U.S.S. Midway*, in the South China Sea. From its deck 100 planes attack Communist fortifications in the Mekong Delta around the clock, day after day after day. The 3,500 men on the crew work 12-hour shifts seven days a week, mostly unloading and loading ammunition. Confidence proceeds from strength, and as we left the carrier I said to the Commanding Officer: 'We're going to win this war, Captain O'Brien!' And he said: 'You know it, Father.' . . . I talked to General Westmoreland about many things while having dinner with him. Before leaving I asked him for a statement to pass on to Americans. This what he wanted me to convey: 'Our G.I.'s here are demonstrating resourcefulness, ingenuity, and courage in the great American tradition, and I could not be more proud than to be in command of them. They are completely the opposite of the gutlessness of many of America's pseudo-intellectuals.' . . .

"Numbers of soldiers complained about the slanted teach-ins held at various colleges back home. My traveling companion, the Rev. Calvin Theilman, of Montreat, North Carolina, asked some soldiers what they thought about the demonstrations for peace back in the U.S. A soldier who had been shot at from all sides spoke up: 'I wish those peace marchers would come over here and march from Saigon to Hanoi. I'd like to see how much peace they have left in them by the time they get there.'

"The number of refugees grows daily. In the past, they've largely been Catholic, driven out by the Viet Cong, who know they cannot trust them. American soldiers soon learn that they are safer in Catholic villages, as the Catholics will not tolerate the Viet Cong. In the Catholic villages, when you ask how far it is to a certain place they will say: 'Seven rosaries.' . . . When you see a Vietnamese refugee woman wiping her tears on her sleeve, having lost everything she owned in the shuffle; when you visit the hospitals and see the sick lying two to a bed, suffering horribly from the ravages of war, you realize that these are human beings with minds as keen and hearts as tender as our own . . .

"Sept. 19: One of the saddest things in Vietnam is the fact that over 200 persons have been arrested since the death of Diem two years ago and never have been given a trial. Most of them are former Catholic leaders. Typical was the unjust arrest of Ma Tuyen, a highly-respected Chinese merchant. His only offense was that he let Diem stay in his home the night before he was assassinated. The man who sees that these people are given a trial will have done a great deal. They languor in a very primitive Vietnamese prison, while American officials and even the American press ignore them. The

> U.S. government is sometimes accused of undue interference, but if we are going to concern ourselves with anything in Vietnam, it should be over the basic right to a trial for these unfortunate people. As long as anyone in the free world can be imprisoned without trial, the free world is that much less free . . ."

Father Dan dealt in issues the way some correspondents covering the war dealt in emotions. They were the stuff of his writing, and his weekly columns gained or lost an audience by how well he reported the facts and how well his readers could identify with his personal observations.

He had a particular aptitude, though, for "getting under the rug" and ferreting out exclusives. For example, in his September 19th dispatch, he wrote: "Since arriving in Taiwan a week ago I have been given a series of briefings on the military and political situation in the Orient. The Republic of China keeps undercover agents in Hanoi and in various places on the mainland. She even has spies who are prominent government officials in Peking. Recent documents from Red China reveal how much unrest there is in that unhappy country. An estimated 40 million people currently work in slave labor camps. The police can sentence anyone to work in labor camps, and they are used primarily for production. Red China's basic policy is to oppose the United States, and she fights us on our home front whenever she can. Since August 8, 1963, Mao Tse-tung has officially backed the Negro dispute in the U.S., considering it a form of 'class war.' Abroad, the Chinese Communists are not only fighting the U.S. in South Vietnam, they continually cook up trouble in such places as

Thailand, Korea, Singapore, Cuba, Africa and Indonesia."

Upon his return home from the war, Father Dan devoted much of the space in his column to exposing and opposing what he knew was a firmly-established Communist movement in America. On October 10th, he warned his readers: "The Cold War is an integral part of the fighting in Southeast Asia, except that the Cold War is conducted *inside* the United States. The only hope the enemy has of winning in Vietnam is through propaganda here at home."

Father Dan's tireless investigation revealed that the Communist plot was highly organized. He told his readers of the countless groups that had been set up by the Communists to help win the Cold War. He named names: The Student Peace Union, the Committee for Nonviolent Action, the Students for a Democratic Society, the Fellowship of Reconciliation, the Women's International League for Peace, the War Resisters League, the National Committee for a Sane Nuclear Policy, the Committee on Racial Equality, the Student Non-Violent Coordinating Committee, and the Catholic Workers.

"America's colleges will be the focal point of the Cold War," he wrote. "The procedure used at Berkeley last year (1964) is to serve as a model for other campuses. Elaborate plans were made during the Summer by Berkeley's *Vietnam Day Committee* to instigate widespread acts of violence and civil disobedience against America's defense of South Vietnam. October 15-16 have been designated as 'international days of protest.' The Communists realize that they can win in Southeast Asia only by getting America to give up. They brag at cell meetings how they shook up the governor of California by their Berkeley riots. They maintain that they can get President Johnson to withdraw from Vietnam by fomenting 20 Berkeleys around the country. Their success depends on how many Americans they can get to cooperate with them unwittingly."

To thwart the rising Communist menace in America, Father Dan gathered together some of the leading experts on Asia and formed the *Asian Speakers Bureau.* Their purpose was to spread the truth about Southeast Asia. The ASB, still very active today, is affiliated with the Free Pacific Association, headed by the Most Rev. Paul Yu Pin, the exiled Archbishop of Nanking. At the time, Archbishop Yu Pin held the distinction of being No. 1 on the list of "Catholic criminals" issued by Red China. He is Rector of Fu Jen Catholic University in Taipei. Another member of the *Asian Speakers Bureau* was Father Raymond de Jaegher, who, like Archbishop Yu Pin, also ranked high on Red China's Most Wanted Criminal list. Few, if any, knew more about Vietnam than he.

Writing in his column about the *Asian Speakers Bureau,* Father Dan explained its mission: "Ten years ago Archbishop Paul Yu Pin started the Free Pacific Association in Taiwan. Since then it has spread to several different countries and done wonderful work in the cause of freedom. The Archbishop, its international President, has asked me to serve as its Secretary General for the United States. Our program is fourfold: (1) an *Asian Speakers Bureau*; (2) an Asian Research Institute; (3) a Free Pacific magazine; and (4) a Pacific News Service. Dr. Stephen Pan and I will be available as speakers throughout the year, as will Dr.

Anthony Bouscaren, Dr. Anthony Kubek, General Thomas Lane, and Miss Juanita Castro, who helped her brother, Fidel, rise to power, but turned against him after realizing that he had sold out the Cuban people to international Communism."

Father Raymond de Jaegher, a Belgian, was also available, through the cooperation of Archbishop Stanislas Lokuang in Taipei. From 1954-1964, Father de Jaegher had rendered extremely valuable service to the late President Diem. His command of languages, his long experience with the Communists in China, plus his knowledge of the people and the problems of Vietnam, were so unique that Diem conferred with him for one or two hours daily during his nine years in the presidency. Diem also used him as his interpreter with the half million Chinese in Saigon, whom Father often befriended.

Other lecturers belonging to the *Asian Speakers Bureau* included Senator Thomas J. Dodd; Dr. Stefan T. Possony, the scholarly Director of International Studies on War, Revolution, and Peace at the Hoover Institution at Stanford; Dr. Robert Morris, the president of the University at Plano and former chief counsel for the Senate Internal Security Sub-committee; Brig.-Gen. Clyde Watts (Ret.), veteran of the China-Burma-India theater; and the Rev. John W. Clifford, S.J., who had lived in Asia for 20 years.

On November 28th, Dan wrote a column titled "Why We Are in Vietnam." It appropriately appeared on the day set aside by Presidential proclamation as "a day of prayer and dedication for all those fighting for freedom in Vietnam." Dan pointed out that in 1964 he wrote a book entitled "Accepting Defeat in Viet Nam" in which he pinpointed the dangerous course American had been taking. "Had we continued on that road," he wrote, "we would have suffered the worst defeat in our entire history. Pearl Harbor was just a single blow, but Vietnam represents a massive challenge of the Communist world against the free. All the world is watching. Had we failed to meet that challenge, or if we yet should fail, the United States will have started on her permanent decline as the leader of the free world. In both World Wars, America resisted aggression by defeating the aggressor nations. Our goal in Vietnam is more restrained. We simply intend to make the Communist forces of Ho Chi Minh cease their savage aggression against the South. . . "

Dan wrapped up America's problems in 1965 in one paragraph. He said it all in 82 words. In his December 19th column, he told his more than a million subscribers: "If the world seems topsy-turvy, it is not the fault of its Maker. The globe is spinning along, right on schedule. If time seems 'out of joint,' as Hamlet said, it is because of our inconsistencies. If life seems more of a paradox than a paradise, perhaps it is because we are weak on basic principles. The world is a wonderland, and life could be so wonderful. Perhaps we need to think things over with the fresh simplicity of little Alice. . . ."

It was a softer Father Lyons talking in "Right or Wrong," January 2nd, 1966. He started out the New Year with a message on the true meaning of prayer. He wrote, in part: "In order to pray well we remind ourselves that God is all about us, that God is 'nearer than the door.' We think of the presence of God, how everything in nature reminds us of Him, how He marks each flower as His own, how He paints the heavens daily and many times a day, lest we tire of them. We remind ourselves how He even puts His rainbow across the sky to tell us that all storms have an ending. The whole creation is a book written by the Finger of God, telling the story of His infinite love. The people we see, the love in children's eyes, the strains of mighty music, the birds and the trees, the clap of thunder, the roar of the ocean surf, all these are the Hand of God, outstretched to greet us. By seeing God in creation we can pray to Him more often. Prayer is the answer to 90 per cent of our difficulties. And humility is the key to prayer. In the words of the Publican: 'Lord, be merciful to me, a sinner.' "

The war in Vietnam, meanwhile, raged on. Father Dan, Dr. Stephen Pan, and Father Raymond de Jaegher kept up the fight. The three of them continued lecturing throughout the United States and Canada. They each averaged about 30 talks a month, including radio and television. They traveled more than 100,000 miles apiece in six months.

On February 15-16, they testified at special Congressional hearings in Washington, D.C., held by the House Committee on Foreign Affairs. Maj.-Gen. Thomas A. Lane (Ret.) and Dr. Stefan Possony also appeared. They each presented about 20 pages of testimony, then remained for questions.

"The fact that the House Committee on Foreign Affairs had sought us out and asked for our testimony made us feel that God had blessed the efforts of our little speakers' bureau," Dan told me.

In testifying before the Committee, Dan pointed out that America's policy in Vietnam was basically correct. It was not only justifiable, he told them, but morally commendable. "Our policy is a combination of Christian charity and enlightened self-defense," he testified. "We failed in the past to apply the Truman Doctrine to Asia, except for South Korea. That failure led to our problems here today."

Father de Jaegher testified at the hearings with Father Lyons. Five members of the Foreign Affairs Committee were on hand to question them, headed by Wisconsin's Clement J. Zablocki, Chairman of the subcommittee on the Far East and the Pacific. The others were Edward R. Roybal, California; Frances P. Bolton, Ohio; William S. Broomfield, Michigan; and Vernon W. Thomson, Wisconsin.

Following the testimony of Frs. Lyons and de Jaegher, here is the dialogue verbatim, February 15, 1966:

> Mr. ZABLOCKI. Thank you, gentlemen.
>
> Father Lyons, in your opening remarks you stated that you were sent to Vietnam last year by the Defense Department. Would you please describe more fully the capacity in which you were sent to Vietnam?
>
> Father LYONS. I was sent by the Defense Department as a journalist to South Vietnam. I was selected as one of four journalists to go to South Vietnam last August. I am in no sense employed by the Defense Department or a spokesman for them. I merely meant to say that I was sent to Vietnam by them.
>
> Mr. ZABLOCKI. Was that a part of the information program?

Father LYONS. Yes.

Mr. ZABLOCKI. Then during this period you were in no way employed as a spokesman for or defender of U.S. policy under the auspices of the Defense Department?

Father LYONS. No; in no way.

Mr. ZABLOCKI. The subcommittee operates under the 5-minute rule. Each member is permitted 5 minutes to ask questions. After all members present have had an opportunity to ask questions, they will be permitted additional questions so long as time permits.

I would like to ask Reverend de Jaegher if he would care to amplify on a statement he made concerning our involvement in the change of government in Vietnam in 1963. Though I realize this is a China hearing, you referred to it in your statement, and I wonder if you would elaborate on it.

Father DE JAEGHER. What would you like?

Mr. ZABLOCKI. To what extent do you think our Government was involved?

Father DE JAEGHER. I think, Mr. Chairman, from what I know, that certainly the Government was implicated in one way. I think the Buddhist question divided the U.S. Government in two groups. One group was for President Diem and one group opposed to him, and from what I heard from the Vietnamese generals, they were called by the Ambassador and were given the green light to start the coup, and the generals had a meeting then, the Vietnamese generals, because these generals did not dare to act, and they decided to postpone. Then the U.S. aid was cut to Vietnam, and later on the generals thought without American aid they could not win, then they began to study the possibility of a coup because they said, "If the United States doesn't back President Diem any more, for our own survival we must act with the U.S. aid," so they started after that slowly to study the possibility of a coup, and they had meetings together, and they made a secret report.

I saw myself that secret report which was shown to me by General Dinh, the general who made the coup, the actual general commanding the coup. He was a very good friend, and he was called the pillar of the regime.

He came to see the President and read that memorandum or gave that report to President Diem, a secret memorandum in Vietnamese . . .

MR. ZABLOCKI. Reverend de Jaegher, you say that not all of the Chinese on the mainland are Communists. Do you see in the foreseeable future any possibility that the Communist regime may change; that it will soften its militant attitude and change its international policies?

Father DE JAEGHER. I think the actual Chinese Red government is still led by diehard Communists who were from the start Communists from the first clique. I don't believe that they will change, and Mao Tse-tung and all the group working with him are getting older, but still they are controlling all China now, and they are very, very strong Communists. They will not change.

But it is possible later on—slowly their successors could change. The younger generation has a great desire for freedom, and so many people escape to Hong Kong; young people. Once I interviewed many of the 20,000 young Chinese from 18 to 20 years old, students who escaped to Hong Kong. I asked, "Why did you come out?" And they said they had never lived under Chiang Kai-shek except as little children, but they said, "We have been indoctrinated all the time, we are all the time hearing the same Communist doctrine—they speak only about communism, and they say the free world is such a dangerous world, the imperialistic world." They wanted to know something other than communism, and they had a desire for freedom, so they came out when they had the chance.

These people said that most of the people have a great desire for freedom, and they don't believe that communism alone can give a solution.

Mr. ZABLOCKI. They have the inborn desire to be free.

Father DE JAEGHER. Yes.

Mr. ZABLOCKI. You do have hope that China may change its attitude?

Father DE JAEGHER. Sure.

MR. ZABLOCKI. Reverend Lyons, in your statement you indicate that you oppose negotiations. Do you oppose all negotiations?

Father LYONS. No, I only mentioned that I oppose any kind of negotiation with the Vietcong. Any war should end up with negotiations, but the negotiation must be based on the fact that the other side is willing to admit defeat. Defeat in this case means to stop aggression. When we go around pleading with them to talk to us, I think that is not effective at all, and this will not bring about their admission that they have to give up.

The only thing to negotiate is for them to get out and stay out. There is nothing else to discuss, and I make it very clear that it would be extremely hazardous to recognize the Vietcong as a separate entity. I am not against negotiation, no, but I say that we can't negotiate for another country. We have done it, but we should not do it.

We are not the Government of South Vietnam. We have no right to say we will negotiate.

Mr. ZABLOCKI. Considering the amount of military equipment, manpower, and other assistance the United States is rendering don't you believe we should have some voice?

Father LYONS. Yes, we should have much voice, of course, but when we say "we" without even taking them in, when we say "we," we don't mean South Vietnam and ourselves, we mean we, the United States, will negotiate. This is the impression. We never say we will try to get South Vietnam to listen to this. We don't even consult them. This is our mistake.

Mr. ZABLOCKI. Mr. Broomfield.

Mr. BROOMFIELD. Reverend Lyons, I would like to ask you what steps would you take to prevent so-called allies from shipping into North Vietnam? I think this is a basic problem. As you know, the French and Canada are shipping into China as well as to North Vietnam.

What steps do you think our Government should take?

Father LYONS. I would certainly consult with the military before making a decision, because you have several choices, e.g., doing like we did against Japan in Haiphong in 1943. We know from experience this will work, and the U.S. Navy told me all this, some of them were around at that time, and they said it was the simplest thing in the world. The harbor entrance is so narrow we simply sank three ships, and the Japanese could not use it for the rest of the war. It was very effective.

That would be No. 1. Another would be to put mines in there, but perhaps the first step would be to ask our NATO allies for a little cooperation. We haven't even had the courage to do that. I say if we expect our young men to have courage to go over there every day—and believe me, I have been on those roads where you get shot at all the time—if we expect our young men at 18 to have that courage, they have the right to expect our Government to have courage to talk turkey to Britain and France.

Senator Dodd came out with an excellent suggestion last week. He said we should buy up the wheat, if necessary, that Canada sells to Iron Curtain countries, buy it all up and tell them they can't have it as long as they are attacking the free world. That is tough.

We have never even complained to Britain about her trading with the north, and it is about time we did. Why did we agree to put an embargo on Rhodesia, and yet we never even said to the British, "In exchange for that, how about you doing something with our enemy?" And people ask me about this all over the country.

Why hasn't the administration the courage to tell the British to cut it out? I think we have to have courage. Fighting a war takes courage. General von Clausewitz, one of the greatest military authorities, said:

"Fighting a war is simple, but not easy. It is simple to know what to do, but it is not easy to do it because it takes courage."

In some respects we have not shown the courage we should show.

Mr. BROOMFIELD. I know—and certainly support your views that this is a South Vietnamese war, and I am sure you are acquainted with the amount of troops the South Vietnamese have there and certainly with the intensified action that our Government is likely to take, we are going to be approaching pretty much a comparable level with the South Vietnamese.

Do you feel there is a danger there of overcommitment in South Vietnam by the American forces, and could this become an American war rather than a South Vietnamese war?

Father LYONS. I think we are relying too much on ground troops. We had the idea—a year ago, that if we sent a lot of troops, China would, also. Many people said that.

We have gotten over that fear. We have sent 200,-000. We talk about sending another 200,000. Somehow we have the idea that now China will let us send troops, but China won't let us bomb the harbor. I think this is the same type of fear. We are afraid to let the Air Force use some of its power.

Mr. BROOMFIELD. You feel that it would be important or necessary to actually use air support. You can't win a war, a ground action war, solely on mainland China?

Father LYONS. I mean we should not grant sanctuary to everything up north that is worth hitting.

Mr. BROOMFIELD. In other words, you don't favor any sanctuaries in the north?

Father LYONS. I think we should adopt a policy of gradually winning the war by hitting the necessary targets.

Mr. BROOMFIELD. With respect to the 1954 Geneva Conference, do you support one Vietnam or two Vietnams?

Father LYONS. I support two Vietnams until there is some way to keep the south from going Communist. I support two Germanies if it means that by unification East Germany would take over the west. I support keeping a country free, rather than having it taken over.

Mr. BROOMFIELD. The Geneva accords spelled out in 1954 that there would be free elections. This was a sticky point in 1956 when they decided not to have the elections.

Father LYONS. But the key word is "free," and the Communists must have a free press, freedom of speech, all these types of freedoms in order to have a free election. They have never had an election in the north, even for themselves—and the key word is "free."

President Diem wrote to President Kennedy in 1956:

We are perfectly willing to have a free election, but they don't know what the meaning of the word "free" is.

First of all, South Vietnam never agreed to have this election. This is something the French agreed to for them. Unquestionably the north would win. The north has 3 million more people than the south, and the Communists always have enormous advantages in an election. They always win by 99 percent—even Stalin did.

Mr. BROOMFIELD. In all your travels and the debates you have had around the country, I am delighted, of course, to see somebody of your ability taking these assignments, because certainly the American people are confused, and a lot of the students in the universities and colleges are dissenting with our present policy.

I wonder if you would comment on the question I often hear of why other Asian countries are not participating more in South Vietnam. We are all delighted to see what Korea is doing, which is a substantial amount for a country as small as Korea, 20,000 men, but I think the total allied forces outside the United States is probably less than 30,000. How do you answer the argument that we ought to have more Asians assisting in the ground action, rather than relying so heavily on U.S. forces?

Father LYONS. Well, the answer is not easy, except Japan, which is the largest country in Asia—we ourselves have forbidden Japan to build up any forces. We still don't seem to realize Communism is our threat.

Japan is not a threat, but we forbid them to build up.

When Formosa offers three divisions, again it is our administration that decided, "Well, China wouldn't like it." This is the policy of fear. We would not let Formosa join SEATO because we thought Red China wouldn't like it, and Red China responded by saying, "SEATO is nothing. Even Formosa does not belong."

It is that policy of weakness where they push us around. We are a great power, a great country, and should not base our policy on that weakness. We should let South Vietnam take troops from Formosa. There are as many troops there as in South Vietnam and North Vietnam, 600,000, that we equipped and trained.

These are not oldtimers, they are young men. All that we have to do basically is convince the north that we are going to win that war, but they still think that we are going to hold back, because we did in Korea.

Mr. BROOMFIELD. In listening to your statement, Reverend Lyons, I get the impression very clearly in fact that you don't feel that there is any flashpoint as far as North Vietnam is concerned where the Red Chinese would bring in ground forces.

Father LYONS. Well, I think this can't be our overriding policy, that if we are afraid to win we have no right to be there, that we have to take the risk. Either we are going to win that war, or we are not going to win that war, but if we say it is bad to win this year, will we be able to say it is not bad next year?

I think that China will be strong in 5 years, and I think that we could not fight two or three wars like this at the same time, sending a hundred shiploads a month of material and men to each place. A city like Washington, D.C., has had to send about 1,200 boys to

Vietnam. We can't do that again and again simultaneously all over the world, and therefore the war can't go on and on.

If we are going to lead the free world, we have to defend this country with dispatch—reasonable dispatch. I don't mean we have to win in 1 month, but we should have a policy of winning.

We read in the press today that the administration says it is neither going to escalate nor pull out. In other words, we are not going to win.

But then we say "Send more troops." That is escalating, but we are afraid somehow that there is something magic against using our airpower, yet that is where we have superiority.

Mr. BROOMFIELD. The other area I would be concerned about is public support in the United States, and certainly I question how long you can keep the maximum public support with a theory of just merely a status quo policy.

I want to compliment you both on your very fine statements this morning.

Mr. ZABLOCKI. Mr. Thomson.

Mr. THOMSON. Thank you, Mr. Chairman. I would like to ask the panel what information they can give us about the formation of other so-called Liberation Fronts aimed at any other southeast Asian peoples. Can you tell us if there are fronts being formed, where they are being formed?

Father DE JAEGHER. I think, Mr. Thomson, there is a front starting already in Laos. They have started already to take over all of Laos. Two-thirds of Laos are already under Communism, and they have started already in north Thailand, where they have a liberation front.

MR. THOMSON: You talk about infiltration. Is it

coming just from Laos, or is it coming from Hanoi?

Father DE JAEGHER. It is coming from Hanoi. In Thailand, we have about 30,000 Vietnamese refugees who came from Hanoi before, very strongly pro-Ho Chi Minh, so they have the basis for infiltration and they are working that way.

Certainly Communism does a slow infiltration in the same way they did in China, a nucleus of a Liberation Front, a liberation army, slowly they expand the zone, and then create a new zone and then unite the two zones together and slowly take over the countryside, isolating the city, and then the city people are angry and they create among the city people a discontent, saying, "the government is bad; we have no food."

Mr. THOMSON. You think there is, then, some validity to the so-called domino theory that seems to be basic in our foreign policy?

Father DE JAEGHER. Certainly the Communists want to dominate.

Mr. THOMSON. The domino theory where when one country falls to Communism—

Father DE JAEGHER. If Vietnam falls, immediately we would have Thailand to defend, immediately, so people who advocate peace in Vietnam say let's pull out of Vietnam to have peace, would have war immediately in Thailand and on a much more difficult position, because the Thai are not as good soldiers as the Vietnamese. The Vietnamese fought for 20 years. I saw that myself, I went on the battlefront very often and saw the fighting myself, and they are really good little soldiers, the Vietnamese. I like them. I saw them fight.

Asian Communists are certainly much more aggressive than the Communists in Europe or the United States, because they are backed by a military force and that is the great difference. It was the military behind the party who controlled China and will control southeast Asia. The people of Asia want freedom, but it is the army who takes and controls, and I have seen that myself when I was in north China since 1937.

That is why, you know, I am so strongly against Communism, because I have seen how despaired the people were under Communism and the desire for freedom of these people. When you have lived 35 years in Asia like myself, you have a love for the people of those countries, and I would like these people to enjoy the freedom that the United States has now.

We know the aggressiveness and the danger of Communism, really, from experience.

Mr. ZABLOCKI. Mr. Roybal.

Mr. ROYBAL. Mr. Chairman, as you know, I am not a member of this subcommittee, but I am very much interested in our policy toward Asia, and I thank you for the opportunity of being present.

Reverend de Jaegher, I was interested in the remark you made to the effect that the people of North Vietnam are happy that we are bombing.

Father DE JAEGHER. Yes.

Mr. ROYBAL. Would they be even happier if we were to bomb the ammunition manufacturing plants in heavily populated areas in North Vietnam?

Father DE JAEGHER. I think all the people who have lived under Communism would be perfectly happy to be bombed to be free. I remember when I was in China during the war, we saw the allies' planes bomb China, and all the Chinese came out and applauded the planes openly, and mostly the Chinese were killed, and very few Japanese were killed.

Still the people seeing the planes, saw the symbol of freedom. I think in North Vietnam it is the same. The people will suffer, and they realize that, but they accept the suffering for the freedom that will come for them or for their children.

I think most of the people who have lived under the Communists—I believe the North Vietnamese are much more strongly against Communism than we are in the United States, or even in South Vietnam.

MR. ROYBAL. It is your opinion, then, if bombing were to take place, followed by troops, that the end result would be that the people then would join us?

Father DE JAEGHER. The people would join if they know that we go for the victory. This would not be just a commando unit—we would stay for the victory. Then they would certainly join. Most of the people would be very happy. They will not dare on a small action to engage themselves because it is too dangerous under the Communists, but if they know we are there, this time in a landing for victory, the people would join certainly and would back it.

Mr. ROYBAL. Do you think that if this were to take place, that Red China then would actively come into the war?

Father DE JAEGHER. No, because Red China would be so afraid to be bombed by the United States. Red China is now preparing her atomic industry, and they know very well that the United States would immediately retaliate by bombing, like President Johnson said, in case of Red Chinese aggression in Vietnam he would bomb mainland China, and we must not forget that the United States has all these allies, like the South Koreans, the free Chinese, and they could wage a war on three fronts.

The Chinese Communists could not last long in a war on three fronts, and the people immediately would work for us, that is assured. I don't believe that Red China would come in. Red China will speak very loudly and she will indirectly send arms and ammunition and maybe people under Vietnamese uniforms—that is possible—but they will not engage themselves entirely because that would be too dangerous for Red China.

Mr. ROYBAL. May I ask a question then of Reverend Lyons? You stated that our present policy contains the following dangerous errors in varying degrees: Fear of China, you said, dominates all of our other policies. The use of Formosan troops, for example, in the bombing area.

Are you advocating then that we use Formosan troops to invade the mainland of China, or are you advocating Formosan troops be used in Vietnam?

Father LYONS. I mean to use them in the same way we used Korean troops. I think psychologically it would be very destructive to the enemy if we had a policy where we took 30,000 troops a month from Formosa. This would be one more nail in the coffin of the aggressor.

I think psychologically this would be devastating. People do say the Vietnamese are against the Chinese, but there are 500,000 Chinese in Vietnam. I meant it only as another ally, and also making it less of a white man's war, more of an Asian war, and so on.

Mr. ROYBAL. You said this war would be settled on the basis of justice. Would you elaborate on that, telling us exactly what it is you mean by justice—justice to whom, and how do you propose we go about it?

Father LYONS. Since World War II, we have not had a policy of defeating our enemy. We have had a policy of driving him back into his own country, and there are pros and cons on this, but under the present circumstances there is no use advocating troop attacks on North Vietnam because I don't think you would get the support of either the Government or the people, who are not geared to that.

Realistically the only thing we can advocate is another Korea, but we have to realize there are great dangers here because it is not a peninsula. We have to be sure we are not relying on some little international control commission and say this little commisison is going to decide whether or not there is any aggression.

We have to have real security when we sign a treaty that they will not attack the south.

By justice, I merely mean that South Vietnam be allowed to live like South Korea lives. To work that out is not easy, but this is what I mean by justice.

Mr. ROYBAL. Do you base it then on some of the points agreed upon in the Geneva Conference of 1954?

Father LYONS. The main point is certainly very just. North Vietnam agreed to leave South Vietnam alone, and that alone would insure justice, if there were no indirect aggression.

Mr. ROYBAL. It was also agreed there would be self-determination, that elections would be held and eventually both would be united. Would you agree with that?

Father LYONS. I would agree with the understanding that until the north changed its policy a great deal, you could not have a free election. In other words, in order to have the conditions that are requisite for a free election in the north, you would no longer have the Communist system, and then it wouldn't matter who won the election.

Mr. ROYBAL. I see that you have disagreed to some extent with the peace offensive of the State Department and the President.

Father LYONS. Well, I think—did I interrupt you?

Mr. ROYBAL. You did, but go ahead.

Father LYONS. I think the peace offensive was largely to quiet critics at home and abroad. I don't think it was conducted like a peace offensive. I don't think we should start a peace offensive without South Vietnam, and so on.

I think it is very difficult for the President's critics—and I am favorably inclined toward this—to say why doesn't he negotiate, why doesn't he turn it over to the United Nations? The answer is he did, and this helps for unity and it helps people abroad who have been very critical without reason, and this is good.

It made us be more realistic. I am not a critic of the peace offensive, but I do say we have to be careful not to just dominate the whole thing and not even recognize the Government of South Vietnam.

Mr. ROYBAL. Thank you.

Father DE JAEGHER. Mr. Chairman, if I may say one word about the Geneva agreement, President Diem each year proposed that there should be free elections in Vietnam under the United Nations, on both sides, but the Communists would never accept free elections in North Vietnam under the United Nations. That is why President Diem said he didn't sign the agreement, but he would accept free elections for a united Vietnam if the election would be really free.

This means under the supervision of the United Nations giving free choice to the people. He said if the election would not be free, then North Vietnam would win a unified Vietnam without a chance for the south.

Mr. ZABLOCKI. Mrs. Bolton.

Mrs. BOLTON. Thank you very much, Mr. Chairman. I have listened here with a great deal of, I find, inner excitement. Both you gentlemen wear the cloth, and you come here with more vivid understanding than any others that I have heard.

Of course your studies have been of human beings. You know how human beings react, and I dare say, although we too feel their mind is strange to us, perhaps it is more like us than we realize because we are all children of the same Father.

I can't tell you how deeply I appreciate every word that has been said. You, Reverend de Jaegher, have your own way of saying it, and Reverend Lyons has his way. I can't tell you, Reverend Lyons, how happy I am to know that you are going in and out, around and about, saying what you feel and saying what you believe. I am thoroughly with you in that belief. I think it is what this country needs to hear.

We have had no policy of winning. I think it was General MacArthur who said there was no substitute for victory, but we have apparently been trying to build one out of some pretty soft material, and of course it doesn't hang together.

I couldn't help thinking at one point in the testimony of Jesus in the temple in Jerusalem when He used a whip to get rid of those who had no business there.

It seems to me unless this country will do something of that kind in the world, we have no business to be there. If we have assumed the responsibilities of freedom, we had better be responsible, we had better have a policy, and we had better make every attempt to carry it out.

I think that the trouble of our country is that some people complain we are not backing the administration, but what do we have to back? I am backing the President, yes, when he issues an order. But some of me is heavyhearted because I do not see any more clearly than you do, Reverend Lyons, that we have any real determination, any real policy.

I have never been able to understand how people in government—and this goes back quite a way—could believe that a Communist was anything but a Communist, with the complete and unwavering determination to rule the world.

We called them agriculturists back in China in the early days and let the dust settle, which to me was an absolutely criminal action. What have we done to the world? What have we done in Cuba, 90 miles from our own shores?

We never got any real satisfaction in the matter of the removal of missiles. I wanted to see the inside of those boxes that were supposed to take them out to sea. Just the shape of the outside of the box meant nothing to me. I don't like halfway measures.

I think we have been weakminded and weakhanded in everything we have done to fight Communism, which is the greatest enemy that humanity has ever had. I really have no questions, but I just wanted to express myself. I have been sitting here all this time waiting to tell you how grateful I am to you both.

Mr. ZABLOCKI. Thank you, Mrs. Bolton.

My final questions are not to be interpreted as being ungrateful, but I do believe in our attempts to assist others we must use discretion, and just because countries do not agree with us does not mean we must use force to transplant our democracies on other shores, for it will never work.

One of the most difficult problems the United States faces is getting across its story to the people in these countries with which we have problems but no contact. During these hearings many of our witnesses have advocated increased contacts; that is, cultural exchanges allowing doctors, scholars, and newsmen to exchange visits and increased trade.

Would the panelists describe in what way they believe we might increase our dialog with Communist China and the other countries in Asia, thereby leading to a better understanding and enhancing the possibility of peace?

Father LYONS. I would say first that we should not feel that we have dialog with the people when we deal with a tyrant regime. The Communist government does not really speak for the people, and our tendency is to give aid, and so on, to the government, and it may not reach the people.

For example, when we have given aid to Iron Curtain countries, we should have been firm about it, insisting that the people know where this is coming from.

Mr. ZABLOCKI. Let's use a specific example. During the drought in the early 1960's, China had a severe shortage of food grains and cereals. Do you believe that it would have been advantageous for the United States to send wheat on a grant basis—under supervision of course—to Red China?

Father LYONS. Well, it is a complicated question to which I don't feel I have all the answers. If we do give help to a people under a tyrannical form of government, we should try to do it in such a way that the people are better disposed toward us because of our help. Otherwise we merely strengthen despotism against the people.

Mr. ZABLOCKI. One final question . . . Why has Prime Minister Ky not asked for the assistance of Formosan troops? Do you think he would accept troops from Formosa?

Father LYONS. Our State Department has not permitted him to take troops from Formosa because, following our same policy of fear—fear of ghosts, fear of shadows, fear of everything—the State Department has decided China wouldn't like it if we let troops go from Formosa.

As I say again, if we expect our soldiers at 19 to have courage, we should expect a little courage here in Washington, D.C., running our administration. The administration is afraid that China won't like it if we let troops go from Formosa. Chiang offered three divisions as a starter to help the war, and save American lives.

MR. ZABLOCKI. It is 12 o'clock.

We thank you, Reverend de Jaegher and Reverend Lyons for your extremely helpful testimony. Thank you very much.

On June 26, 1966, Father Dan's "Right or Wrong" column greeted his readers with this headline: "BACK TO VIETNAM." The story under his by-line announced that President Johnson had asked him and Rev. Calvin Thielman to go to South Vietnam and look into some of the civilian problems caused by the war. Wrote Father Dan:

"Few people realize how much the United States is doing to help the people adversely affected by the fighting. Both government agencies like AID (Agency for International Development) and private agencies such as the Catholic Relief Services, are doing a great deal to help the Vietnamese. Every month more than 100,000 people flee from Communist tyranny in the Viet Cong areas of South Vietnam. All over the world, the traffic from Communist territories to free areas is always one way.

"Dr. Thielman, who used to do research for our mutual friend, Billy Graham, and I are to report to the President on our return. We hope and pray that our mission to Vietnam will shed some light on helping the Vietnamese more effectively. We both realize, of course, that the greatest thing America can do for South Vietnam is to press on to an early victory over the forces of Communism. We also realize that meanwhile every compassion must be shown to the casualties of war.

"We are meeting with officials in Washington, D.C., before we depart. Our hearts are full as we prepare to take off in a military jet. The words of Pope Paul on May 22 come very much to mind, when he described Communism as 'a blindness which man and society will have to pay for in the end with the gravest consequences.' "

Father Lyons and Rev. Thielman picked up their travel orders at the Pentagon, and the following day they flew to San Francisco, accompanied by Captain Lloyd Young, of the U.S. Navy. Capt. Young, a veteran of the Pacific since 1941, was assigned by the White House to serve as an aide to the two clergymen. He would be their escort, expediter and guide all the time they were in Vietnam.

En route to the war zone, Father Lyons used the time to write a column:

"It is a beautiful summer evening as we cross the blue Pacific. We have just left Travis Air Force Base, bound for Saigon. In retrospect, we are moving from one phase of the battle to another, from the cold-war phase that is being fought within the United States to the battlefield itself. Many people underestimate the psychological war, the propaganda war at home, but our enemies base most of their hopes on it. They can never defeat us militarily unless they can destroy our will to win. . . . There is no such thing as the inevitability of history. Human events are shaped by human beings. The policy of conciliation, appeasement and indecision has never been effective against an aggressive dictator. Communism is masterful at sowing confusion, division and dissension. But we have a weapon that it can never produce: the weapon of spiritual values. Communism is atheism reduced to its logical conclusion, just as democracy and freedom are the natural result of Christianity."

Shortly after his arrival in Saigon, Father Lyons and Dr. Thielman had breakfast with General Westmoreland, who gave them lodging in his home. Dan had come to know the General quite well on his previous visits to Vietnam, and had the deepest respect for him. In his July 10th dispatch back to *Our Sunday Visitor,* Father Lyons told his readers:

"General Westmoreland is not only a very good man, he is one of the truly great men America has produced since World War I. Yesterday he spent four and one-half hours visiting the crews of the Air Force B-52's in Guam. When he met a young soldier from Worcester, Mass., in the hospital there, he noticed that the boy was Italian, and figured he must be from Father Smith's parish. He was right, so he instructed the soldier to write a letter to his pastor 'within 24 hours,' giving his personal regards to him.

"The incident brought to mind something that happened as I was leaving Saigon last September. General Westmoreland was reviewing some troops when he noticed the rough face and graying hair of a veteran

> Army sergeant. 'Bliven!' he cried. 'What are you doing here?' And the sergeant replied: 'I'm fighting the enemy, sir!' General Westmoreland turned and said: 'I knew this man in World War II and in Korea. This is the best soldier in the United States Army.'
>
> "The sergeant stood at perfect attention, while a non-military tear rolled down his cheek. The rest of the day was filled with important matters for the commander of our American Forces in Vietnam. But that night, before he went to bed, he said to me: 'I can't get over seeing old Bliven today.' "

While Father Lyons' primary purpose was to study the civic action of the military, and later report back to President Johnson on how his proposals were being carried out, he did find time to get out into the bush for some side trips of his own. At Cam Ranh Bay, for example, a Protestant chaplain put him in a Jeep and the two of them drove off into the jungle. The road they traveled was nothing more than a trail, with five-foot-high brush on either side of them. The area was infested with Viet Cong; so much so that the military traveled from nearby Nha Trang to Cam Ranh only by heavily-armed convoy.

The chaplain drove at breakneck speed, with the scorching sun beating down on them in the open Jeep. "Tough country out here," the chaplain laughed, "in spots. And you want to be sure of the spots, before someone beats you to it!"

There would be a civilian once in a while on the trail. He'd see their dust cloud long before they'd see him and he'd hurry off the trail into the thick brush and hide until they passed.

Rough country and unpredictable in the best of days.

They pushed on deep into the jungle brush. As they drove, Father Lyons noticed for the first time a fresh bullet hole in the windshield on his side. He said, "Why don't you keep the top up? That's what they did with the Jeeps in Saigon."

The chaplain grinned. He said, "We like to know who's shooting at us."

He gripped the steering wheel tighter and pounded on down the trail.

Father Lyons said, "Where exactly are we going?"

"I want to show you this ancient monastery," replied the chaplain. "It was founded by the French but has since been turned over to Vietnamese priests."

Father Lyons scanned both sides of the road. It was obviously a very easy area for snipers to stay out of sight.

He asked, "Does anyone ever get shot at out here?"

"All the time. We call this road Ambush Alley."

The chaplain was young, husky and fearless. Father Lyons, whose formidable Jesuit Order has had to contend with enemies inside as well as outside the Catholic Church for more than 400 years, decided then and there that if his genial Protestant host was so willing to face the danger of enemy automatic weapons, while they, themselves, were unarmed, he was darned if he was going to say anything.

Exactly as if they had had an appointment, fifteen miles further down the road they pulled up at a clearing and stopped in front of the monastery. In it there were a handful of priests, one of which wore a crownless straw hat and a freckled tonsure sticking out through it like a great wen. His cassock was black and white, as spotless as you could find in any monastery.

They lunched on green fruit and stale bread. They talked the afternoon well down, and finally they were done. They shook hands all around, and our visitors got back into their battered old car and drove off whence they came, their hands waving in farewell.

They made it safely back to Cam Ranh Bay, and on the way Father Lyons kept remembering the World War II signs the government used to post in railroad stations back in the U.S.: "IS THIS TRIP NECESSARY?"

It was amazing what courage could be.

Later, Father Lyons was with a group of war correspondents flying into Laos. As the pilot prepared to land, rumors spread throughout the plane that they were the target for Communist gunfire.

One of the correspondents said, "Could Father Lyons walk up and down the aisle while we're landing?"

"I'm in sales, not management!" said Father Lyons.

They made it down unmarked, but the very next day, when they went up again, their plane was hit in mid-air by a spray of bullets. No one was hurt, but there were some anxious moments. Even then Father Lyons found something to laugh about. Turning to one of the correspondents, he said, "A good landing in the war zone is when you walk away."

With a journalist's pride, Father Lyons was pleased to discover that all over Vietnam there were those who faithfully read his column in *Our Sunday Visitor*. Many of the chaplains received copies by mail, he learned. It usually took two months for the paper to arrive, but if it was sent by first class mail at domestic rates to the A.P.O. in San Francisco, it would be flown the rest of the way.

There was something very special about Father Lyons. To his readers, he was their personal link to the war. For example, Mr. and Mrs. Blake Huttula in Elma, Washington, phoned him in New York several years ago just as he was leaving on another trip to Vietnam. They wanted him to know that their 18-year-old son, Carl, had been reported killed in the war, and that they were unable to obtain any details. Could Father Lyons help them? He promised to do all he could.

A few days later, Father Lyons arrived in Saigon and immediately arranged with President Thieu to have a Vietnamese Air Force plane fly him to Can Tho, in the Mekong Delta, where the tragedy occurred. Within a week, he wrote to the Huttulas and gave them the facts. Infantryman Paul Huttula had died while saving the life of a fellow G.I. The details meant a great deal to the parents.

Many of the soldiers received Father Dan's column regularly in letters from home. Among those who did was a young Marine named Timothy Votaw, whom Father Dan met in the hospital at Chu Lai, near Da Nang. Tim had been only a boy the year before when he was graduated from Central Catholic High School in Portland, Oregon, but he became a man in a hurry in June, 1966, when he stepped on a land mine, blowing off both of his legs completely. The Italian boy from Brooklyn who had been with him paid with his life.

On the eve of visiting Infantryman Tim, 19, Father

Dan had dinner with General Louis Walt, Commanding General of the Marines in Vietnam. It was arranged for Father Lyons to formally present the Purple Heart to Tim on behalf of President Johnson.

When Father Dan was introduced to the boy, Tim's face lit up immediately.

"Oh, Father," he beamed, "my mother sends me your columns from *Our Sunday Visitor* every week. Our family reads you all the time."

Several years later, Father Dan visited Tim in Portland. Tim was by this time married and studying journalism at Portland State College—but still hoping he would one day get back with the Marines, even though he was a double amputee.

At the hospital in Da Nang, Father Dan autographed a copy of his *Vietnam Crisis* for Tim. The book was written in collaboration with Dr. Stephen Pan and had been out for less than a month. It was a 350-page paperback, selling for 75 cents. The authors spent 18 months preparing it. The book is not a reporter's diary but a systematic approach to the Vietnam problem. It is far more than the personal observations and subjective experiences of the authors. Before writing it they painstakingly consulted hundreds of documents in the Library of Congress, in the New York Public Library, in the British Information Service Library, and in the various divisions and missions of the United Nations. Present and former officials of both the Vietnamese and Chinese Governments furnished them with many other valuable documents.

The authors felt the book filled a very serious need,

in 1966. With many American soldiers being killed every week, and numerous more being maimed, they believed Americans at home should have been making every effort to understand the situation. Father Dan told his readers: "In a democratic society the government cannot act without a consensus. A democratic government has to have informed citizens in order to act wisely."

All over Vietnam Father Dan was asked by servicemen for copies of the book. The military command agreed to distribute copies for him. Subscribers of *Our Sunday Visitor* were able to buy two copies for a dollar, and have them airmailed in their name by the paper to the men in Vietnam. Within a month after the offer was first made orders were received from 43 states and four Canadian provinces. The first printing of 100,000 copies was sold out.

In his column of August 7, 1966, Father Dan made some very prophetic observations:

> "We can still win the war in Vietnam. We have missed the boat, but we have not missed the last one. The bombing of the oil storage tanks was a very important step in the right direction. The next step should be to mine the harbor at Haiphong. The North will not give up until we do. Instead of sending another 300,000 servicemen, we should make better use of planes. Nor do we need to send more Americans as long as there are 700,000 soldiers on Formosa. Some argue that the Vietnamese might resent the entry of Formosan troops, but at least we ought to try. Surely we could use some of the planes and pilots from Taiwan. There is no way that the war can be won quickly on the ground. Our superiority is in the air.

"After the closing of the harbor, the industry around Hanoi should be hit. So should the hydroelectric plants along the Red River. Without industry, without electricity, without supplies, North Vietnam could not carry on the war. This is the quickest way to win. It is also the most humane. Only by winning can slaughter on both sides be prevented. Victory against aggression is the only key to world peace."

Though President Johnson ignored the advice, President Nixon finally acted upon it—six years later! In a banner-line story carried by *The Seattle Times*, on Wednesday, August 23, 1972, I felt that Robert Heilman, veteran reporter and an old family friend of Father Dan's, handled it well:

"PRIEST HAD A PLAN: MINE HAIPHONG, HE TOLD NIXON"

"The Rev. Daniel Lyons, S.J., may be the most qualified person in the United States to say to President Nixon:

" 'I told you so.' What the priest told Mr. Nixon six years ago, Mr. Nixon did last spring—mine the harbor at Haiphong.

"In 1966, Richard M. Nixon, then a man in no official capacity, spent a few hours talking to Father Lyons, a native of Seattle and a widely-known priest-journalist, when both were in Taipei.

"Father Lyons then was in Taiwan after a long visit in Saigon—during the past 10 years he has visited the beleaguered nation 17 times. 'Haiphong Harbor should be closed by mining,' the Jesuit priest told the future President. That's precisely what Mr. Nixon did—in the spring of 1972, when, Father Lyons said in Seattle, it was politically expedient. 'Better late than never,' he said. Father Lyons had no trace of I-told-you-so in

> his voice, but he did express regrets that White House action wasn't taken long ago.
>
> "He said, 'Nixon's withdrawal of troops is all the more reason for keeping supplies from the enemy. It is no longer possible for the enemy to wage a major offensive against the South.' Father Lyons described President Nixon's 1972 action as 'the first decisive action in 10 years to bring the war to an end.' "

When Father Lyons first urged our government to bomb the munitions plants of Hanoi, he was attacked in an editorial by *America*, the official Jesuit magazine. "BOMB HERE, BOMB THERE," cried the editors in big, bold type. And Monsignor S. J. Adamo, another Catholic columnist, blasted him for his stand on the war.

Pressure to tone down the hawkish priest came from many sides. Once, when Father Lyons was spearheading the effort back in the U.S. to help the Biafran people during their civil war, Father Pedro Arrupe, the General of the Jesuit Order in Rome, applied for a visa to visit his missionaries in Nigeria. His application was denied.

"But why?" Father Arrupe wanted to know.

"Because you belong to the same Order as Father Lyons."

Today, as I write this chapter, the mailman brings me a letter from Don Dornan. Don is one of the nation's leading free-lance photographers. His news and human interest pictures have appeared in virtually every major news magazine in the world. *Time* and *U.S. News & World Report* have often employed his services.

With headquarters in Los Angeles, Don's letter was postmarked Taiwan, August 6, 1972. He wrote, in part:

> "Father Lyons has a big following even way out here.

Dr. Chien, head of the Government Information Agency's visitor's section, talked very fondly of him. Everybody who is anybody either has met him or knows his name. Strangely, I did meet one—an American business executive—who didn't like him, but, then, he displayed his views and went over with me like a lead balloon.

"The meeting with Cardinal Yu Pin was very memorable. He let me take a great number of pictures of him, many with the students and university in the background. He also invited me to lunch and has helped me in every way.

"The experience out here has left me with deep respect and admiration for the Nationalist Chinese. What I am trying to say is that I am crazy about them. They simply grow on you. I have never felt so strongly about doing whatever I can to save this freedom-loving country. I wish the U.S. would wake up to what's happening in Asia."

Amen!

CHAPTER 16

"Shake Hands Now—and Come Out Fighting"

Father Dan is a great debater. Even his enemies will admit to that, sometimes as they lick their wounds. He prefers a formal debate, but he is not particular. The Gannett newspapers asked him to join them in a symposium, in the fall of 1972, entitled: "Why Should Catholic Priests Marry?" The wording of the question irked him, and he was quoted in the press as follows:

"The Catholic Church, like many organizations, finds many critics telling it how it should be run. When I polled all of the Catholic pastors in New York state two years ago, 91 percent replied that it is better for the Church if priests not be allowed to marry. The trouble with our critics is they do not want to ask the question: 'What is better for the Church?'

"It is better because we are more free to dedicate ourselves to our work. One has only to look to the example set by the twelve apostles. Or take the Eastern Church, where there are married clergy. They have never been the missionaries. Historically the married priests have been considered second-class clergy. The leadership in the Eastern Rite has come from the Religious Order priests, who do not marry.

"From the financial standpoint alone, it would cost an additional $500 million a year to pay every U.S. priest a living family wage. And this at a time when a third of our schools are closing for financial reasons.

"The Catholic Church has been the missionary Church par excellence. We are far more mission-minded than any other Church, and always have been. A missionary without a family can do far more and take greater risks. So can the priest at home, following Christ's example."

Sometimes it is others who rise to Father Dan's defense. When he ran an ad in *Twin Circle* for a book by Arlington House entitled "The Jew In American Politics," Monsignor George Higgins attacked *Twin Circle* for being "anti-semitic." But Neil McCaffrey, President of Arlington House Publishers, came to his defense. In a letter-to-the-editor, he wrote: "I see where that croaking old voice of the Catholic Left, Monsignor George Higgins, has accused you of being anti-semitic." He then explained that Higgins had obviously never seen the book, did not know it was written by a Jew, and that it had received good reviews in a dozen Jewish publications. "Monsignor Higgins often jumps into the pool without looking, whether there is water in it or not," commented Father Lyons. "The facts seldom bother him."

When the Gallup Poll announced, in the spring of '72, that "56 percent of U.S. Catholics favor abortion," Father Dan knew the poll was wrong. "When you take a poll, one or two percent may make a mistake, and one percent may vote for the devil, but I am certain that more than 95 percent of U.S. Catholics are against abortion."

He polled 1,000 readers of the National Catholic Register, selected at random by the computer in 50 states. On October 20, 1972, he sent out the poll as follows: "Dear Register Subscriber: The Gallup Poll claims, on the basis of a recent survey, that 56 percent of U.S. Catholics believe an expectant mother should have the right to take the life of her unborn child for any reason. Do you agree? Do you disagree?"

The question was fair enough. He wanted to know if America's Catholics favored abortion on demand, if they thought it should be simply a matter between the mother and the abortionist, as Gallup claimed. The result? By the end of October he had nearly 50 percent returns. Six agreed. Four hundred and forty-eight disagreed. By November 1st, 1972 the story was being fed to all the wire services, as well as prominently written up in the *Register* and *Twin Circle*.

Father Lyons touched off an ecclesiastical storm in the hierarchy when he blasted Bishop Robert Tracy, of the Baton Rouge, La., diocese, for setting up a good-conscience committee to regularize the process of bringing certain remarried Catholics back to the sacraments.

Wrote the Religion Editor of *Time* magazine (Oct. 2, 1972):

"Jesuit Daniel Lyons termed the good-conscience practice a 'scandal' and questioned how any divorced Catholic who attempted remarriage could be considered to be in good conscience. Lyons' view is known to be shared privately by many U.S. prelates, including the president of the National Conference of Catholic Bishops, John Cardinal Krol of Philadelphia. In August, Cardinal Krol consigned the good-conscience cause to limbo. . . and forbade all practices 'contrary to current discipline.' "

In the November, 1972, issue of *St. Anthony's Messenger,* Father Lyons had a letter-to-the-editor in which he accused Bishop Dozier of Memphis of "talking through his mitre." The letter reads:

> "In his interview in *St. Anthony Messenger* (8/72), Bishop Dozier of Memphis claims his views on the Vietnam war are 'in the mainstream of Catholic thought.' But when he advocates peace at any price, he certainly does not speak for his fellow bishops in this country, who made it extremely clear in their annual statement a few years ago that 'a nation has the right to defend another nation against aggression.' The U.S. bishops also quoted the Vatican Council to prove that soldiers who fight against aggression are 'instruments of security and freedom on behalf of their people.'
>
> Nor does the bishop speak for his fellow bishops in South Vietnam. Unlike his excellency, I have talked at length with the South Vietnamese bishops. There is not one bishop in South Vietnam who agrees with him. Nor does he speak for the clergy and laity in this country. Nearly 90 per cent of the readers of the *National Catholic Register,* for example, agree with President Nixon's closing of Haiphong harbor, which

As America's leading priest-journalist, and an expert on Asia, Father Lyons gets around. He is shown here with, left, Father Raymond de Jaegher, President Chiang Kai-shek, and Thomas Chow at Taipei, in 1966.

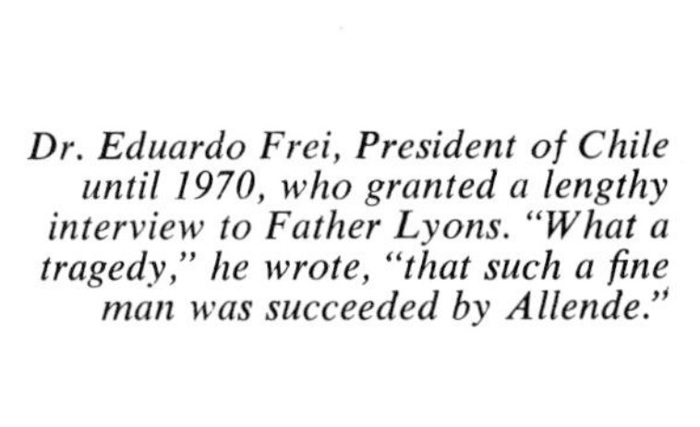

Dr. Eduardo Frei, President of Chile until 1970, who granted a lengthy interview to Father Lyons. "What a tragedy," he wrote, "that such a fine man was succeeded by Allende."

Father Lyons interviews C. K. Yen, Vice-President of Taiwan.

Father Lyons, left, and Rev. Calvin Thielman get the lowdown on Vietnam directly from General Westmoreland at his Saigon headquarters.

Texas millionaire Ross Perot, hands on hips, and Father Lyo and Father Matt Menger, Texas missionary in Laos (white shi lower left), and several newsmen tour the war zon

To find out about the Vietnam war first-hand, Father Lyons has gone to the war zone 17 times in ten years. "The children will steal your heart away," he says.

ather Lyons and General Tom Lane (Ret.) tour the old mperial Palace in Hue with Vietnam interpreter and G.I. escort.

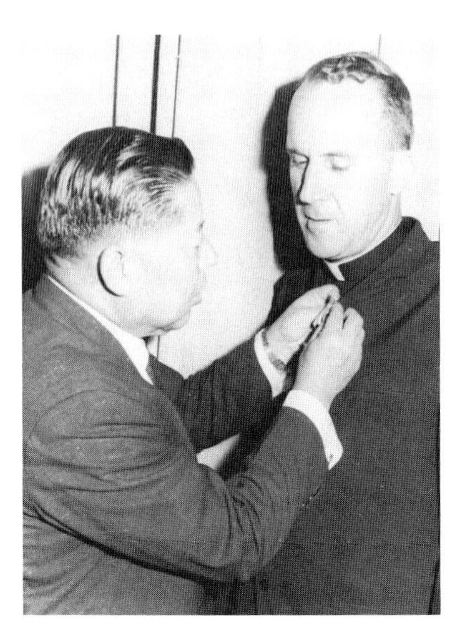

The Minister of Education, Republic of China, pins medal on Father Dan, whose best-selling book, "Vietnam Crisis," had just been translated in full into Chinese. Photo right, Cardinal Paul Yu Pin presents plaque to Father Lyons in behalf of the Republic of China at Taipei.

Father Dan interviews General Creighton Abrams, Commander-in-Chief of U.S. Forces in South Vietnam.

This is St. Christopher's Catholic Church in the heart of Taipei, Taiwan, where Father Lyons offers Mass when he is in Free China. It is the main parish church for the families of U.S. servicemen and was built partly by the late Cardinal Spellman. (Photo by DON DORNAN)

Cardinal Paul Yu Pin, who did much to interest Father Lyons in Asian affairs, stands in front of the campus of Fu Jen University, where he is president. (Photo by DON DORNAN)

Father Lyons, center, and Dean Manion relax and enjoy Guatemalan scenery after lectures at Chamber of Commerce seminar in Guatemala City. With them is Mrs. Manion.

On an inspection trip throughout Asia together, Father Lyons and Congressman "Buz" Lukens (R.-Ohio) met with President and Mrs. Marcos of the Philippines at Manila.

Eugene Lyons, author, lecturer, and colleague of Father Lyons. For 20 years, he was also Senior Editor of Reader's Digest.

Upon arriving in Poland in the Fall of 1972, Father Lyons called to see Cardinal Wyszynski, above, who has fought long and hard to defend the Catholic Church there against Communist persecution.

Father Lyons (circle) awaits his turn to meet Pope Paul.

Dr. Anthony T. Bouscaren, political science professor, lecturer, and one of Father Lyons' co-authors. Says Dr. Bouscaren: "Father Lyons is demonstrating what one man can do. He is an inspiration to thousands of people."

Dr. Stephen Pan has a rich and varied background in Asian affairs. He co-authored Vietnam Crisis *and* Voice of Peking *with Father Lyons.*

Dr. Stefan Possony, distinguished lecturer for Father Lyons' Asian Speakers Bureau, and contributing editor of Twin Circle.

> involved both mining and bombing. Half of the 2,000 polled were priests.
>
> When Bishop Dozier says that President Nixon 'never faced the question' of whether the war is 'morally right or wrong,' he is talking through his mitre. How does he know?
>
> Bishop Dozier has the obligation to tell us if he advocates surrender of the whole world, or if there is any part of it he thinks we should defend."

Father Dan does not like to quarrel with a bishop. He does so only when he sees that even bigger issues are at stake, such as the surrender of 17 million people. He does so only when he sees that a particular bishop, like Bishop Dozier on the question of Vietnam, has not done his homework, that his facts are wrong, that he is out of line with his fellow bishops. Father feels strongly that men like Bishop Dozier, and Bishop Gumbleton in Detroit, are seriously at fault for not consulting with their fellow bishops. That the truth may out, he has tried to debate both bishops, but neither one is willing to take him on. They are not willing, he is convinced, because they could not defend their positions before a knowledgeable person in a debate.

Nor does he like to challenge people who have made mistakes in the past, unless they persist in those same mistakes. One of the architects of our disastrous policy that led to the loss of China's Mainland was Philip Jessup, then a U.S. Ambassador. Father did not challenge him—until Jessup came out strongly on August 29, 1972, advocating the surrender of Vietnam.

Father Dan then challenged him publicly to a debate—

"Or have you retired since August 29?" CBS-TV and radio heard about it, and invited both contestants to have a go, prime time. They pre-empted Bill Cosby at 10 p.m. in the Connecticut market.

He kept insisting throughout the debate that Jessup's policies, which had so much to do with the fall of China, had led to the Korean war and to the war in Vietnam. "Your same policies now," he said, "will lead to war in the rest of Asia. Your most important obligation in this debate," he said to Jessup, "is to tell us where, if anywhere, you would draw the line. How much of Asia do you advocate we should surrender? What about Africa and Latin America? Is there any part of the world you would consent to see defended against Communist attack?"

Jessup never answered. He simply quoted form letters from Eisenhower, the Connecticut Bar Association, and other groups commending him. "What a confused mind, what a Patsy for the Reds! And yet, he was our Ambassador at the United Nations, he was our judge on the World Court, he was a very close advisor to Secretaries of State and even Presidents," said Father Lyons afterwards.

The CBS station in Hartford, Connecticut, where the program was carried, did not take sides. But one of the officials commented privately later that it was too bad Father did not have a stronger opponent. The trouble with a lot of the Leftists, said Father, is that "they have never been challenged."

On one occasion he was on a TV program in Los Angeles with ex-Father William DuBay. Father Patrick Peyton was also on the program. When DuBay tried to say that the Church had restricted him too much as a priest and not allowed him freedom of movement, both Father Dan and Father Peyton mentioned how many times their work had taken them to the far corners of the globe, that the Church had not restricted them. DuBay could not have had two worse examples of living contradictions to his point.

Father Lyons has debated the issue of Vietnam many times since he first founded the Asian Speakers Bureau, in 1965. He has repeatedly let it be known on most of the college campuses that he will debate anyone who is opposed to the basic U.S. policy of defending South Vietnam. He has accepted every offer, whether it be a formal debate or a panel discussion: in person, on the radio, or on TV. It is doubtful whether anyone has had more confrontation with the doves.

He told me, "If the doves had compelling arguments I think I would have heard them. I have publicly debated many excellent speakers: Authors, professors, clergymen, Monsignors, college deans, attorneys, businessmen, former U.S. congressmen, and dozens of Ph. D.'s. I have never felt, nor have I ever been told, that I lost the majority of the audience. The better the competition, the better the debate, because the facts will out.

"*Doves that I have Met* could be the title of a book. They all have one or two traits in common. They are are either uninformed or unrealistic or they have a different set of values. Among the professors it is not the Asian experts who decry our role in Vietnam. Among the clergy it is not the missionaries in the field who clamor for *de-escalation.*

As the late Senator Dodd once pointed out, there seems to be 'a law of diminishing understanding,' depending on one's intellectual and geographical distance away.

"A group of 19 experts who justifiably identified themselves as constituting 'most of this country's small nucleus of specialists on Vietnam' pointed out that they have never seen the name of even one acknowledged expert on Vietnam among the thousands signing ads in the *New York Times* protesting against U.S. policy. Of 6,000 professors who signed such ads in 1968, only four were in the field of international relations.

"The hardest problem for the doves is to come up with some sort of realistic conclusions. On March 11, 1968, I debated on the Barry Gray radio program in New York City. My opponent, Professor William Pepper, kept insisting we should 'get out of there.' When you ask, 'Get out of where?' you get no answer. To be realistic, the advocates of such a policy should tell us where they would draw the line. They should tell us what countries, if any, they propose to defend. They should also explain why they think that getting out of South Vietnam would contribute to world peace, and why it would not encourage other wars of liberation by the Communists against free countries.

"On the Barry Gray show, Professor Pepper kept urging that the United States get out of Vietnam. But when I said he urged 'surrender' he objected to the word. When I debated Father John Sheerin, C.S.P., the editor of the *Catholic World*, on March 6, 1968, at Westfield, New Jersey, he insisted that Ho Chi Minh was 'a patriot' and that our defense of South Vietnam was immoral. But when I asked for his alternative, he denied that we should leave. The war is immoral, he maintained, but we should keep on fighting.

"The third point about many of the doves is that they have a different set of values. Many of them would settle for peace at any price. They are more concerned with peace than they are with freedom or justice. They see some good in Communism. War, they argue, is too much of a price to pay. The fighting is not worth it. They ignore both the realities of history and the aggressiveness of Communism. The Communists do not want to take over the world, they say. Or if they do, they will gradually change. We should appease and not oppose them.

"There are also those who act like doves and serve their cause because they are crippled with indecision. Such citizens in a democracy are a burden to their friends and a blessing to their enemies. Lastly, there are those who want a firm policy of winning. I am sure that we are the majority.

"As far back as November 12, 1965, I was writing in my column that we could easily have won in Vietnam, but we were not winning. As long as we kept granting sanctuary to the enemy, I said, he could continue to make us bleed. We deliberately avoided a policy of winning because we felt we didn't have to win. We thought that all we had to do was 'negotiate.' Do you think that aggression has changed since Hitler's time? Do you think that aggressors do not have to be defeated any more? Do you believe that all we have to do is get them to sit down at the conference table? Those were some of the questions I have been asking.

Americans forgot that we negotiated with this same aggressor in 1954 and again in 1962. In 1954, we found Hanoi so unfair in its negotiations that we refused to sign the treaty. Ho Chi Minh signed, promising to leave South Vietnam alone. Bue he never kept his word, and the eight nations of SEATO condemned him for aggression each succeeding year.

"In 1962, we met with Ho Chi Minh again. He promised to withdraw his troops from Laos, and we were so eager to be fair that we withdrew our troops. The result was another broken treaty, the Ho Chi Minh Trail, and a bigger war in Vietnam. No, negotiation was not the answer then. All that was needed for peace in Southeast Asia was for Hanoi to keep the agreements it made with us before. But Hanoi had no intention of doing so. Thus negotiations are meaningless unless there is good will."

Father Lyons was a staunch and vocal battler against the noisy "teach-in" movement of the wild 1960s. To combat it, he printed up an attractive brochure, promoting his Asian Speakers Bureau, and each year mailed it to every college and university in the U.S. The mailing piece listed the names of a number of prominent speakers who were available for lectures and debating. The most sought was Father Lyons, himself. Subsequently, he appeared at more than 200 campuses during the height of the teach-in movement.

Father Dan was asked to debate a professor at Wayne State College in Detroit a few years ago. The professor backed out, so the radical black clergyman, Rev. Albert Cleague, showed up to debate, complete with his black militant henchmen who stood in the aisles of the auditorium. "You will be lucky if you get out of here unharmed," someone warned.

The debate started, and as Father discussed Vietnam, the radical Reverend referred to the war as an excuse to get black soldiers in the front line, so they could be shot by their fellow white Americans. Father Dan soon had all he could stomach, so he denounced Cleague as a black racist, told him his arguments were a farce, and stomped off the stage, down the center of the aisle and out the rear door of the auditorium, leaving Rev. Cleague all alone on the stage and the audience still seated. "If I were a white racist, I would expect to be treated the same way," Father Dan said.

Three of Father Dan's most famous debates have been made into a best-selling record entitled "The Fight For Freedom."

The first was with Dr. John Oliver Nelson, the former Yale professor and head of the Presbyterian Peace Fellowship. At one point, Dr. Nelson called South Vietnam a "swampy little enterprise," and Father Lyons was quick to take advantage of the slip. He said, "I don't consider it that. I value the lives of sixteen-million people." Later, Dr. Nelson needled Father Lyons for something he said. "You sound just like J. Edgar Hoover!" he snapped. The padre's comeback was typical: "I've always considered Mr. Hoover a good American. And I have always felt he was pretty well informed."

The debate was held in St. John's Lutheran Church, an historic house of worship at Easton, Pennsylvania. Father Lyons' chief points were these:

"There are two ways to get out of Vietnam. We can win

or we can lose. Hanoi knows we can win. The problem is winning the cold war here at home. War must be a last resort. Every other means must first be tried. But when it is necessary, the role of a soldier fighting in defense of his or another's country is like that of a policeman. You cannot solve crime by firing the policeman. You can call it a 'dirty war.' A policeman has a dirty job. But, thank God, he does it.

"In 1947, President Truman proclaimed the Truman Doctrine in this manner: 'One of the primary objectives of the foreign policy of the United States is the creation of conditions in which we and other nations can work out a way of life free from coercion. If we falter in our leadership we may endanger the peace of the world, and we shall surely endanger the welfare of our country.' This was one of President Truman's most important policy statements. We should mark it well, and learn from it. It was the Truman Doctrine of containment that stopped Communist aggression in Central Europe, when the Soviets were threatening to conquer Greece and Turkey.

"Secretary of State Dean Rusk said to Senator Fulbright and the Senate Foreign Relations Committee: 'Last time, only two members in the entire Congress voted against the defense of South Vietnam. If you wish, let us have another vote. But before the members of both Houses vote, let them first retire to consider this: If we tell the other side that we will give up, that we will let them take South Vietnam, that is not the road to peace. That is the road to war.'

"Year after year, 13,000 village leaders are assassinated

by the Viet Cong. After serving as our Ambassador to South Vietnam, Maxwell Taylor said, 'No one has ever been know to voluntarily go from the free areas into the Communist areas.'

"Forty-one nations have helped South Vietnam. Only two have helped the North: Moscow and Peking. In the South they have freedom of religion, speech, ownership. It is no solution to let the Reds take over. They want to know how far we will let them go. Compared to the threat of a Communist takeover, our Founding Fathers had nothing to complain about concerning England. Yet who will condemn George Washington? Who will condemn Lincoln for fighting to preserve the Union?

"Neville Chamberlain did not get peace by taking the easy way out. He thought he could turn his back on his responsibilities when he said, 'Czechoslovakia is a tiny country far away.' Forget the Czechs, he said. Well, today, the United States cannot forget the 42 countries it has pledged to defend. If we abandon Indochina, our defense treaties won't be worth the paper they're written on. We will only be inviting war."

Father Lyons has debated Father Philip Berrigan, S.S.J., several times. The first was at Notre Dame, then at the University of Cincinnati, and then at Purdue. The latter was a knock-down, drag-'em-out alive clash, witnessed by 1,300 students in a jammed hall.

In his opening remarks, Father Lyons said, "The free world will rejoice if we keep South Vietnam free. The world is afraid only that we will not honor our commitments." Then, turning directly to Father Berrigan, he added. "You can dream all you want. But don't fool yourself. If you are unwilling to defend yourself, you'll get stepped on. Your country sooner or later will be overrun. When I interviewed the foreign minister in Thailand, Thanat Khoman, he told me his country would not have been able to preserve its independence if we had not taken a stand in the defense of Indochina. The leaders of Indonesia, fifth largest country in the world, say the same thing."

Once on the offensive, Father Lyons never let Father Berrigan regain the attack. Now he fired his 16-inch guns: "What alternative do we have? We can defend just part of the free world. Father Berrigan is in opposition to our present policy. He has an obligation, therefore, to give us an alternative. I have called on him to do so. The reason he has not is that there is no reasonable alternative."

When he debates, Father Lyons seldom uses notes. He comes mentally armed for war. He is fired up like a steam engine, pistons pumping, ready to roll.

A debate they still talk about at Duquesne University, in Pittsburgh, was the one in which he methodically took Monsignor Charles Rice apart. Fully aware of how the Steel City felt about Communism—many of the citizens had their roots in central Europe—and knowing that the Monsignor took a very soft line against it, Father Lyons held his firepower in reserve until he had relaxed the audience. He started out by saying, "I was a little concerned to be on the left of this podium tonight. But I see that from where you sit out in the auditorium, I am on the right, and Monsignor Rice is on the left." Twelve hundred people laughed, relaxed, and settled down for a sparkling debate.

Father Lyons then reviewed the Monsignor's arguments, point by point, like a surgeon performing an autopsy.

He said, "I am not interested in inconsequential details or distorted criticisms. The Monsignor has said, 'I do not know if we will defend Mexico or not.' He is the Affirmative in this debate. He is proposing the change from our present policy. He is obliged to come up with a solution that is better than that.

"If the United States is defeated in Vietnam, it will be the biggest defeat in the history of our country. Regarding his point that this is a civil war, let us recall that the eight nations of SEATO unanimously condemned the aggression of the North against the South. Regarding Walter Lippman's argument that 'no non-Asian country can win a war in Asia,' I don't think Walter realizes we defeated Japan some years ago. We cannot surrender the rest of the world without being defeated ourselves.

"While I am at it, I'd like to correct the thinking of my opponent regarding Pope Paul. He is not against armed defense. He has merely said that 'no one ought to force his neighbor to resort to armed defense.' Regarding the Monsignor's blind faith in the United Nations, it is of no avail to count on the U.N. when it comes to stopping Communist aggression. The Communists in the U.N. favor aggression against the free world. That is what 'liberation' is all about. We can only count on organizations like NATO and SEATO.

"As for the Monsignor's claim that 'the Church in Hungary and Czechoslovakia is in pretty good shape,' I leave it to this audience to decide whether your friends and relatives behind the Iron Curtain are better off since the Soviet Union took over central Europe.

"Granted, elections in Saigon are not run as well as ours. But it took fifteen years after the Revolutionary War was over in America before the first election was even held. Because of World War II, England, with all her experience in democracy, didn't have elections for nine years. So if you are looking for an excuse to turn South Vietnam over to the Reds, you can use their elections as an excuse. But you can be sure of one thing: Once the North takes over, there will be no elections.

"Another point the Monsignor has tried to make here tonight is that of the alleged patriotism of the Viet Cong. Well, no South Vietnamese has ever been a leader in the NLF (National Liberation Front), except known Communists. We should therefore keep in mind the words of Pope Paul to the government in Saigon, in which he urged it to work 'for a just solution to the conflict, while preserving the freedom of South Vietnam.'

"Monsignor Rice has further indicated that he does not know whether we should ever defend Japan, if necessary, or anywhere else. I can assure him that the other side has made up its mind. It is determined to go on taking over other countries. It is far less brutal to win a war with dispatch than to drag it out. It is the doves, with their confused thinking, who have dragged out the Vietnam war."

Father Lyons then supported his position by quoting Bishop Duhart, the Prefect Apostolic of Thailand. The bishop had recently stated that it was too simple a solution to let the Vietnamese decide for themselves. He said, "They are too overburdened with daily threats. Unless the U.S. helps them, they are not free to decide. The Vietnam war is the most moral war in which the United States has ever been engaged."

Father Lyons added, "Bishop Duhart said that because he knows."

To make another point, Father Lyons quoted some statistics cited by Hubert Humphrey, then Vice-President. He said, "The Vice-President announced after his visit to Vietnam that 62,000 civilians had been killed by the Viet Cong. A thousand a month, apart from any war activity. In 1954, when the country was divided, 900,000 went South and only 23,000 went North. It is the same old story. Nobody goes to Havana any more. Nobody goes to Red China. Nobody goes to East Germany. Nobody ever got shot climbing over the wall to get into East Berlin. It is always one-way traffic. No free country ever has to build a wall to keep people *in*. The only time we build a wall is for a prison.

"But summing it up, I don't think we are so soft or derelict in our duty, or so far from our Christian commitment, that we are going to abandon today's free world."

Several years later, in 1970, Father Lyons heard the sequel to his debate with Monsignor Rice while visiting Rome. He was having dinner with Cardinal Wright and his secretary, Father Donald Wuerhl, in their apartment. To Father Dan's surprise, the Cardinal recalled how Monsignor Rice had phoned him after the debate. Cardinal

Wright was the Bishop in Pittsburgh at the time, and he had asked the Monsignor, "How did the debate go, Charley?"

"Terrible!" Monsignor Rice replied. "I had a lot of trouble."

"What happened?"

"That big hall was full of little old ladies in tennis shoes. And they were all against me."

Cardinal Wright told him, "You just met up with the silent majority, Charley. That's what happened to you."

"They weren't silent at all," Monsignor Rice said. "That was the trouble."

Several years ago, Father Lyons was debating at a state college in New London, Conn. His opponent was so pro-Communist in his views that Father was unable to get him to say one word of criticism against anything the Communists had done anywhere. The debate grew so heated that the opposing professor lost his temper and shouted at Father to "go to hell!"

The audience was both shocked and sympathetic, but this mood was quickly turned to laughter when Father replied in mocked solemnity:

"Thank you, Sir. Thank you very much. That is the first time I have ever been invited to Communist Headquarters."

CHAPTER 17

Twin Circle: The Facts

I trimmed the broiled fat from around my steak. I was a patient man; I had spent thirty of my forty-eight years trying to locate facts and then reduce them to words. We were having dinner at the New York Athletic Club, Father Lyons and I, and I wanted a lot of inside facts about *Twin Circle*, the national Catholic weekly that he and Patrick Frawley launched in 1967.

"Why did you leave *Our Sunday Visitor*?" I asked him. "I heard rumors—"

"What rumors?" he said.

"That you and Monsignor Yzermans didn't see eye to eye."

Father Lyons sipped tea and nodded. He said, "The Monsignor's views were too far left of mine. He could not, for example, understand how any Catholic—namely, *me*—in clear conscience could be in favor of the ABM, our defensive missile program, and he said so in his editorials shortly after he replaced Monsignor Joseph Crowley as editor of *OSV*."

"Had you gotten along all right with Monsignor Crowley?"

"Monsignor Crowley was an excellent editor to work with. He had been a captain in the Army before entering the seminary, and had a realistic view of the world situation. I was dismayed when he stepped down as editor."

"Where is he today?"

"He has since been made auxiliary bishop of the Fort Wayne, Indiana, diocese, which owns *Our Sunday Visitor*."

"Let's talk about *Twin Circle*. What's the history behind it? You have been involved in the paper up to your neck."

"We founded *Twin Circle* in the spring of 1967."

"By *we*, you mean Patrick Frawley and yourself."

"Yes. We already had the Twin Circle Publishing Company, Inc., and I headed it as president. We then hired four experienced staff members from the *National Register* chain in Denver. One of these was Frank Morriss, who only recently had resigned as news editor of the *Register*. Frank was brought in to serve as Editor. Assisting as Associate Editor was Clement Zecha, who had for years served the *Register* as editor of its local editions. Coming with them was John Murphy to work as our Advertising Manager, and Julia Boggs, Circulation Manager. Waiting in the wings was Dale Francis, the veteran Catholic newspaper columnist and editor."

"Wasn't Dale writing for *Our Sunday Visitor?*"

"He wrote a column for them and had been acting editor there, but then Monsignor Yzermans replaced him as editor.

Over the years, Dale and I had become close personal friends. We had worked together under the editorship of Monsignor Crowley and had a deep respect for each other. We held similar views on domestic and world problems. Both of us agreed that *Our Sunday Visitor,* in 1966, was too far to the left of our thinking and totally unacceptable to our long-range aims. It sickened us to think that the largest Catholic newspaper in the U.S. had taken such a sharp turn at a time when our country was faced with the military might of the Soviet Union. Dale and I met and consulted with one another several times about the danger. He had also grown very concerned about the shift to the left of the *Register* in Denver. The *Register* was the second largest Catholic paper in America. And to compound our worries, the No. 3 Catholic paper, *National Catholic Reporter,* with a circulation of nearly 100,000, had gone radically left. It was so bad, in fact, that Bishop Helmsing, in Kansas City, where NCR was headquartered, said the paper should drop the word Catholic from its masthead."

"Who was the editor of *National Catholic Reporter?*"

"Robert Hoyt. He was well-known for his anti-clericalism since the days when he was with the *Register*. But even *NCR* got fed up with his radicalism and finally fired him."

"What precisely did he do to provoke his dismissal?"

"He was out to build circulation, and to do this he attacked the Church satirically. Some of his attacks were in very poor taste. This caused a lot of confusion within the ranks, particularly in the convents. Young nuns would read Hoyt's paper and be upset for days. I called it the *Non-Catholic Reporter*."

"What sort of influence does the paper have today?"

"It has lost much of its former punch. The sensationalism is mostly gone now—and with it, most of its circulation. It's questionable whether it can even continue publication much longer."

"Were there any other Catholic newspapers on the national scene that worried you?"

"The only other one was the *Wanderer*. It had been in existence for more than a century."

"What was its position politically?"

"It was much more conservative than the others."

"Is it still that way?"

"It is still pointedly conservative. Al Matt and his son, Al, Jr., are the editors and are doing an important job in defending the policies of the Vatican. It's ciruculation is about 40,000."

"What you're saying, then, is that the leading Catholic newspapers in the United States were either too liberal or too conservative for your thinking, and you felt the time was perfect to launch a newspaper better attuned to your views of Catholic faith and American freedom. Is that correct?"

"Yes, but not just to our views—to the views of the majority of U.S. Catholics."

"Well, how did Mr. Frawley get into the picture?"

"During 1966 and '67, Patrick and I spoke frequently about the possibility of starting a new Catholic paper some day. As the chairman of Eversharp, Inc., his company often gave financial support to the publishers of conservative Roman Catholic newspapers. He was just as concerned as Dale Francis and I were over the shifting editorial policies of the *Register*. A glance at the paper's front pages in those days told us who their Catholic heroes were: the two Father Berrigans, Father Groppi, and all the other radicals. They simply were too negative for us to swallow. Certainly, we felt, they were no help to America in these troubled times."

"When did you first meet Frawley?"

"In 1966. At the Cardinal Mindszenty Conference in St. Louis. I knew very little about him. And when he invited me to meet with him on his boat a few weeks later, I knew even less about his boat. Were we going to sleep on shore? Should I bring a sleeping bag? The *boat* turned out to be big enough to sleep 17, with a crew of five. *Fortune* magazine published a major article on him a few months later entitled, 'The Frawley Phenomenon.' The writer who wrote the article used such terms as 'evasive' and 'elusive' and 'inaccessible' to describe him. He said Pat was an 'enigma, unknown and misunderstood.' He said his management methods were preposterous, but admitted that there were clear signs that he knew what he was doing. The writer confessed that Frawley's business empire 'somehow works just fine.' "

"So much for *Fortune's* view of Mr. Frawley. What is your own personal opinion?"

"Over the years, I have found him to be less of a phenomenon than a friend. He is not evasive. He is not elusive. He is not inaccessible. Nor is he an enigma, unknown, or a preposterous business manager. I will admit, however, that he is misunderstood by many.

"I had met him only twice when he suggested sending 'Vietnam Crisis,' the 334-page book I co-authored with Dr.

Pan, to every priest in the U.S. He asked me, 'How many priests are there?' I told him there were 59,000. He said, 'Well, let's send them each a copy. How much would it cost?' I took my pencil out and did some quick figuring. I then told him, 'It will cost about $35,000.' I quickly added, 'But we don't have to send a copy to every priest. We could leave out the parish assistants.' Patrick said, 'Oh, no, don't do that. Send it to *every* priest—all 59,000. And send along a letter to each priest on the list.' He must have been very interested in Vietnam, I thought. But it wasn't that at all. He said, 'I want all the priests to know *you*.' What an excellent calling card that was. Every priest in the United States was sent a copy of 'Vietnam Crisis.' For several years afterward they kept identifying me with the book."

"Now you know what *Fortune* meant when it called him a *phenomenon.*"

"He is truly one of the great promotion men in the country. Consider the facts: Here was an immigrant from Nicaragua, where his father had emigrated from Ireland, and with the $4,000 his dad had given him for college he started the Paper Mate Pen Company. He began preempting sales from his competitors, until one of them told him, 'You can't get anywhere in the ballpoint pen business here in California because I've got Melvin Jacobs. Mel grew up with all the managers of the big drugstore chains.' So Pat's gloating competitor told him, 'You can't get anywhere without Mel. You're going to have to merge with me.' That was the wrong thing to say to Patrick Frawley, Jr. He is very independent and no one pushes him around.

So what did he do? He went out the very next day and convinced Mel Jacobs they should join forces. One obstacle after another was overcome, and Patrick climbed to the top of the pen business, while his competitor folded. *That's* Pat Frawley."

"Didn't Mr. Frawley recently sign up Mark Spitz, the great Olympic swimming champion, to a lifetime contract for promoting some of his products?"

"Yes, and Mark turned down larger offers, including a reported $1 million from Anheuser Busch, to work with Patrick. Mark also turned down a beer distributorship. He joined Mr. Frawley, he said, because he liked his program of fighting addictions.

"Patrick has a way of attracting other people. When he hired a refugee chemist named Fran Seech some years ago he was told that Seech was very hard to get along with, that he was a neurotic. Pat replied that 'Cecil B. DeMille made a lot of money handling some of the nuts in Hollywood.' "

"Did he succeed in keeping Mr. Seech?"

"He managed to hang on to him for three years, largely by playing chess with Seech rather regularly. But when Patrick's sister-in-law heard about all his arguments with Seech, she recommended he contact Dr. Fred Seyer, a top scientist at U.C.L.A. Within a few years, Seyer's three sons had gone to work for Patrick. Frank, the eldest, developed what Seech had first come up with, an ink for ball point pens that would not leak. Frank later became president of Schick Safety Razor Company under Patrick, a position he still holds, though Patrick sold the company.

"Patrick picked up two other talented inventors who

have been with him ever since, Clarence Schrader and Hartley Sears. These two men were principally responsible for solving the intricate problems of making ball point pens. The ball point pen was originally patented in 1896, but was never made to work successfully until Schrader and Sears developed a method for making it work. There is a tiny ball in the point that must be held in place by a paper-thin thickness of brass. The ball must be held firmly but revolve freely to permit an even flow of ink.

"Under Frawley's direction these two men also developed the first cassette projector in America, which meant the teacher or housewife operating it did not have to thread the film. Under his leadership Schick Safety Razor Company became the first American firm to introduce the stainless steel blade. These were three great contributions to better living in America and around the world: the stainless steel blade, the cassette projector, and the first ball point worth writing with. Frawley looks to these men and others to make further significant contributions for his companies. Frawley's latest product is a new type of electric razor that shaves you as close as a razor blade without any discomfort. It is called the Schick Flexomatic, and is the first electric razor that eliminates the need for another shave later in the day.

"In the United States, amidst all the talk about fighting discrimination, you will still find some firms are predominantly English, German, Italian, Jewish or Irish, depending somewhat on the types of business they do. But one can see from the management of Frawley's companies that the executives are selected on their personal character and the ability to get the job done.

"Patrick was one of the first American employers to hire a Negro vice-president in the person of Cage Johnson. Cage has long been active in Catholic circles in Los Angeles, and is the father of a prominent medical doctor there. Another man whom he acquired along the way is Edward Ettinger. A member of the Jewish faith, Ed was operating a small restaurant in Los Angeles when he met Patrick. He sold the restaurant and joined Mr. Frawley. A skilled executive, he is now chairman of the board of Schick, and Frawley's right hand man. When Frawley first met Ettinger he was impressed by his sense of fair play and his practical approach to business problems. Patrick is a great believer in taking special night-school courses and in the use of libraries. He was impressed when Ettinger followed his suggestion and took courses in English and public speaking.

"His vice president for finance is Mr. William Humphreys, a Scotch Presbyterian who formerly worked for Internal Revenue. He has been with Frawley for twelve years now. Another man, now retired, who worked closely with him for many years is Thomas Welsh, an Irish Catholic whom Patrick met in Nicaragua. Welsh left Lever Brothers to help Patrick build up his companies.

"At age 51, Patrick has given a couple of million dollars to Catholic causes, and to other causes, along the way. When people tell him he does not understand something, he listens. But when they tell him he does not know how to make money, he smiles politely. As we sit here discussing him, his stock has doubled in the past six months. He can afford to smile."

"How did he acquire the Schick Safety Razor company?"

"He sold Paper Mate to Gillette and used the money to buy Schick.

"I told him one day I was going to have 'Vietnam Crisis' reprinted. Pyramid Books offered me a contract involving any future books I wrote. Patrick asked, 'How long will the contract run?' I told him three years, and he said, 'Don't tie yourself up for that long. Let's start our own book publishing company. I've already got the name for it: *Twin Circle.*'

"Twin Circle? What did it mean? He said, 'It is a good symbol. Two circles are easy to remember. I just happened to think it up one day while I was driving around, so I had it incorporated. I've never used it.' That is how Twin Circle Publishing Company was born. We first reprinted 50,000 copies of 'Vietnam Crisis,' and followed this up with 100,000 copies of Eugene Lyons' 'Workers Paradise Lost,' one of the finest books ever published about the menace of Communism. The condensation originally ran in *Reader's Digest.* Eugene Lyons is a former senior editor of the magazine. Another paperback we published was 'Dagger In The Heart,' by Dr. Mario Lazo. It's all about the fall of Cuba and the Bay of Pigs fiasco, and, to date, we have sold about 80,000 copies. It was also condensed in *Reader's Digest.* It is the best book ever written on the subject."

"So you and Frawley started *Twin Circle,* the newspaper, as a Catholic conservative force to combat the radicals."

"That's right. We felt we needed our own organ—a voice to answer the leftists."

"Is Mr. Frawley a very religious man?"

"Very. He is for anything that helps religion, society, and the family. He is wholly against those forces that would destroy them."

"Such as what?"

"Such as pornography, abortion, state control of our private lives, and Communist takeovers of other nations. For example, when a Protestant clergyman named Richard Barnes, a member of the California Assembly, came to Pat and asked him to back a bill against the state's wholesale pornography, Pat gave him his answer by running full-page anti-pornography ads in almost every Sunday paper in California. The advertisements stressed the virtues of Christian family life."

"Father, what was there about Patrick Frawley that attracted you to him? What convinced you that you wanted to work with him?"

"One of his traits that attracted me to him was his dedication to helping people who are addicted to alcohol. We both belong to the Pioneer Total Abstinence Society, and have vowed never to touch liquor. I admire those with the same philosophy."

"But Mr. Frawley confesses he was once an alcoholic himself."

"I don't like the term alcoholic. He was addicted to alcohol for some years, but he was one of the lucky ones. He was directed to a hospital in Seattle that saved his life."

"How?" I asked.

"A Father John Fitzgerald told Mrs. Frawley about Shadel hospital in Seattle. You've heard of it. Shadel specializes in breaking the addiction to alcohol. So when Mrs.

Frawley talked to Patrick about taking the treatment, he agreed to go. At the hospital he lost all desire to drink. He became indignant at the liquor industry for having addicted him. The result: He *bought* the hospital, and later built another at Fort Worth, Texas. They are now called Schick Hospitals. A third is being started at the Sisters of Charity Hospital in Los Angeles. It will be called the Schick Clinic at St. Vincent's Hospital."

"Who's in charge of the hospitals?"

"Dr. James Smith is the Chief of Staff in Seattle. Dr. Robert Dunn is the Chief of Staff in Fort Worth, and Dr. Todd Bailey will be in charge in Los Angeles.

"At my suggestion," Father Lyons continued, "Mr. Frawley authorized me to write to every bishop in the U.S., telling them about Schick, and offering to take any priest with a drinking problem to Seattle at cost or for free, if necessary."

"What was the response?" I wanted to know. "Were many priests sent as a result of your offer?"

"Only about thirty-five," he said. "It has been Mr. Frawley's experience in business that when people have been misinformed most of their lives by the media, it is impossible to overcome this misinformation by a single letter, or an advertisement, or a news story. He discovered that the liquor industry had purposely confused people into thinking that alcohol addiction is really a mysterious disease or illness, and that excessive drinking is only a symptom of this disease. The liquor industry does not like the term alcohol addict. Those who attend Alcoholics Anonymous meetings are being told, 'Pray for a return to sanity.' The only sanity involved is the determination to break the addiction, and the realization that they can never drink again. It stands to reason that those thirty-five priests who were sent to Schick had no mental problems. Otherwise, they could not have been cured in ten days.

"There is an excellent Catholic psychiatrist on the Schick staff, Dr. Frederick Lemere. He has been there for nearly 20 years. Dr. Lemere told me that the percentage of people addicted to alcohol who have mental problems is virtually the same as the percentage of people with mental problems who have no addiction.

"When I studied in Ireland I was much impressed with the work of the Pioneer Total Abstinence Society, which is run by the Irish Jesuits. They had 500,000 members. The majority of the membership had joined the PTAS between the ages of 16 and 18. They all wear a Pioneer pin, a small white badge outlined in gold, with a picture of the Sacred Heart in the center."

"I notice you wear a Pioneer pin on your lapel. You're never without it."

"Both Mr. Frawley and I wear the pin. Membership is based on the idea that alcohol is not wrong in itself, but is so addictive for some people that we members made the voluntary sacrifice of never drinking. In this way we never risk the danger of addiction, and our sacrifice is to remind others that alcohol produces an addictive reaction in some people. I became a member of the Pioneers in 1950, after my second year in Ireland. To say I have never taken a drink since then isn't saying much; I rarely had a drink before then.

"I liked Patrick's approach to the problem. He wasn't blaming the addict. He simply wanted to help. That's the way I feel. I often write articles about Schick. I cite the facts: 17,000 addicts cured; 70 per cent of those who go to Schick are cured in 10 days; half of the others become cured by being treated a second or third time. It is impossible to calculate the damage to health caused by alcohol. Sales last year were 24 billion dollars. The addicts alone drank 12-billion dollars worth. The 12-million dependent drinkers consume another 8-billion dollars per year. So a relatively small percentage become dependent, or slaves to this drug. Each addict is a complete slave. He drinks as much as 200 moderate drinkers, or 12 heavy drinkers. He is largely responsible for auto accidents and accidental fires."

Statistically, Mr. Frawley points out, the susceptibility points to those whose genes were formed in areas of the world where there is an abundance of water. The Eskimos who started drinking at 18 are sometimes dead within three years. The American Indians from Siberia have been victimized by this drug since they first encountered it. So have the fair-skinned Irish, the Scots, the Scandinavians, the Celtic people in France, and the black people from the rain forests in Africa.

The reason for this is believed to be the dieretic action of alcohol which forces fluids out of the body. This action precipitates a thirst somewhat like a sailor who tries to drink seawater. Perhaps as many as 20 percent of the Irish have this reaction to alcohol. The rest, of course, do not. Only about one percent of the Mediterraneans have this susceptibility to alcohol. For the others, alcohol is a straight sedative. For the highly susceptible, alcohol is a sedative-irritant. Those are the ones who become excited. They are the life of the party.

"We hear a lot about drugs like Antabuse," I said. "Do the Schick hospitals use that for curing alcohol addiction?"

"No," said Father Lyons. "The Schick Centers believe that drugs like Antabuse are based on a misconception of the nature of the addiction, which is physical, involving the memory—rather than mental depending on reason. The reasoning mind, already aware that alcohol has caused serious difficulties, also understands that the body will have an adverse reaction to taking alcohol when Antabuse is administered. It knows Antabuse is dangerous. Because the reasoning mind fears the reaction more than the alcohol, it will refuse Antabuse so that drinking can be resumed. By the same logic, a chain smoker could not be persuaded to take a pill that would make him violently ill in case he smokes a cigarette."

I said, "Alcoholics Anonymous and others speak of an addict stopping drinking when he 'hits bottom.' What do they mean?"

"When a drug such as alcohol is taken it usually causes an immediate sensation that is pleasant, like any sedative. The irritating effect to the addict is delayed. But the irritation may finally occur immediately on taking the drug. When this happens to the alcohol addict, the addiction soon ends. That is what is known as 'hitting bottom.' The problem is: Will a person live long enough to experience this sort of involuntary salvation? Hitting bottom is unpredictable. When the reaction changes, it may be too late; the organs may have been incurably damaged. The advantage at the Schick hospitals is that there is no need to hit bottom.

"We have a massive job ahead of us. There are more than 7,000,000 addicts in this country—7,000,000 slaves to alcohol. At least Patrick Frawley recognizes the challenge, and is doing something about it."

"But he isn't stopping there. The other day I visited one of his smoking clinics. Now he's going after the smokers."

"Dr. Alton Ochsner really got Pat to thinking."

"Dr. Ochsner?"

"Dr. Ochsner, who serves on the board of Schick's hospitals and smoking clinics, is a giant in the field of medicine. When 6,000 physicians were surveyed in 1971 on five leading U.S. clinics (Mayo, Ochsner, Lahey, Cleveland, and Scott and White), the Ochsner clinic was rated No. 1 in accuracy of diagnosis and in effectiveness of the treatment. He is the former president of the American Cancer Society and of the American College of Surgeons.

"Listen to what Dr. Ochsner has to say about smoking: 'I'm convinced that all heavy smokers will contract lung cancer, unless they first die from another disease. The insidious part about lung cancer is that by the time it is diagnosed, it is usually too late to arrest it.' Dr. Ochsner now serves on the board of Schick hospital and of Patrick's smoking clinics. He recently told us that smoking is still his most important and most accurate means of diagnosis. He said, 'If I have a patient with a suspicious lung shadow and he is a smoker, I know he has lung cancer.' He has also found that smoking causes ulcers, and he will not treat any ulcer patient who refuses to quit smoking. He said it is impossible to cure a smoker's peptic ulcer. Do you want more evidence? Well, the death rate from coronary diseases is from 50 to 100 percent higher among smokers. Medical researchers have found that those who average two packs of cigarettes a day run a 241 percent higher risk of dying from heart disease. The statistics are awesome."

"Do filters help much?"

"No. The doctors I have talked to tell me that only a very costly filter could eliminate the 40 poisonous chemicals found in cigarettes. The only guarantee is to keep the tobacco out of the lungs. The average victim of lung cancer lives only 10 weeks after his cancer is diagnosed. Of all the common forms of cancer, lung cancer is the most deadly."

"Was Mr. Frawley a heavy smoker?"

"Yes. And after he cured his alcohol addiction, he decided to get rid of his addiction to cigarettes. The result was the birth of his Schick Centers for the Cure of Smoking. He started them in California, Oregon, and Washington. They are built around the technique used at Shadel. It is called 'aversion therapy,' a Pavlovian treatment that eliminates unwanted habits by linking them to unpleasant stimuli. With alcohol they consist of a physical aversion caused by taking a medical substance, under a doctor's care. With nicotine, the aversion is caused by harmless but mildly irritative electric stimuli. Pain is not necessary because the instinctive memory is so sensitive. That is how a person becomes addicted without warning. He does not feel the addictive urges. But his instinctive subconscious memory does, and those recordings will later control his behavior. The Schick therapy simply causes the instinctive memory to make new negative associations with cigarettes."

"What are the early results from these smoking clinics of Frawley's? Are you optimistic?"

"More than 2,000 nicotine addicts have been cured, and thousands more are signing up. These clinics are still very new, remember. The public must first be educated. Frawley plans a national program later, but right now they are confined to the West Coast. The rate of cure is about 70 percent the first time around. The essential thing is that a smoker must *want* to stop if he is to be cured. It is not enough simply for your family to want you to stop. Frawley has also learned through his clinics that *will power* is not enough, either; that it only induces hopelessness and is generally ineffective. You have to out-smart the addiction. No one becomes addicted voluntarily. You have to reprogram the memory.

"Frawley told me: 'If an addict thinks you are trying to say he is smoking too much because he is mentally ill, he will persist in trying to do it *moderately,* but without much success. The minute you tell him not to smoke because of the chemical reactions taking place and it will make him sick, you will have a greater chance of getting him to stop. That's how Schick succeeds in breaking the fixation that alcohol helps to relax—that smoking helps to relax—that they are beneficial.'

"In the Catholic tradition, Frawley is not a prohibitionist. His concept is to educate, not prohibit. But for anyone who is addicted he feels there must be voluntary abstinence.

His chief interest is in saving lives. Is there any wonder I like to work with him?"

"How would you define your working relationship with Mr. Frawley? Since he has invested great sums of money in your various enterprises, would you call it an employer-employee kinship?"

"No, we are not that. We are more like close advisors to each other. We consult with one another quite a bit. But as *consultants,* not as employer and employee. That's the only role I have ever had with *Twin Circle* or any other Frawley-controlled business. It is the only role I want. We have a lot of respect for one another."

"What will be your next big project? Do you have anything on the drawing boards?"

"Recently, I said to Mr. Frawley: 'You have the answer for alcohol addiction. You have a good start on nicotine, with your chain of smoking clinics. Now the next big problem in America is overweight. Americans eat improperly and too much. You ought to begin thinking about buying some existing company in the field of weight control. We could study it, improve it, and then promote it.' Frawley said, 'We'll do it. We will use the same technique as we're using on liquor and smoking—the aversion method. And I'll be our first customer. I must lose 10 pounds.' "

"Let's go back and talk some more about *Twin Circle.* After all, the paper serves as a vital instrument in the promotion of your many activities. Tell me about your staff. How did you manage to hire Frank Morriss?"

"In May of 1967, I was out on the Coast visiting Frawley at his home in Los Angeles. On the table was the latest copy of the *Register* and I saw where Frank had just resigned as the paper's News Editor of the national edition. I figured the resignation was probably at the request of Father Flaherty. This indicated to me that the *Register* would veer even more sharply to the left. When I brought Frank's resignation to the attention of Frawley, I said to him: '*Twin Circle* should publish a national Catholic weekly of its own.' He agreed, and told me to look into it. I phoned Dale Francis, who was still writing for *Our Sunday Visitor* but wasn't happy with the new editor's left-wing policies there. He said the situation at *OSV* was intolerable. He explained that editor Yzermans hadn't talked to him for months, even though they shared the same corridor. I suggested he resign, but he said he had a loyalty to the paper as its former editor and felt he should stay on as long as there was any chance of salvaging it.

"Next, I called Frank Morriss. I told him that Frawley and I wanted to start a new national Catholic weekly. He was very interested and cooperative, and I arranged to fly to Denver for a meeting with him. Out of that conference grew the nucleus of our staff: Frank Morriss, Editor; John Murphy, Advertising Manager; and Julia Boggs, Circulation Manager. I personally handled the promotion. We quickly picked up 35,000 direct-mail subscribers by placing ads in *Our Sunday Visitor,* the *Register,* and about 30 other Catholic publications. Frawley worked closely with me on this intensive subscription campaign.

"The paper set up its headquarters at Wheatridge, Colorado, near Denver, and was printed at the Hirschfield Printing Company. Sample copies of that first edition were mailed to all the pastors across the U.S. In June, 1968, the printing was moved to *Our Sunday Visitor's* plant in Indiana, as part of an economy move; and we switched our editorial and circulation operations to 86 Riverside Drive, New York City. Frank Morriss stayed behind in Denver, however, but continued to write his column for *Twin Circle* and other Catholic papers.

"I stepped in as Editor. Jack Murphy ran the advertising from there until his untimely death, in 1971. Julia Boggs moved to New York for a few months, long enough to teach the circulation operation to Rose Reid, a native of Ireland who had been teaching on the West Coast and joined our New York office in 1967. Elizabeth Schmitz, executive secretary to Jack Murphy, replaced him as Advertising Manager after his death. Others who hold down important jobs for the paper's circulation department are Kathleen Rooney, also from Ireland, and my sister, Noreen Gilkey. Bob Miller joined us about this time as our accountant. He also played an important role in keeping our staff working smoothly together."

"When did Dale Francis join the staff?"

"In the spring of 1968 he left *Our Sunday Visitor* to serve as columnist and consultant for *Twin Circle*. More than anyone else I relied on him for making policy. Later, Clement Zecha also joined the staff in New York from Denver as Assistant Editor, but after several months was replaced by Vincent Ryan. Vincent is now the Editor, assisted by Edwina Bowe. Bob Morris, who was Editor for awhile, is Publisher. Archbishop Robert J. Dwyer of Portland, Oregon, serves as chairman of the editorial board and columnist of both *Twin Circle* and the *Register*. We are very indebted to him."

"I notice that Father Cletus Healy, S.J., is today listed on the *Twin Circle* masthead as Contributing Editor. How did you pry him away from the Wisconsin province?"

"I arranged for him to be loaned to us. The same is true of Father Walter Dimond, who joined *Twin Circle* as Associate Editor in 1972. He has been loaned to us by the Detroit Province."

"It must have been quite expensive soliciting new subscribers by direct-mail and newspaper ads. Are you still doing it?"

"No, it was getting too costly. Father Healy and I came up with a unique plan. Why not have our circulation workers phone pastors long-distance and sell them on the idea of taking a hundred or more copies of *Twin Circle* free for a three-week trial. What we wanted was exposure. This would be followed up with another phone call after the trial period to see if they'd like to subscribe regularly to a bundle of perhaps 50 copies. We talked to Frawley about the program, and he was enthusiastic. He said, 'The idea of phoning the pastors directly is a stroke of genius.' "

"When was the phone campaign launched?"

"Father Healy, a very capable organizer, started the campaign in June, 1969. He used one and sometimes two WATTS lines, figuring how to get the top value out of the long distance phones. He had a staff of part-time women making the calls. They worked about three hours apiece daily, and kept the phones busy regularly over a 12-hour period. The gamble paid off handsomely. We shot our

Twin Circle circulation up over 100,000 within the first year, and later, when we started publishing *National Catholic Register,* we followed the same plan to boost its circulation up to 95,000."

"I notice that *Twin Circle* moved its newspaper office to Los Angeles in 1969. Why?"

"*Twin Circle* is owned by the Schick Investment company. Frawley felt it would be more convenient for the staff to be closer to the business offices of its parent company. We had been getting pretty crowded at our 86 Riverside Drive address."

"It was about that time you started searching around for a second Catholic newspaper to buy."

"I can see, John, you have been doing your homework. The history behind that is this. During 1968-69, I met with the head of *The Catholic Digest,* Monsignor Terrence Murphy, and talked to him about the possibility of buying it. No conclusions were really reached, however. Then Dale Francis and I talked to the board of *Our Sunday Visitor* about a merger. We offered to take over the newspaper in still another proposal—minus their physical plant and other business—but the *Visitor* preferred talking merger. Their plan was to split up the 16-page format into two sections. Eight pages would be *Our Sunday Visitor,* and eight would be produced by *Twin Circle*. According to their proposal, Dale would edit the *OSV* section, and I would be in charge of the *TC* half. We would be given 10-year contracts to serve as co-editors."

"Where would this leave Monsignor Yzermans?"

"On the strength of the negotiations, he resigned as editor of the *Visitor.*"

"Were you in favor of the merger?"

"While everyone else felt we should merge with the *Visitor,* I fought against it."

"Why?"

"Because I knew it would have been the end of *Twin Circle.* I had very little faith in the 10-year contract that the *Visitor* was offering Dale and me. I felt it could be broken at any time. That could have meant leaving the Catholic world without a newspaper to defend the Vatican and the Magisterium of the Church."

"At this time, where was Mr. Frawley?"

"In Europe."

"But when he heard that you were opposing the merger, what was his initial reaction?"

"One of mild disagreement. Yet when I was able to show him that we were operating moderately in the black, he agreed that it was better not to lose control of the paper. The merger was killed."

"Who replaced Monsignor Yzermans as editor of the *Visitor?*"

"Father Albert Nevins. He is a veteran Maryknoll priest who keeps *OSV* soundly on the side of moderation and orthodoxy, which its board had always wanted."

"That still left you without a second Catholic newspaper."

"Not for long. Since 1968, I had been sending feelers out to the *Register* in Denver. My contact was Archbishop James Casey. I let him know that *Twin Circle* was also interested in buying the *Register*. Whereas we wanted only the paper, he wanted to make it a package deal. He would sell us the *Register* if we would agree to take over the entire plant, building and grounds. Price: about $1,500,000. I studied his offer from all angles. Finally, on June 15, 1970, I wrote to Frank Wieck, whom the Archbishop had named to represent him. I told him, 'Your physical plant in Denver is too big an anchor for our little boat.' Wieck replied: 'Would you like to buy just the newspaper, without any of the equipment?' I immediately called Frawley. He told me to continue with the negotiations."

"How much did they want now?"

"The new asking price was $500,000. I felt it was fair. The *Denver Register,* as it was formally known, had a good reputation, and by owning its national edition we could help all 18 diocesan editions. We felt it was a golden opportunity to help the Church. Also involved was our promise to bring our printing from the *Visitor* plant in Huntington, Indiana, to Denver. The *Register* badly needed the extra income.

"Another meeting was arranged. Dale Francis, Bob Miller and I flew to Denver and met with Archbishop Casey, Auxiliary Bishop George Evans, Father Richard Hanifen, the chancellor of the diocese, and Father Bert Woodrich, director of public relations. Dick Casey, attorney for the archdiocese, was also there. Our attorney was Irvin Woodland.

"That evening I flew back to Los Angeles to confer with Mr. Frawley. He gave me two checks totaling $250,000 to tie up the deal, and I returned to Denver on an early morning flight. Within two hours after I returned, the contract was signed. We now owned what was to become today's *National Catholic Register*. I strongly recommended that Dale Francis be named editor-publisher, which he was, and we agreed to have *Twin Circle* printed in the Denver plant. We also moved our *Twin Circle* editorial and circulation offices to Denver in order to combine their operations with the newly-purchased *Register*. Dale has improved the *Register* immensely. In fact, when Cardinal Yu Pin and Father de Jaegher called on the Apostolic Delegate in Washington, D.C., in 1970, Archbishop Luigi Raimondi told them: 'The most important thing that happened to the Church in America in 1970 was the acquisition of the *Register* by *Twin Circle*."

"You had a pretty big operation by this time. According to my notes, you were serving as editor of *Twin Circle* that year, and were also producing and appearing on your own radio and TV programs, lecturing on college campuses, writing books, and a dozen other things. The answer is you must have been assisted by some pretty capable people."

"I had a great staff. Vincent Ryan was Managing Editor of *Twin Circle*. Frank Malina, Tom Davis and Bernie Belson, assisted by Christine Lawler, Claire Nelson and Lillian Victorero, looked after our affairs at 86 Riverside Drive in New York, and every few weeks I commuted between the West Coast and New York to make 10 or 15 Twin Circle radio programs, and a couple of Twin Circle TV shows in Washington, D.C. I also kept up my fact-finding trips overseas."

"Shortly after that you were accused of attacking the bishops' committee on the grape dispute. What was it that you objected to?"

"I did not like the way an ad hoc committee of five bishops, which was dominated by auxiliary bishop Donnelly of Hartford and Monsignor George Higgins in Washington—both champions of compulsory unionism—I did not like the way this committee acted independently of all the rest of the bishops, yet appeared to be acting in the name of all of them.

"I did not like to see the American bishops favoring one union against another, which the committee of five bishops did when it backed Cesar Chavez' union against the Teamsters. The U.S. bishops had no business getting that deeply involved in partisan unionism—and I said so in my column. I sent a letter to all the bishops about it, and several replied that they agreed with me. I kept insisting that Chavez did not really have a union; that if he had, he would not legally be able to use a secondary boycott, as he did whenever he advocated a boycott of grapes or lettuce at the foodstores. I kept insisting that Chavez had no right to represent the grape pickers unless the majority of the pickers voted for him to do so. Instead, Chavez used the boycott to force employers to make their workers join the union without a free election."

"*Newsweek* has written that *Twin Circle* owes much of its militancy to you. How do you answer these charges?"

"If by militancy they mean I am forever ready to combat liberal Catholics who either question church dogma or erode absolute moral standards—if by militancy they mean

I am a firm believer in the Pope as the chief teacher of the Catholic Church—if by militancy it is meant that I am pro-America in the fight against Communism—if by militancy they mean I am against those who would take self-determination away from the people—then I am guilty as charged."

"Father Hawk?"

"Suit yourself. I have been called a lot worse."

CHAPTER 18

Summing Up

There are disorderly scraps and threads snarled through every man's life, that begin nowhere and end nowhere, and it ought not to be so for the ultimate peace of biographers. For a sense of incompleteness is depressing and a sense of frustration is an indeterminate burden that can become dangerous with the passing years.

Out of the stacks of notes, memories, dispatches and official records that were at my disposal during the writing of this book, it was apparent that a single volume could only touch the highlights of a personality so vibrant and absorbing as Father Lyons. Now, as I look back over what I have so far written, I can see that all I wanted to tell about him is not all here, and so this chapter comes down to being a potpouri of those missing parts.

Most of what I am putting down here was drawn from a long talk I had with Father Lyons on his last visit to my home at Tacoma, Washington, in August, 1972. We were sitting at the breakfast table, drinking our morning tea, and I sipped at my cup and listened.

"A book such as this," he said, wiping his mouth with the napkin, "should give a picture of the times we are writing about."

I asked, "How would you describe our times?"

"We are living in rather exciting though troublesome times," he said. "Sort of like a ship at sea. You remember the storm more than the calmness. The period following Vatican II came at a time of turmoil and it allowed some people to run in the wrong direction."

"Do you still fear Communism? We have had a lot to say about it in this book."

"It's a very real threat," he said, solemnly. "We are living in an era when the United States, for the first time in its history, has been eclipsed militarily by a rival power. Next time we will not have a couple of years to prepare ourselves as we did in the past in the event of war. We are living in an enormous propaganda period, simply because our enemies are very clever at propaganda. One of their obvious propaganda feats is the selling of socialism. Socialism is nothing but a power grab, when a government decides to take over all the schools, suppresses the churches, takes over all ownership, all businesses. By pretending to do this in the name of the people it is called a Peoples' Republic, even though there are no elections. The only difference between Communism and socialism is that one is by rape and the other by seduction."

"There has been a lot written about Vietnamization,"

I said. "Do you feel it has proven a success?"

"Oh, yes. Definitely. Mining the harbor at Haiphong and destroying the bridges, railroads and industrial centers in North Vietnam have made it virtually impossible for Hanoi to carry on any large scale aggression against the South. In 1968, when we had 500,000 U.S. troops helping Saigon's forces, the North conquered the former capital of Hue. But four years later, when we hardly had any combat troops over there, the North was unable to take Hue or any other important town."

"In your opinion, what was the main difference between the way President Johnson ran the war and the way President Nixon handled it?"

"Well, Johnson waged a stalemate. He acted on his oft-expressed philosophy that 'some day Hanoi's leaders will meet with us at the conference table.' His assumption was that when they did they would listen to reason, and bargain fair and square. Such thinking was disastrous to decisive action."

"In other words," I said, "you didn't have much faith in the Paris negotiations."

"The negotiators in Paris didn't have the authority to make decisions. In time of war, declared or otherwise, the peace table is merely a place for tallying the results between the armed forces. North Vietnam may keep the aggression going for years, but it can do so only on a small scale, as long as Haiphong is closed and we deny her access by rail, road or pipeline. She may let the war peter out gradually. Or she may bargain with us in exchange for our POWs and other concessions. Her only hope is to talk us into getting rid of President Thieu. She would then try to put in a coalition government. An alternative would be for her to assassinate Thieu, as well as to continue killing village chiefs. But the one thing we must keep clearly in mind is that Hanoi wants nothing except to take over South Vietnam. So our positions for negotiations are entirely irreconciliable. We can only work for another South Korea."

"You have been to Vietnam numerous times. You know the people. You know the leaders. You have seen the war with your own eyes. If the war drags on what steps would you take?"

"If I had no other choice, I'd threaten to make the war seriously risky for the North Vietnamese."

"How?"

"By stepping up the bombing. Or threatening an invasion from the South or from Laos and Thailand. I would also break off trade with Moscow and Peking, if that would help stop the war. This is the way to peace with justice and freedom for South Vietnam. This is the way to discourage aggression there as well as any place else."

"Well, let's talk about your work for a while. John O'Connell, who is one of the top Executives of The Hearst Newspapers, and before that was Editor-in-chief of *Cosmopolitan* and *American Weekly* magazines, told me that he feels you have brought more vitality, interest and plain good writing to America's Catholic press than anyone else in the past ten years. Are you personally pleased with your work?"

"I enjoy it very much."

"Do you find it essential to live in New York, the hub of mass communications?"

"I live where I can best do my work. It doesn't make much difference whether I live in New York or Seattle or Los Angeles or Boston. I have always enjoyed any place I have been and enjoyed anything I have done. Perhaps the thing I least enjoyed was the dry courses we often had to take in philosophy and theology."

"Are you saying that you didn't particularly like life in the seminary?"

"I didn't say that. I said I considered my courses in philosophy and theology too dry. I enjoyed seminary life. It was a rather quiet period for me—an interlude—a time of preparation."

"Your work today seems so unpriestly. If you didn't wear the collar and the garb of the priest, one would take you for a regular journalist. Or, as Bob Considine would say, 'one of us working stiffs.' "

"Well, I am a working stiff. But I have been luckier than most people. I have been given a lot of freedom, especially since I left teaching, though I enjoyed teaching immensely. I feel that the work I am doing today has to be done."

"You make it sound as if the years are running out on you."

"Well, aren't they? They're running out on all of us. The minute you are born you start growing old. When a person is 20, he thinks he is going to live forever, if he doesn't get hit by a car. Oh, he realizes that some of his classmates are going to die, and he is going to miss them. He figures that some day they will be getting older. But not he. He is like the Irishman I met at Dublin airport, waiting to meet his brother who had been away for 50 years. 'My dumb brother,' he said to me. 'How does he expect me to recognize him after all those years? He didn't even send me a picture!' I asked him, 'Do you think he'll recognize you?' And he said, 'Of course. I haven't been away.'

"My point is that a person of 20 thinks five years is a very long time. He can hardly remember back that far. But I am now 52, and I know that the next five years will pass quickly, just as the last five have. And the next five after that."

I said, "When you were 20 and studying at the seminary, did you know what you really wanted to do with your life as a priest?"

"I thought of many things. I wanted to teach, I wanted to preach, I wanted to write. I wanted to start a chapel for poor men on Seattle's Skid Road. I wanted to do all those things."

"But if someone had asked you if you wanted to spend all your life doing any of them, what would you have said?"

"I would have said, No, not all of it. I, too, thought I was going to live so long that I could never spend all those years at one job."

"Perhaps you have been fortunate."

"I have not had to spend my life at one job. I have found myself working my way out of jobs and moving onto the next. I enjoyed every job. But always something unfolded, beckoning me on to something else."

"What do you consider middle-age?"

Father Lyons smiled.

He said, "Ten years beyond where you are now."

I said, "Edgar Eisenhower, the President's brother, once told me we can't put an age on brains. He said age shouldn't stop us. A man past 65, he said, isn't too old to set the world on fire."

"What did he base his facts on?"

"A study made of 400 famous men of achievement in history. It showed that 65 per cent of their greatest work was done past 60."

Father Lyons smiled again.

He said, "On the other hand, the most-written-about man in history is Christ. The second is Shakespeare. The third is Abraham Lincoln. And none of them lived to be 60! So what it adds up to is that it is what you do that counts, not the age at which you do it. How old was Edgar Eisenhower when he told you that?"

"About 75. He swore he did better work at 50 than at 40, and he claimed he never slowed down at 60. He was still playing golf three times a week and going to his law office regularly—at 80!"

"Perhaps he had something. Now that I have crossed the half-century mark myself, I am discovering I can do more work than before."

"Why is that?"

"Because I no longer have to recreate. I can find recreation in a change of occupation. Most of what I do I do not consider real work."

I said, "You're fortunate to be able to live in the same building in which you work."

"That's right. No one bothers me at night, and I can work as late as I want while the big city is asleep and everything is quiet. The same is true on Saturday. The mail sack arrives, and so does Bernie Belson, our faithful office manager. Father Paul Chan, the Cardinal's secretary, is always there, too, looking after the scores of Chinese students he helps get scholarships for each year."

"How many Chinese students would you estimate that Father Chan and Cardinal Yu Pin have put through American universities?"

"More than 2,000."

"What is their primary purpose?"

"To some day play a vital role on a free mainland China."

"You feel very strongly about that, don't you?"

"It was Cardinal Yu Pin who first taught me how the fate of Asia depends on the outcome of the cold war in the U.S. Just as it was the false propaganda in America after World War II that brought about the fall of mainland China to the Communists, so the truth can help America bring about the conditions that will sooner or later undermine Communism there."

"You appear to be a man in a race against time. Your schedule would kill most men your age."

"Now that I am past 50, I am far more conscious that time is running out and that I must do all I can in the next year, in the next 10 years, in the next 20 years, if God gives them to me. All we know for sure is that He rations the years out to us, a day at a time.

"A person in middle age should have more perspective, more sense of striving to achieve, and less need for play and recreation. Living in New York, and having learned how to reach the media, it becomes more important to appear on television programs, radio newscasts or talk shows than to give a lecture in a parish hall, or even on a college campus. In this manner you can reach many more students, as well as thousands of other people. Then, too, we have access to the U.S. Press Association. A year and a half ago, we took over its editorial management. This gives us the opportunity to supply the 1,240 subscribing editors with six or seven editorials a week. The USPA services newspapers in one-third of all counties in the country, and is a powerful instrument in helping to keep editors informed. Our editorials also go out to some 450 subscribing business executives and public relations men."

"How does John V. Hinkel figure into your organization? He's the former *New York Times* writer, isn't he?"

"John worked for the *Times* for years. A very competent writer. He now lives in Washington, D.C., and is a public relations specialist. His specialty is dealing with the press. By hiring him, we found he could spread our editorials nationally and even internationally. He writes up our columns, articles and speeches in the form of an expert press release, and then hand-carries them around to everyone in the National Press Building, where his office is located. He not only covers the U.S. press, but the Asian, European, and Latin American press as well."

"What are the results?"

"We know we're getting wide coverage. Our friends in Buenos Aires or Lima or some other far-flung place send us the newspaper clippings showing the space we received. The Communist *Daily World* sometimes repeats a blast at us that first appears in *Pravda* or *Izvestia*. I recall an incident several years ago that indicated our messages were getting through. Father de Jaegher was visiting with Father LaDany in Hong Kong. Father LaDany is a noted Jesuit scholar who publishes the *China News Analysis,* which is recognized as the best information distributed about mainland China. He said to Father de Jaegher, 'I am trying to lie low in Hong Kong. I don't want the Communists here to bomb my office. Tell Dan Lyons to change his name. He has to take another name!'

"The problem stemmed from the fact that the Chinese in Formosa had given me an official name the year before, based on 'Lyons, Daniel.' It came out in the Chinese translation so close to the one held by Father LaDany that when my name kept appearing in the Hong Kong papers, blasting the Chinese Communists, the people there thought it was Father LaDany who was attacking them. The only solution was for me to take another Chinese name, one which sounded more like 'Lyons' than 'Lyons, Daniel.' But it was some time before we cleared the problem up for Father LaDany by informing the Chinese press of my new name."

"With all this emphasis on newspaper writing and press releases, does this mean that you are cutting down on your famous campus debates? Are the college lecture halls going to see as much of you in the future as they have in the past."

"Of course, my time is growing more limited. But I still feel that a red-hot debate on campus is very much worthwhile. It usually draws a big crowd, gets a good play by the local press and radio-TV, and gives me a chance to discredit the local leftist professor I tangle with."

"Do you find other organizations wanting to work with you?" I asked.

"You mean groups who support our philosophy and aims?"

"Yes," I said.

"Well, let's cite the de Rance Foundation."

"Where are they located?" I wanted to know.

"Milwaukee."

"That's Harry John's foundation, isn't it? The millionaire?"

"Yes. Harry is the president. Dr. Donald Gallagher is vice president. Harry John put his family fortune into the foundation in order to carry out his vocation in life."

"What exactly does he consider his—quote—'vocation in life'—unquote?"

"To promote the welfare of the Catholic Church. He has been of considerable help to contemplative religious Orders."

"Where does the name de Rance come from?"

"De Rance was the one who led the 17th century reform in the Trappist Order."

"And Harry John and Dr. Gallagher want to see the Church keep on an even keel."

"That's right. They want to strengthen the spiritual elements."

"Give me an example."

"Well, Mr. John bought a magnificent painting of the Sacred Heart of Jesus. He paid $30,000 for it. By putting a full-color reproduction of it on the cover of *Twin Circle,* we were able to sell a thousand copies of it. In this way a lot of Americans were able to have a very inspiring piece of religious art in their homes and thus help unite their families under the Fatherhood of God, as seen in the Sacred Heart of His divine Son."

"You were quoted recently as saying that the big crisis in the world today is spiritual. Would you care to elaborate?"

"On the one side you have the forces of faith; on the other, you have the forces of disbelief. The conflict between the two grows sharper and more vicious by the day. God is being left out of religion, even by some clergymen. They call it the *social gospel,* but it is the Gospel according to Marx. Instead of extolling man's virtues, a civilization that is secularized actually degrades man and enslaves him. Only when man has improved himself will he be able to improve society. You cannot help the lot of man by destroying spiritual values. The idea that you can put in a tyrannical system, with no checks and balances, and make it work better than what we already have is totally absurd. The idea that you can do away with religion and yet make everybody honest is a farce. The idea that you can destroy man's incentive by doing away with the profit motive, that you can do away with free enterprise and neglect the most talented and best-trained members of our economic and industrial society and replace them with know-nothing bureaucrats—

wrap everything up in red tape and still increase production—is preposterous."

"Father, in recent months you have been very vocal on the subject of zero population growth. Who do you feel is behind the movement?"

"The atheistic elements, basically. They are so pessimistic they despair of any progress being made. But, then, why shouldn't they despair? According to their religious philosophy, man has no hope of reward, no future life, no moral value. According to them, there are no laws of nature because there is no law-giver. According to them, it will only be an accident if the sun should rise tomorrow. By refusing to honor God they bring dishonor on us all. We could do with a zero growth on atheism. There is too much of it now, especially among the university professors."

"Do you remember what Whittaker Chambers said back in 1952, after bolting the Communist Party? He said that without God, man is just what Communism claimed he was: the most intelligent of the animals. Man without God, he said, is a beast—never more beastly than when he is most intelligent about his beastliness."

Father Lyons said, "Chambers also said that the crisis of the Western world exists to the degree in which it is indifferent to God. Faith, he said, is the central problem of this age. He wrote: 'The Western world does not know it, but it already possesses the answer to this problem—but only provided that its faith in God and the freedom He enjoins is as great as Communism's faith in man.' So the biggest problem of all, it seems to me, is recognition of God, and therefore the absolutes: truth, good, and evil. Or lack of faith in God, and therefore a blindness to such things as right or wrong, truth, good or evil. The new hypocrisy is that of the sinner who will not admit he sins. A noted psychiatrist told me: 'The trouble with 90 per cent of my patients is that they sin too much. They only come to me to find some excuse, so that they can go back out and sin some more. They don't need me. They need God.' "

"I remember a particular column you wrote two years ago. In it you replied to the alarmists in the Church who were concerned about the decline in the number of converts to Catholicism in America. You pointed out that this was due more to false notions of ecumenism than anything else. You said, 'Tolerance is a virtue, but indifference is not. Nor is spreading the faith to be confused with feeding the hungry. In the long run our spiritual welfare is all that counts, for in the long run we will have to shed our mortal frame.' "

"I remember the piece. What I was saying was that in addition to a weak faith, many Catholics have no sense of history. Too many of them have forgotten the historical facts. One hundred and thirty years ago, when Catholicism was barely tolerated in England, and when Catholics were rare and very poor, the most popular historian of his time, Lord Macaulay, was asked to write an essay on Ranke's History of the Popes. He thought of how little the Catholic Church in England amounted to, how the mighty British Empire was the greatest the world had ever seen, and how the Protestant cathedral of St. Paul's in

London represented the growth and power of the Church of England, to which he belonged. But Macaulay had a keen sense of history, and although he had no use for the Catholic Church, his historical sense led him, in 1840, to make this magnificent pronouncement:

"He wrote that there was not, and there never had been on this earth, a work of human policy so well deserving of examination as the Roman Catholic Church. The history of that Church, he wrote, joined together the two great ages of human civilization. No other institution was left standing at that time which carried the mind back to the times when the smoke of sacrifice rose from the Pantheon. He said that the proudest royal houses were but of yesterday when compared with the line of the Supreme Pontiffs. He marveled at that line which could be traced back in an unbroken series, from the Pope who crowned Pepin in the eighth century; and far beyond the time of Pepin the august dynasty extended, until it was lost in the twilight of fable. Then came the Republic of Venice, which was modern when compared with the Papacy; and the Republic of Venice was gone and the Papacy remained.

"In his essay, Macaulay wrote: 'The Papacy remains, not in decay, not a mere antique, but full of life and youthful vigour. The Catholic Church is still sending forth to the farthest ends of the earth missionaries as zealous as those who landed in Kent with Augustine, and still confronting hostile kings with the same spirit with which she confronted Attila. The number of her children is greater than in any former age. Her acquisitions in the New World have more than compensated for what she has lost in the Old. . .'

"Macaulay confessed that he did not see any sign that the end of the Catholic Church's long dominion was approaching. What he was saying was simply this: The Church has been around for a long time, and it is going to be around for a long, long time yet. I like what Mrs. Roberts Blount, whose nephew served recently as U.S. Postmaster General, said. She said that if the Catholic Church had held strong in the sixties it could have converted half of America. 'Society,' she said, 'has been in such a state of confusion and turmoil that if the Church had remained firm it would have attracted countless thousands to its ranks. But instead, what do we see? The unholy spectacle of priests and nuns deserting their sacred calling in a so-called 'crisis of identity.' "

I said, "I thought Mrs. Blount was a Protestant."

"She was. And so was her husband. They were surrounded by Protestants. She lives in Tallassee, Alabama. Both came from prominent Southern families of long-standing: socially, financially, and politically. But before he died, they both joined the Catholic Church and built their parish church and rectory. A few years ago, Mrs. Blount told me, 'I am glad that my husband didn't live to see the Church he loved so much become so shattered.' "

"Father, do you agree with Mrs. Blount? Do you believe that the Church is in as shaky condition as she does?"

"Well, in the past several years vocations have dropped off. Our school system is in jeopardy because so many lay people—and even some of our clergy—put so little value on it. There is an attack within the Church on Sunday Mass and even on the Mass itself. Confession in the hands of today's modernists is largely falling by the wayside. Divorce is being advocated even by some Catholic clergy. The doctrine on sin is becoming passe, and the whole range of spiritual life is being weakened and undermined. I only hope that we can learn from our mistakes. I hope that society at large will once again be able to see the Church as the backbone of our civilization, rather than something that resembles a reed shaken by the wind."

"What was that you said to Father James Kavanaugh on the Barry Farber radio show, in 1969?" Father Kavanaugh was the priest from Lansing, Michigan, who gained national prominence, in 1966, after writing an article for *Saturday Evening Post* entitled, "I Am A Priest—I Want To Marry." Father Kavanaugh had written it under the pseudonym "Father Stephen Nash," but it soon became known as the work of Father Kavanaugh. He later wrote a book that sold more than 100,000 copies in hardback, and more than a million in paperback. The title of the book was, "A Modern Priest Looks at His Outdated Church."

Father Lyons clearly recalled the debate he had with Father Kavanaugh on the Barry Farber show.

He said, "I asked Father Kavanaugh in the middle of the broadcast if he believed in the divinity of Christ, and his immediate reply was 'no.' I pointed out to him that Christ was crucified for insisting on His divinity, but it made no difference. This former priest was too far gone.

The erosion, the cancer, the cry of the rebel in the Garden of Eden—*'non serviam,* I will not serve'—had been repeated once too often in the mind and heart of this poor priest, as it has by thousands of other rebels and revolutionaries for 2,000 years."

"Did you ask him if he believed in God?"

"Yes, of course."

"What was his answer?"

"We were still on the air when I put the question to him, and he shook his head and said, 'It took me 21 pages to discuss that in my book. I cannot answer it so briefly.' "

"And how did you answer that, Father?"

"I told him, 'If you really believed in God, you could give me a simple yes. That's all.' "

"What was his comment on the question of prayer?"

"He said he no longer prayed."

"Why?"

" 'Because,' he said, 'to talk to Him would be like talking to myself.' All you can do for a man like that is to pray for him—at least, until he can pray for himself."

I said, "Father Dan, on the subject of Catholicism in America, who would you pick as the one man who did more to bring American Catholicism to the attention of the world, and for making it a major factor in church councils, than any one else?"

Without hesitation, he replied, "Cardinal Spellman. He was a priestly priest and a man after God's own heart. He spent the last 25 years away from the comforts of home at Christmas time in order to bring comfort to troops around the world. Despite his infirmities he had hoped to do the same in 1968. Instead, God took him Home for Christmas."

"Did you know Cardinal Spellman?"

"Not well. I last met him in Taiwan, and so was at the airport to meet his plane. By then he was not a well man. His legs were far from steady as he walked off the plane, but he carefully walked around to meet each of the 50 Chinese children in the band that greeted him. At noon, he offered Mass at St. Christopher's Church in Taipei, which he had helped provide near the American base. Afterwards he asked that everyone in the church come up to meet him in the sanctuary. He met them all, kindly and patiently, with no thought of his own fatigue.

"I had dinner that night with the Cardinal at the residence of President and Madame Chiang Kai-shek. He told his hosts and long-time admirers how much he had always enjoyed visiting the Far East and spending Christmas with the troops. He explained slowly, with simple and touching eloquence: 'I thought I might not be able to come this year. My legs are no good, my hearing is no good, and my eyes are no good, and I did not want to embarrass anyone or cause any inconvenience to anybody by dying on the journey.'

"President Chiang then stood up at dinner to give a toast. But he was much too diplomatic to toast the Cardinal first. He said, 'I want to give a toast to Pope Paul VI!' That, he knew, would please the Cardinal most. When dinner was over, Madame Chiang hurried to take his right arm, while a servant took his left. Cardinal Spellman remarked simply and pleasantly: 'I just need about three more assistants!' As I left that night, Madame Chiang said to me with tears of admiration: 'You certainly have a wonderful Cardinal!'

"Father, much of your newspaper journalism in the past several years has largely concerned Communism in Asia. What about Communism in Europe? What are you going to do about that?"

"I've been considering a trip behind the Iron Curtain for more than a year now," he told me. "I applied for a visa to Russia and its satellites and it has been approved. I'm flying over for sixteen days in mid-September (1972)."

I said, "Over the years, you have been pretty rough on the Communists. You've been attacked by *Pravda,* and *Izvestia,* and *The Daily World* in New York. Aren't you surprised that your visa came through?"

Father Dan smiled. "Maybe," he said, "they want to prove to me that I have been wrong about them."

"Maybe," I said, "they want to put you in prison."

Postcript 1972:

Father Lyons Behind the Iron Curtain

At precisely 3 p.m. on Monday, September 18th, 1972, Father Lyons and Father Cletus Healy, a fellow Jesuit, boarded a plane in New York, buckled their seat belts, and settled back for the long uncertain journey behind the Iron Curtain. This was a trip that Father Dan had been thinking about for more than a year and a half. When he first told me about it, I tried to talk him out of it.

"Don't go," I had told him. "Once they get their hands on you they'll never let you out. They will throw you in jail for the slightest error."

"Granted it's a calculated risk," he said. "But it is a *reasonable* risk. It is a risk I feel I have to take. As a journalist, I have to go and see for myself."

There was no chance of changing his mind. Sure, he accepted the fact that he was going into a police state. Yes, he knew of the Red attacks made on some visiting clergymen. For more than a year he had put off the trip because he had his doubts as to whether he would see more than a regular tourist would. But now that he was going, his reservations quickly dissolved into excitement. His sister Pat told me, "I've never seen Dan so excited."

Several hours before his plane took off, he phoned me long-distance. I wished him God speed and cautioned him to be careful. I said, "Don't take any unnecessary chances. They will have someone on your tail all the time you're over there. Don't give them any excuse to put you in jail."

He said, "I have left instructions with my staff as to what to do if I don't come out. Both Father Healy and I have signed an affidavit swearing to our intentions. I am having a copy sent to you. Don't worry, I will be all right."

And then he was gone.

A day later, the mailman dropped the following note in my mailbox:

"To Whom It May Concern:

This is to certify that Father Cletus Healy and I, Father Dan Lyons, are going to abide by all the rules and regulations while we are in the USSR countries. We will make no dealing in the black market or in any other way make ourselves liable for fines or imprisonment. We are not going to pass out any literature.

If we are accused of the contrary and do not come out as scheduled, please inform Senator James Buckley that we are being unjustly detained, falsely accused, and that any confession to the contrary will be untrue and made only under severe duress.

We hereby swear to the truth of the above.

Sincerely in Christ,
Daniel Lyons, S.J.
Cletus Healy, S.J."

Their first stop was Czechoslovakia. The plan was for them to stay together through Czechoslovakia, Poland, and Russia. In Moscow, they would part. Father Lyons would travel on to Rumania and Hungary alone, while Father Healy would go to West Germany, to take photos of the Iron Curtain.

For sixteen days we heard nothing. And then on October 4th, my phone rang. It was Father Lyons, phoning from New York.

He said, "Well, I'm back, thank God. But the trip was worth it. I found out what I wanted to know—even more. I managed to bring out two-and-a-half notebooks filled with quotes and facts and figures. I never once dared leave them in my hotel. I always took them with me. Now I am sending them on to you. I also took a lot of pictures. Perhaps you would like to have this stuff to finish out the book."

So here they are. Fresh from behind the Iron Curtain. Father Lyons' personal notes. They represent still another glimpse inside the man himself—perpetual motion under fire:

"For the past several weeks I have been traveling behind the Iron Curtain. I was never sure whether they were going to let me in, and once they did, I was far from certain they would let me out. I did not tell them I was a journalist. But as the Communist newspapers have attacked me in recent years, I am sure they knew who I was, so there was always the very real threat I would be brought in for questioning.

"That can be a rather indefinite procedure. As several priests behind the Curtain told me, they are sometimes asked to stop by police headquarters with the remark: 'Just come by and answer some questions. If you don't recall the answers, well, there is no hurry.' They are willing to wait, and to have you wait—in jail.

"Until the last member of the secret police looks you over for the last time—until the last soldier inspects your passport—until your plane at last starts down the runway for Zurich and the free world, you never know whether you will be allowed to leave.

"I learned a lot of facts behind the Iron Curtain. From extensive discussions with many priests and others I was able to find out information about the Church in countries like Poland and Hungary that officials in the American Embassies admitted they were not aware of.

"My first stop was Czechoslovakia, a country 70 percent Catholic. The Church is in a semi-dying condition there, but it is not dying out. As in all of the countries behind the Iron Curtain, Czechoslovakia is ruled with a tight fist by the one million members of the Communist Party. There are 14 dioceses, but only two bishops. The government will not permit any more to be consecrated.

"About 3,500 priests are active. Another 500 must work as laymen, since the government does not recognize them as priests. Approximately 35 priests are ordained each year. No Catholic schools are permitted. Most of the nuns have recently been confined to work as staff in mental institutions.

"Still, the people have preserved a sense of humor. The Czechs gathered around when their 45-foot statue of Stalin was being carted away from the middle of Prague and said with a smile: *'Sic transit gloria mundi.'* They recalled with a laugh how the Russian soldiers sent to quell the uprising had asked: 'Where is the Suez Canal?' That is where they had been told they were being sent.

"I met a nun the first day at a local church who was as happy a person as you could find, happy because she was able to work around the church, an example of things we take for granted but which mean so much to persons living under those conditions. I met a man who was free to work around the church because 'I am being punished,' meaning he was not allowed to work. That happened to tens of thousands of persons in Czechoslovakia after Dubcek was ousted a few years earlier.

"Remember how Stalin used to call it 'changing the guard' when he had a purge of Party officials? It still goes on. Three hundred thousand members of the Communist Party have been purged in Czechoslovakia in the past four years. Forty percent of the writers have been forced out of their profession. Fifty thousand union members were purged. The remaining writers hew the Commie line, attacking the clergy in that 70 percent Catholic country as 'fascists' and 'Nazi.' Monasteries have been closed at a great rate, and priests have been forced into early retirement to make them scarcer.

"The police are not much in evidence. Nor are there Russian soldiers on the streets. But everyone knows there are 80,000 Soviet troops stationed 30 miles away. One of the first buildings I saw was a training school for future members of the Party. It is the Party members and they alone who get all of the good jobs and who run every facet of government. Only they can be candidates; only they can hold trusted positions. Only they have all the power.

"Prague is still a very beautiful city, steeped in history as few other cities outside of Rome. It is the former city of good King Wenceslas, who is buried in the cathedral; of St. John Nepomocene and St. Procopius. It was also the city of John Hus, who protested the policies of Rome a hundred years before Luther in Germany. Hus was rector at Charles University in Prague, a follower of Wycliffe in England. The Hussite Protestants inaugurated the election of bishops and started the distribution of Communion under both species, big innovations in those days under the pretext of democracy. The university there was founded in 1348 and named after King Charles IV.

"In the 14th century, when only Rome had a population of 50,000—Prague was second with 40,000. London was third, with 35,000. The 13th-century cathedral and palace buildings overlooking Prague are one of the most beautiful and interesting collections of edifices to be seen anywhere. The second largest building in Prague was formerly a Jesuit college. It is now the university library, housing 1.5 million volumes.

"Like any other job, there is a knack to gathering information, and I worked diligently at it, fifteen hours a day. If my references seem vague, it is to avoid retaliation against any of the persons I interviewed by the Communist governments involved.

"There are four kinds of visitors that travel behind the Iron Curtain: 1) Those who go to visit relatives. They find out what conditions are like in a certain area, but cannot publicize it for fear of reprisals on their relatives and for fear they will not be allowed to make another visit. 2) Tourists who stay at foreign hotels, do not know the language, and talk only to their official guides and to their fellow tourists. They learn little about the repression in the lives of the people. 3) Businessmen who may or may not learn some of the facts, but who prefer not to say anything because it would be bad for their business. 4) Journalists who may find out the facts, and who may or may not report on what they see, once they have left.

"This is the sort of information the tourist does not pick up. He is told that apartment rents are cheap, and sometimes they are as low as six percent of one's income. But the average family spends 48 percent of its budget for food. Clothing is about two-thirds as high as in the United States. Yet the average income is only about $125 per month for men and $100 for women.

"The birthrate is understandably low, so the government is encouraging people to have more children. A wife can stay home for a year or so when she has a child, drawing her salary all the while and applying the time toward her pension. The government also pays an allowance of about $12 a month for each child, up to a maximum of $30 per month.

"People with foreign currency such as tourists, or relatives who receive such currency in the mail, as well as Party officials, can get special money (crowns) known as "tuzex" crowns. These crowns can be used in special shops where only special items are for sale. Ironically, "tuzex" is also the name applied to prostitutes who walk up and down the main streets late at night. Let it not be thought they do not exist in Communist countries. As for other types of crime, stealing cars for 'joyriding' is an increasing problem, though they cannot be resold without great danger. Stripping cars is also common.

"The Czechs were formerly called Bohemians. Their western borders were known as the Sudetenland, which Hitler invaded at the outset of World War II.

"No Catholic schools are permitted in Czechoslovakia. There are two or three bishops for the 14 dioceses. Two seminaries are in operation: one for the Czechs called Litomerice, and one for the Slovaks. There are about 150 seminarians in the Czech seminary, with about 35 ordained each year. Not many for 10 million Czechs, most of whom are Catholic.

"The government must approve where each priest is sent. About 1,660 parishes have no resident pastor. Instead of bishops, in 12 of the 14 dioceses there are priests who are vicars. They are chosen largely by the state. The other seminary, which has about 200 seminarians, is in Bratislava. There is no Slovak bishop.

"Among the very beautiful and historic buildings in the city which are still very much in use is the Tyl theater, built in 1770. Mozart first played his Don Giovanni opera there in 1787. More aware than ever of the need for tourist currency, the government is sparing no expense to keep up the historic buildings, most of which are Catholic churches.

"The countries behind the Iron Curtain are considerably

more prosperous in the cities than most Americans think. Yet as I look back on our country's worst year, 1933, the Communists are not as prosperous as we were then. Compared to today's Reds, we had large houses, ample food and clothing. The main thing that we did not have, which they do, is full employment. Yet even there we had an advantage, and still do: most American mothers do not have to work. There it is a basic economic necessity. More basic, of course, is that we have our freedoms: of religion, of speech, of ownership, of movement, and of the press.

"There are no strikes, no student uprisings, and there is no drug problem, although it seems to pose a serious threat in Moscow, judging by the way the papers there are attacking it. Alcohol, however, is a very serious problem in some of the Iron Curtain countries. Most of the auto accidents in Czechoslovakia, I was told, are due to drinking.

"On leaving Czechoslovakia I flew to Poland. Warsaw has little visible history, as the city was systematically leveled to the ground by the Nazi in World War II. There are 440 markers, each one indicating where 10 or more people were executed. After the Russian troops had taken part of the city, they encouraged the people to rise up against the Nazi forces, which the people did on August 1, 1944. The Russian troops then sat idly by for 60 days while the city was destroyed and the people slain by the tens of thousands. The Russian troops then 'liberated' the city with hardly any opposition, after it had been destroyed and the people massacred.

"Poland also has bitter memories of the slaughter of its Jewish residents by Hitler. He built a ghetto in the city, walling them off from the outside except for shipment to Auschwitz and the gas chambers. Ten percent of all the Jews killed by the Nazi forces were from Warsaw.

"Poland is the only Communist country (the Communists prefer the word 'socialist' countries) where the farms have never been collectivized. Eighty-three percent of the farm land consists of small farms, privately owned. There are also a few small privately-run stores and businesses, none of which can have more than five employees.

"As in the other Communist countries, Polish troops do not serve outside their own country except in an emergency, such as when Hungarian troops were forced to help in the invasion of Czechoslovakia, in 1968. Nor is there any conscription for university students, except part-time while at school and during one summer.

"The importance of the Voice of America broadcasts cannot be over-emphasized. Many of the people do listen, as their own newspapers are limited to the Communist line. Radio Free Europe is also effective, and one can easily hear both in the various countries. The main distinction between them is that the VOA broadcasts are officially the voice of the U.S. government, whereas RFE are not.

"Unofficially, Radio Free Europe is a CIA operation, partially financed by private donations. Iron Curtain peoples can also pick up our Armed Forces Network broadcasts, as well as the BBC from England and broadcasts from several other countries, depending on what languages they understand.

"When I asked a Polish journalist how many people were killed during the riots over food price increases in 1970, he replied: 'They never give us such figures. We hear about killings in Uganda, but not about casualties here.' The black market in foreign currency is very strong in Poland. Most of the taxi drivers I encountered, and perhaps half the waiters in hotels, are actively soliciting illegal currency. Our U.S. press keeps attacking black market operations in Saigon, but seldom mentions the extensive black market or corruption behind the Iron Curtain.

"Father Healy and I offered Mass together every day. We found a Carmelite monastery flourishing near where we stayed. At huge St. Anne's Church there was a large display against abortion, including life-size photos of unborn children. The clergy in Poland are proud that ultra-liberalism from Holland and elsewhere has never infiltrated the Church in Poland. The late Robert Kennedy was a big success with the students when he spoke in Warsaw, and I was delighted to hear that Cardinal John Krol of Philadelphia was about to visit Poland. A Polish speaker, he was bound to be an inspiration to those people—a light in the darkness of persecution.

"The average wage in Poland is 2,000 zlotas—$60 American. The average rent would be $15 a month, though one of our guides was paying $30. In all of the large cities in socialist countries, the people have two- or three-room apartments, and are lucky if there are not two generations of the same family living together.

"There are 36 million people in Poland. Nearly 99

percent of them are Catholic. The Communist Party, with its two million members, rules everything and everybody. Some of the Party members receive the Sacraments occasionly, but not in an area where they are known. The Church discourages Party membership, but has not attached automatic excommunication to it. To do so would be like a declaration of war against the government. Some would deserve it, but not all.

"There are almost 700 Jesuits in the two Polish provinces, with about 150 of them working on missions outside the country. One Province has 28 Novices, the other, 21. Conditions were much stricter under Stalin, and there seems to be a trend toward a limited understanding with the Church. Jesuits are not allowed to teach in schools, but they give missions, run some parishes, and conduct catechism classes. There are some Catholic publications such as a newspaper and the Apostleship of Prayer periodical, but the government has the final say on all printed matter. Even sermons are often taped and are controlled by the state.

"I was assured by a knowledgeable Polish priest: 'The Communists will not succeed in destroying the Church—not in Poland.' Cardinal Wyszynski is a vigorous 71, and his probable successor, Cardinal Wojtyla in Cracow, is only 51. Said an elderly Jesuit: 'Communism is like a carrot: red on the outside, but white inside.' A western diplomat in Rumania assured me in the same vein that Communism is 'a very thin veneer,' meaning that it does not have much of a foundation, and is desperately trying to preserve its own life.

"One priest told me how priests are forbidden to give lessons, so he gave 'conferences' to students. He could not give them Retreats, so he formed hiking clubs and took them off to the mountains on camping trips to accomplish the same thing. He was finally fined about $50, but he fought it to the highest court. He had to pay the fine, but went right back into business at the same old stand. Another priest told me how he had taken 2,000 students on a pilgrimage to Our Lady's shrine at Chestahova.

"In Poland, unlike the other Communist countries, the priests are not supported by the government, which of course is an advantage. They keep no record of who attends catechism classes, so the government does not know who attends. Parents do not hesitate to teach catechism to their children. Nor does the government have any control over who is to be ordained. If they know ahead of time that a boy wants to enter the seminary, the government will try to discourage him. But the number of vocations is high, particularly in Galicia; that is, in Cracow and below. The government does demand the right to approve who is appointed as a pastor. The parishes are free to take up collections at Sunday Masses. That seems true in every Communist country.

"There are about 17 dioceses in Poland, with approximately 150 seminarians in each diocese. Visiting the churches there and elsewhere behind the Iron Curtain reminded me of our Catholic churches before the second Vatican Council. They have beautiful choirs, Benediction of the Blessed Sacrament, Latin hymns and a number of Latin Masses, plus statues to our favorite saints of yesteryear, particularly St. Theresa of Lisieux, St. Anthony of Padua, the little man of Assisi, St. Elizabeth of Hungary, and the newest saint in that area, Father Maximilian Kolbe. One wonders what we have done to replace those dear people whose replicas are resting unceremoniously in the basement of so many of our churches.

"The Polish government has done a remarkable job of rebuilding Warsaw, with hundreds of thousands of new apartment units. As in all Communist countries, however, their rebuilding problem was not half as bad as West Germany's. Nor did they recover half so quickly. Unlike free-world countries, family apartments are almost all limited to two or three rooms.

"Fifty percent of the tourists to Poland are from the United States, mostly Polish-Americans like Mr. and Mrs. Stanley Traczewski from New Jersey, whom we happened to meet in Warsaw and who helped serve as interpreters for us. I say 'we' as Father Cletus Healy was still with me on this part of the journey. We offered Mass daily, occasionally in our hotel room if an early departure made it impossible elsewhere. But we usually went to a nearby parish and had no trouble anywhere in using church facilities.

"In Poland, the government permits 10 Catholic schools to operate, but none for boys. Some of the Communist Party bosses send their daughters there with the excuse: 'It is my wife's decision.' Unlike the other Communist countries, 83 percent of the farm land consists of small, privately-owned farms. Poland is the only country that has succeeded in toppling a Communist regime, after the people struck and rioted when food prices were increased two years ago.

"When I asked a priest in the old-town section of Warsaw whether they had any modernist theologians, he said 'No!' He then explained to me in Latin: 'A group of such theologians reportedly got together (somewhere) and thought they were Christ. The Christ child appeared and told the people: 'I am Christ. But don't tell them.'

"The Poles told me: 'We are the freest of the socialist nations, but we are the poorest.' The Church is strong because the bishops, priests and lay people stick together. Under such conditions there are always some who will turn against their religion; and many more, perhaps half, who will slip away because they are weak and need all the help that the Church in a free society can give them. But persecution breeds greatness as well, and unites the truly faithful. In Poland, they do not have the problem we do with leftist theologians and disgruntled malcontents.

"As we were leaving Poland an alert native spoke with us of our going to the Soviet Union. I joked that we might be spending 60 days as a guest of the state—free room and board in a Soviet prison. The Warsaw resident replied very seriously: 'You will be lucky if it is that short a stay.' We learned in Moscow that even for a very minor transgression, such as speaking your mind to the wrong person or selling an item of clothing to someone who requested it, a sentence of from seven to ten years is normal, if the government decides to prosecute.

"We flew from Warsaw to Moscow on Aeroflot, the Russian airline whose seats were apparently made for midgets.

Whereas nearly every guide and taxi driver in Poland was involved in the black market, tourists do not encounter that in the Soviet Union. The Russian people are under much more severe discipline. They also identify with their government more than the satellite countries do.

"The Czechs, Poles, Rumanians, Hungarians and others feel that their country is a colony of Russia, and they resent it. They particularly resent the universal persecution of religion by the U.S.S.R. The only country where the people look on the Russians as their friends is in Bulgaria, which was rescued by the Russians from the Turks as late as 1878.

"A big distinction must be made between the satellite countries and the Soviet Union. Nearly 50 percent of the population of the U.S.S.R. is not Russian. Outstanding examples are the former countries of Lithuania (predominantly Roman Catholic), Latvia and Estonia. I say 'former countries' because the Soviet Union has gobbled them up. They have no governments of their own and no foreign legations. They have literally disappeared from the map. The U.S.S.R. has made every effort to see that they cease to exist. I do not include them as satellites.

"By satellite nations I mean countries like Poland, Hungary and Czechoslovakia. A more accurate description would be to call them Soviet *colonies*. This identifies Moscow as head of an empire, which she is; the only sizable empire in the world today. That makes Moscow 'imperialistic,' despite the propaganda she creates and which is faithfully parroted by the Left, that only the United States is an imperialist. If you think in terms of the Soviet Union and her colonies you will find it easier to grasp an extremely important fact: that those countries resent the government in the Kremlin far more than the Russian people do.

"I was told that many millions of Russians are rather satisfied by now with the progress being made by their government. That is infinitely less true of the people in other countries living under Russian rule. Despite an abiding resentment of the police-state, particularly the ubiquitous spying on the entire population and the suppression of religion, the Russian people tend to identify with the government. But to a very large extent, non-Russians reject the government's legitimacy. They do not consider breaking a law or stealing or cheating the government in any way immoral. In their minds, it is the leaders, posing as their rulers, who are illegal and immoral.

"On the entire trip I wore my clerical suit and Roman collar. It meant special questioning at the airport in Moscow. They particularly wanted to know: 1) Did I come on business? 2) Did I bring any literature? But the Roman collar made it easy to get a friendly response out of many non-officials. The lady at the money exchange asked: 'Why did you come here?' 'To see you,' I said. 'Oh, thank you very much!' Then she added, as did several others later, that we should see this monastery and that. 'Be sure to go to Zagorsk,' they urged, 'to see the monasteries there.'

"I was told there were 40 open churches in Moscow, a city of eight million people. There is only one Catholic church, St. Louis, a small place that was formerly used by the French and now serves mostly Poles and Germans. There is one Jewish synagogue, and two Baptist churches attended by Russians. About 150 students from the United States study in the Soviet Union. The majority of people, reportedly, are still Christian, but as in other countries, a maximum of 10 percent rule the country and hold down all of the responsible positions: in this case the 25 million members of the Communist Party.

"Few people approach foreigners for black market dealings, and in the Soviet Union you can presume such people work for the government. The American Embassy explained to me that sometimes the government convicts foreigners for some slight misdoing, metes out sentences of seven to ten years, then perhaps tries to exchange them later for Russian spies in U.S. jails.

"Conditions are so tight that occasionally a taxi driver will refuse to take 'imperialist' money as a tip. I refer, of course, to rubles. The ruble is pegged at $1.20 but is worth about half that amount. The average wage is 120 rubles a month. About one-fourth of that goes for rent, half for food, and the rest for clothing and a few other items. Clothing prices are about two-thirds as high as in the United States. Food is cheaper, but many items are often not available. It is estimated that 80 percent of the Russian diet is starch.

"Medical doctors are poorly paid. They earn not much more than a factory worker. Eighty percent of them are women, though the head doctors are usually men. Public transportation is good; so is mass public housing, though two or three rooms are all any family has, except for the favored few. Those who earn $1,000 or more per week pay only 13 percent income tax. (The average person pays

Archbishop Robert J. Dwyer, Portland, Oregon, is chairman of the editiorial board for Twin Circle and the Register.

Frank Morriss, columnist and Editor of Twin Circle, *1967-1968.*

Rev. Kenneth Baker, S.J., former president of Seattle University, and now editor of Homiletic & Pastoral Review.

The Rev. Pedro Arrupe, General of the Jesuits, is the first Basque to head the Order since its founde St. Ignatius Loyola. After meeting him, Fathe. Lyons said: "He is very kindly and personable. H is just as I imagine St. Ignatius to have been."

Dan Lyons, S.J., meets the long-time friend of his late father's, President Eamon de Valera of Ireland.

Key people in Father Dan's journalism career. Left to right, Father Lyons, Dale Francis (editor-publisher of National Catholic Register*), Mrs. Patrick Frawley, Cardinal Yu Pin, and Patrick Frawley.*

Father Lyons is also popular with many Protestants. He is shown here with Dr. Billy James Hargis, after his speech at Dr. Hargis' annual religious conference, Tulsa, Oklahoma. They are close friends.

Father Lyons addresses annual convention of Archdiocesan Council of Catholic Women at Mobile, Alabama, in 1968. At the dinner that night, Archbishop Toolen, then 83, condemned the Jesuit College there, Spring Hill, for planning to bring Timothy Leary to the campus. "They are paying him $1,200!—$1,200 for one lecture!" said the grand old Archbishop. Then turning to Father Lyons at the head table he said aloud, "Don't get any ideas, Father Lyons!" Later, Leary was cancelled.

One of Father Lyons' and Patrick Frawley's chief projects is Schick Hospital in Seattle, designed to cure people with drinking problems. Says Father Lyons: "It is impossible to calculate the damage to health caused by alcohol. There are nearly 7,000,000 slaves to alcohol in the U.S. Schick is the best answer to the alcohol problem."

Father Lyons has interviewed many world-famous people for his Twin Circle *columns, but none more beautiful than Princess Grace of Monaco, shown here in the Palace gardens. The former Academy Award-winning motion picture actress from Philadelphia is a regular subscriber to* Twin Circle *and often orders books through Twin Circle Publishing Company to send to her friends. Father Lyons had a lengthy interview with her at the Palace in 1971. In a speech to the world-wide convention of La Leche League, Princess Grace said of Father Lyons: "A friend of mine, Father Lyons, a Jesuit, once made a remark I have never forgotten. He said, 'We have been deluded into thinking that knowledge is a substitute for discipline. No age has ever tried to avoid discipline as much as ours.'"* (Photo by DON DORNAN)

Father Lyons' "Twin Circle Headline" was a popular program on television in 40 U.S. cities for several years. He conducted a similar syndicated program on radio in nearly 600 cities and towns. Shown here with Father Lyons is announcer Tom Davis, center, and Senator Strom Thurmond, of South Carolina, a former Army general and expert on national defense.

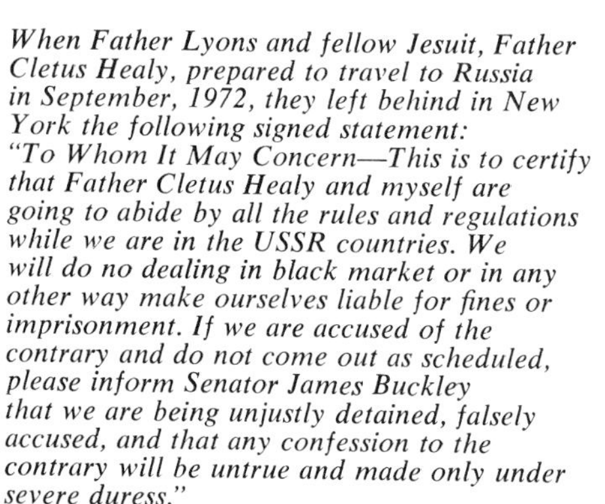

When Father Lyons and fellow Jesuit, Father Cletus Healy, prepared to travel to Russia in September, 1972, they left behind in New York the following signed statement: "To Whom It May Concern—This is to certify that Father Cletus Healy and myself are going to abide by all the rules and regulations while we are in the USSR countries. We will do no dealing in black market or in any other way make ourselves liable for fines or imprisonment. If we are accused of the contrary and do not come out as scheduled, please inform Senator James Buckley that we are being unjustly detained, falsely accused, and that any confession to the contrary will be untrue and made only under severe duress."

One of Father Lyons' hosts in Rumania during his 1972 visit was this orthodox monk. Said Father Lyons: "I spent about an hour in this monastery, where 43 monks live together. The monk shown with me here was a gentle, friendly priest and answered all my questions. To communicate, we spoke Latin, English and Rumanian through an interpreter."

In Budapest, Father saw this group of little boys and snapped their picture. He later explained: "The little boy, second from left, who is being taught atheism in a state school, folded his hands in prayer when he saw my Roman collar."

A great help to Father Lyons during his 1972 fact-finding journey behind the Iron Curtain was this government-guide and interpreter in Bucharest.

This beautiful 13th century church in Budapest was another subject for Father Lyons' camera. He said: "The finest art in any country are the memorials to God left by our ancestors. Nowhere behind the Iron Curtain where I traveled did I see where the Communist regimes added anything to creative art."

One of the Russian orthodox churches in the Kremlin, Moscow, that Father Lyons caught with his camera on his September visit in 1972.

St. Josef's Roman Catholic Church, Bucharest, where Father Lyons offered Mass in October, 1972. It is one of five Catholic churches in Bucharest still open.

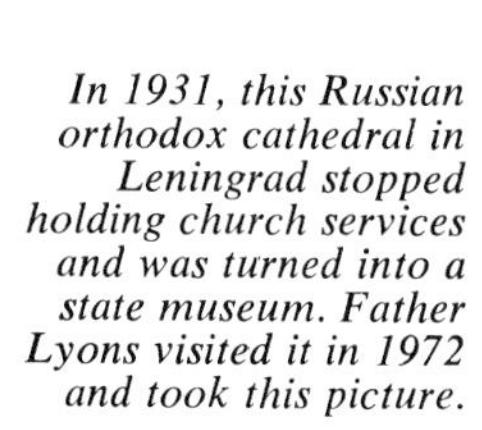

In 1931, this Russian orthodox cathedral in Leningrad stopped holding church services and was turned into a state museum. Father Lyons visited it in 1972 and took this picture.

none.) Communal kitchens exist only in older apartments. In a rare burst of candor, an Intourist official explained to me the government admitted communal kitchens were a failure and that their construction was discontinued.

"The government literature boasts of an eight-hour day, but we kept meeting the same Intourist people on duty up to 9 p.m. whom we met at 9 a.m. the same day. They admitted they were working a 12-hour day. Nor was the end of September the height of the season. Tourism is increasing 22 percent per year. Our hotel, the Rossiya, has 6,000 rooms.

"There is a second priest in Moscow, Father Joseph Richards, an Assumptionist Father. He is there in accordance with the Litvinoff agreement whereby the United States is permitted to have one priest in Moscow to look after Americans. He has a nice but tiny chapel in his apartment, where about 30 persons attend Mass on Saturday night. He offers three Masses in the cafeteria at the American Embassy on Sundays, attended by Catholics from various legations.

"Having served in Moscow seven or eight years before, he knows the ropes and is the essence of prudence. Had he met Solzhenitsyn? No, he did not think it would be proper, unless he chanced to meet the Russian author at a reception or cocktail party. A woman who cleaned the chapel once asked him if he could visit her family, but he felt it would be unwise to do so. 'It is their ball and their bat and their playfield,' he explained. It is also their umpire and their scorekeeper, I might add.

"When his predecessor, Father Bissonnette, wrote a critical book entitled, 'Moscow Was My Parish,' after serving there for two years, the Kremlin got even. It did not allow anyone to replace him for four long years. Father Richards is right. He is there to work with his little flock of foreigners and to teach catechism to their children, not to get ousted.

"I asked at the U.S. Embassy how well the phone system worked. The reply was that it worked fairly well but was sometimes *weak* 'because of all the tape recorders tapped onto the line.' A diplomat there expressed astonishment at the enormity of the surveillance that goes on, remarking that the cost of snooping in the Russian budget must indeed be colossal. It puts no food on the table, however.

"Russian officials will not visit any residences of American diplomats. There has been no improvement in such matters, and the U.S. Embassy made it very clear to me that people can still be sent to Siberia, or jailed for many years. Still, this is the best time in several years for visiting the Soviet Union. They need many of our other products as well as our wheat, and as long as tourists bring in so many dollars, and as long as our government loans them the money for much of what they buy from us, as is our wont, they are not so quick to let our people rot in their prisons. Yet the situation can change, as it so often has in the past.

"It is anything but a classless society, and those who have special influence with the government, or who get money from abroad, are permitted to shop at special stores that are reserved for foreigners or people with foreign currency. Even Peking demands Swiss francs for the taxes it levies on any Soviet goods unloaded at Red China's ports en route to Hanoi. Communists, more than anyone, know what the ruble is really worth.

"Our first Mass in the Soviet Union was that of Christ the King. Our second was of St. Michael the Archangel, asking him to defend the interests of God. We visited the magnificent St. Isaac's cathedral in Leningrad. It is one of the world's greatest examples of Byzantine architecture. Sadly, it is just a museum, not having been used as a church since 1931. I thought of those words of author Solzhenitsyn: 'These churches represent the finest heritage our ancestors have given us.' But not as *museums*.

"Near the former cathedral in Leningrad we visited the Ermitage, one of the best art museums you can find anywhere. It was the former winter palace of the Czars. There are 23 original paintings by Rembrandt, including his magnificent Prodigal Son. There are more than 40 by Peter Paul Rubens (most of them partially finished by his associates). Hundreds of paintings by Russians over the last few centuries were also outstanding.

"We visited the marvelous Tretiakov museum in Moscow, with its many fine paintings, including priceless ikons painted 650 years ago by Rublev. The people in Moscow enjoy the museums very much, and also the wonderful music heard on the radio.

"In Russia, the wives all have to work, no doubt to the disadvantage of small children. No nursery worker or teacher has the time or interest in bringing out the personality of a child like the youngster's mother. It is sad to see so many women sweeping the streets in inclement weather.

I also saw younger women mixing cement on a construction job.

"Father Healy and I parted in Moscow. I wanted to check on Rumania and Hungary, and he went on to West Germany to take photos of the Iron Curtain from the Baltic all the way south to the Adriatic. It is a worthwhile project. How the liberal press has 'gotten used to'—yes, even forgotten—about the Iron Curtain, fencing in those hundreds of millions of people, guarding the walls with machine guns and dogs trained to kill.

"When we asked a well-informed person in Prague how many people would want to leave if there were no wall, he laughed heartily at the thought. His only doubt was whether it would be a majority. As he thought about it, his doubt seemed to be only how great a majority it would be. Yet how the doctrinaire liberals in the U.S.A., who never mention The Wall, would scream if Franco or Thieu or the Greek colonels put up such a structure! In non-Communist countries, such walls are put up only to keep people in prison who have been convicted of crime. But the Communists can imprison everyone, for they have done away with due process for hundreds of millions of citizens.

"But some people must like the system. Yes, all you have to do to join the Party is have a father or a friend who can get you in and be willing to turn in your friends and relatives as well as strangers. Above all, you have to condemn God and actively attack Him. That is all right, some would say? All you had to do under Hitler was to condemn a certain race. It depends on your sense of values.

"As I left Moscow, the customs woman going through

my luggage dug out a rosary, held it up and asked if it were the only one I had. It was a foolish question, since I was *leaving* the country. I pulled another rosary out of my pocket. Did she want me to leave them in Russia? Hardly. She seemed to have forgotten whether I was coming or going.

"With that parting question I was let out, and flew to Bucharest, the capital of Rumania. On the plane I sat next to a Rumanian student in his fourth year of college. He asked me what were the facts about Vietnam. In turn, I asked him if his country was run by the Communist Party, like all the others. 'Yes,' he replied, very simply. No need to elaborate. Like others I was to ask later, he had never heard of the great Russian writer, Solzhenitsyn.

"Rumania derived its language from Latin, when the Romans took over that country in the first century. The Rumanian government has a reputation of differing with Moscow, which it does. It denies the Brezhnev doctrine that a socialist country cannot break away from Moscow. It condemned the Kremlin severely for invading Czechoslovakia in 1968. Yet it had no use for Dubcek. It is strictly orthodox in its Communism at home. It considered Dubcek to be very dangerous, convinced that you cannot have freedom of the press or much of any other freedom without damaging Communism irreparably.

"Rumania is somewhat tolerant of religion. Like other Communist countries, it tries to keep religion weak, yet has a special department for it, the Ministry of Cults. The heads of the churches are listed as government officials. Such governments cannot understand anything existing that is not a part of themselves. As in the other countries, the only outside organization that operates within their country with their people is the Roman Catholic Church.

"In Communist countries, a signal from the regime is all-significant. When the father of Ceausescu, the head of the Communist Party (and therefore head of the government) died last year, he was buried in the Orthodox Church—not secretly, but with TV and newspaper publicity. It meant a great deal. It meant that henceforth anyone can have his relatives buried in the Church.

"The state religion has traditionally been Orthodox. Roman Catholics are just 10 percent of the population. There used to be two million Jews in Rumania before World War II. Now there are only 100,000—most of them elderly. About 500,000 have migrated to Israel, and the majority of young Jews go there to live.

"The Catholic primate of Rumania is Bishop Jacob Antal, now 80 years old. He is located in Alba Julia, in the western part of Rumania called Transylvania. In February, 1972, the Vatican arranged with the government to consecrate Bishop Aron Marton as the future successor to Bishop Antal, an important and encouraging step.

"There are four or five Catholic parishes in Bucharest, each one with a resident pastor and a total of about 20 priests. There are two seminaries with 160 seminarians in the country; not many for more than one million Catholics. The various embassies are not allowed a resident chaplain, and the Italian church remains closed most of the time. But the government permits the Vatican to send a priest,

Padre Molinari, from Rome five times a year. He comes at Christmas, Easter, and on three other important occasions. The Italian Embassy notifies the other foreign legations.

"I visited a beautiful monastery not far from Bucharest, and was surprised to find 43 Orthodox monks living there. So in answer to the question: how is religion doing behind the Iron Curtain? It is different in each country. As good an estimate as any would be to say it is about 90 percent suppressed, yet it is not dying out. When the time comes—when freedom has returned—the people will be brought back rather quickly. They will need more instruction than conversion. And instruction is easy, while conversion is usually slow and difficult.

"Experienced men in our foreign service point out that Communism blows hot and cold, that a thaw will not necessarily continue. It never has in the past. Communist power is so arbitrary. It seems to exercise the antiquated 'divine right of kings,' though even such kings were to be bound by God's law. There may even be a certain degree of benevolence in the despotism. But it is a throwback to a centuries-old system, compounded with the viciousness of atheism.

"From Rumania, I flew to Budapest, that beautiful city on the Danube. More than 70 percent Catholic, it remains one of the most charming cities in Europe. Hungary was the first country where the people rebelled in droves against the system, in 1956. As the statue of Stalin was torn down, the Catholic primate, Cardinal Mindszenty, was forcibly taken out of jail and placed in the American Embassy for sanctuary, where he remained until 1971, when he went to Vienna.

"The rooms where he lived for those 15 years are now the Ambassador's office. One of our foreign officers there who used to walk with the Cardinal in the courtyard of the Embassy told me he asked him one day: 'Your Eminence, you have been in Fascist prisons and in Communist prisons. What would you say is the difference?' Cardinal Mindszenty replied very briefly: 'In Fascist prisons they *feed* you.'

"There is considerable truth to the saying that America is better liked by the peoples behind the Iron Curtain than in western Europe. One of the reasons they liked us is because they detest their system. A Russian remarked they would never get ahead of the U.S. because if they did 'you would see the hole in the seat of our pants.' A Rumanian told me he heard the reason Israel won the six-day war is that the United States had given better equipment to Israel than Russia had given to the Egyptians. They like to think such things.

"They go to any length to criticize Russia. When Khrushchev visited the United States, they still say in Rumania, he told President Eisenhower he heard there were a lot of alcoholics on the streets in New York. President Eisenhower said it was not true, and finally told Khrushchev he could shoot anyone he saw drunk on the streets that night. 'The next day,' went the story in Rumania, the New York papers carried a front-page story that 'a fat man, a gangster, went around the streets of New York and shot everyone who works at the Russian Embassy.' Farfetched, of course, but that gives you an idea of what Rumanians think of the Soviet Union.

"I looked up some of the priests in Budapest and visited the magnificent 13th-century St. Matthias Church overlooking the city, where members of the state opera sing in the choir at the request of the state. It is good for tourists, figure the Communist leaders. It is also good for the Church. It gets more Hungarians to Mass. I offered Mass downtown at the overwhelmingly beautiful basilica, and at the popular little chapel of St. Rita's.

"I learned that there are 210 Jesuits in Hungary, and that all but 10 of them must work full time in factories instead of as priests. None is permitted to teach, and when priests who are not recognized by the state are put in jail, there are still no priests in jail as they are *workmen,* not priests. It's something like the baseball umpire who says 'they're nothing until I call 'em.'

"Hungary is so rich in history: St. Stephen, who died 1,002 years ago; St. Margaret, St. Elizabeth and many others. There are eight Catholic schools in operation, all of them secondary. Six for boys and two for girls. Of the boys' schools, two are run by the Piarist Fathers, two by the Benedictines, and two by the Franciscans. There are no Protestant schools left open. In a conciliatory gesture they were offered to the state, and the state took them over.

"A bishop's secretary is always a Red agent who opens all letters in and out. The bishop cannot change a pastor. The churches have lots of strangers in attendance on Sunday, people from other areas who do not want to be seen in church by their associates. Sometimes they drive 20 miles to church, only to find their boss also there.

"So it goes. And so the system will finally break down. We must pray for that day, and as the free world's leader the U.S. must remain militarily strong, avoiding war by being prepared for it.

"The only country in the Soviet bloc that likes the Russians historically is Bulgaria. But even the Bulgarians resent the militant, senseless atheism of the Soviet. How ironic it would be if the U.S.S.R. were to break down because of its persecution of religion!

"That is exactly what is eventually going to happen. Meanwhile, the Communist Party in each country is preserving many of the church buildings and pieces of religious art as museum pieces for tourists—preserving them unwittingly for the day when their own people will once again be able to worship God in peace and freedom.

"It may be a hundred years from now. But it will come. The future does not belong to those who hate a God they say does not exist.

"The future belongs to those who love the God Who made them."

THE END

Index

D

E

F

G

H

M

N

O

P

R

S

T

U

V

W

Y

Z